WE WERE INNOCENTS

WE WERE INNOCENTS

An Infantryman in Korea

William D. Dannenmaier

University of Illinois Press

Urbana and Chicago

© 1999 by the Board of Trustees of the University of Illinois
Manufactured in the United States of America
C 5 4 3 2 1

This book is printed on acid-free paper.

Library of Congress Cataloging-in-Publication Data
Dannenmaier, William D. (William Deal), 1930–
We were innocents : an infantryman in Korea /
William D. Dannenmaier.
p. cm.
ISBN 0-252-02449-4 (acid-free paper)
1. Dannenmaier, William D. (William Deal), 1930–
2. Korean War, 1950–1953—Personal narratives, American.
3. Soldiers—United States—Biography.
I. Title.
DS921.6.D36   1999
951.904'2—ddc21   98-25403

CIP

To Ethel Dannenmaier Van Cleve, the finest sister and friend a person could ever have, who insisted on saving the letters I refused to accept or read for forty years—the letters on which this memoir is based.

And to the 54,246 Americans who died in the Korean conflict, the 103,284 wounded, the 8,174 missing in action, and the 7,000 known to have been prisoners of war, more than half of whom died.

• • •

CONTENTS

Unknown and undecorated except for the Combat Infantryman's Badge, I was an anyman, an everyman. There were tens of thousands of me. As infantrymen in Korea, we fought and sometimes died. My story, a citizen-soldier's story, is the story of thousands. I have done my best to tell it truthfully and accurately for all those who have lost the ability to speak.

—W.D.D.

ACKNOWLEDGMENTS

To my nephew, John Walter Van Cleve, who pushed me into writing this book and then painstakingly edited every page. To my wife, Sheila W. Dannenmaier, my brother, Joseph H. Dannenmaier, and my daughter Laura K. Stearman, who proofread and critiqued every page. To Professor John Newman at Colorado State University, Dr. Joan Brune of Peoria, Mr. Kenneth S. Gallagher, senior editor of Combined Books, and the members of my writers' group, all of whom encouraged me to continue a sometimes difficult work.

I also wish to thank members of the University of Illinois Press. To Richard L. Wentworth, director and editor in chief, and David M. Perkins, director of marketing, for their continuing encouragement; to Emily Rogers, acquisitions editor, and Stephanie Smith, formerly publicity manager—both of whom won my affection by saying nice things about essays I sent to accompany messages; and to Theresa L. Sears, managing editor, for forcing me to re-read and reconsider every single line.

PROLOGUE

I had a strange dream. Someone told me my father had died. Then I was in a car with a woman, perhaps my wife, and three of my children. Someone else was driving. We arrived at a large field. People were coming from everywhere for the burial. I cried. I cried inconsolably. Finally, as people came closer, I controlled myself and began talking to them. Then I awoke. My eyes were wet.

It may not seem strange to you that I cried over my father's death, but my father died in 1954, more than forty years before my dream. It was the first time I had cried.

He died just a few months after I returned from Korea, where I had served as an infantry scout. I shed no tears in 1954. In fact, his funeral made little impression on me. My feelings were those of a driver who passes a minor car accident: a slowing down of necessity, indulging curiosity, and then full speed ahead. I had seen too many dead men. During my year in Korea, life had become a transient acquaintance, death a companion. One could not, must not, be upset by death.

Thinking about, and planning for, this book finally unlocked that sealed compartment in my mind, that immunity to grief. It took more than forty years for that door to open.

I'm sorry, Dad. I loved you then, and I love you now. But I saw too much.

This book is about my life in Korea, the life that left a part of me frozen for forty years. It is about being an infantryman, being expendable, and about having dreams that continue to trouble my sleep. Dreams that will probably continue as long as I live. At my death they will end unless, as I have sometimes thought, I died as a young soldier. Then, those dreams are my eternity.

I remember precisely where I was when I heard that the United States was sending troops to Korea. I was standing on the pathway approximately thirty feet in front of the entrance to the main lodge of the Cedarledge Girl Scout Camp, about thirty miles outside of St. Louis, Missouri. After working more than forty hours a week, at night, for four years to be able to attend college, I had spent the summer before my last semester working as a biologist at the camp. There I fell deeply in first love with one of the counselors. I was looking forward to graduating in January from Harris Teachers' College in St. Louis and beginning my real career, perhaps even going on to graduate school in conservation at the University of Missouri.

The announcement of the "police action" changed everything. At the time, I had no true appreciation of how much it would alter my whole world. It was a police action, not a war, and everyone knew what police did. Police actions, unlike wars, are not dangerous. A few men may be hurt, but not tens of thousands. I had missed World War II by one year because of youth. Now it was my turn.

In 1992, presidential candidate Bill Clinton justified his avoidance of military service during the Vietnam War by saying that opposing opinions concerning the merits of a war should be accepted. In 1950 it was different. We debated our differences but accepted our responsibilities. I fully expected to serve in the armed forces, as did my friends. We were innocents. We knew nothing of the reality we faced. Fortunately for them, many of my friends never had to learn. They served their nation in peaceful areas.

I have spanked my children when I considered it necessary, but since leaving Korea I have struck an adult only once. I was trying to tell my first wife about a particularly troubling "M*A*S*H" episode on television. She laughed at me, then stretched out on the sofa and closed her eyes as I talked. Her disdain and disinterest in what may have been the beginning of the thawing of my emotions pushed me beyond my limit. I slapped her.

I have enjoyed many "M*A*S*H" shows, laughing along with Hawkeye as war was neutered—humanized—and roles caricatured, but that particular show opened old wounds. Each of the characters had been asked what troubled them most, and each had answered, correctly, that it was boredom. On the front line in

Korea, boredom dominated our lives. There was no toothbrush to use, no razor to shave with, no books to read, no television to watch. We just waited. Hour after hour, sometimes day after day, of waiting for moments of action.

Don't, however, get the idea that this was like lingering for a salesperson, a spouse, or even, perhaps, a fish to bite. Neither irritation nor peace, much less relaxation, lurked in this waiting. Always there was tension. Always. Like springs in a tightly wound stopwatch, we had to be ready.

The hours of waiting didn't anger us. They weren't annoying. In unspoken communication, we hoped they would last. The alternative was always less pleasant. True, sometimes you believed you knew the end of the wait, as when you were told that you had a patrol as soon as it was dark. But the people who were interested in killing you also had the power to determine when you must work—whether work meant diving off a wooden box that served as a toilet to avoid artillery fire or leaping from a state of semisleep in anticipation of a real or imagined foe. Living—in the sense of surviving—meant staying alert, and tense, twenty-four hours a day, seven days a week, from the moment you headed for the front until you were safely away from it. And like tightly wound springs, sometimes men snapped.

You couldn't relax even if trucked back to the shower point. Some rear echelon hero might steal your belt or rifle or wallet as you stripped and walked through the monthly shower. Thus, you set a guard, a buddy, who watched while you hurriedly showered so that he would also have a chance for cleanliness before it was necessary to return. Or, as many of us learned to do, you simply skipped those monthly showers.

Combat time, time when you were in the trenches or dugouts of the front line, was unremitting, relentless tension whether or not there was actual gunfire. Carelessness was unforgiven. For me, line time lasted about seven months—not very long in a civilized world. Still, those seven months gave me more memories than I care to have. And they were the end of a lifetime for some of my friends.

I should make one thing very clear, right at the start. Tension does not equal fear. After getting out of the army, I was a teacher for more than twenty years. Then I went back to work for the army, doing research and conducting war games. I once sat through a meeting during which a colonel described what he called the "trembling, fearful infantryman." The man didn't know what he was talking about; I wanted to tell him to keep his mouth shut. He hadn't been there, he wasn't infantry. We were always tense, seldom fearful. You can't live with constant fear, not day after day. In our minds we were normal, just careful. We laughed and joked, not always about things civilized people would find pleasant. We played games, stole any food we could find—or any other thing that might make those days remaining to us as comfortable as possible. I saw lots of bravery, too much stupidity, and some insanity, but very little fear.

I had an opportunity to respond to that colonel, and I was glad to take it, though it isn't wise to embarrass an officer when you work for him. I was furious at the time and am still discouraged at the memory of his description of the men I knew. In my response I said that those who hadn't been there shouldn't judge. The word to use was tension, not fear.

I used quail hunting as an analogy. A patrol is rather like going on a quail hunt without a dog and using a single-shot shotgun. I did a lot of that as a youth. You walk through a meadow with your gun up and ready, knowing that at any moment a quail might burst up from under your feet. You get only one shot and it has to be good, otherwise no quail.

When you're out on patrol, the quail also has a shot, so you've got to be quick or lucky, or both. I was generally both.

You pay a price for that tension. For years after I came home I continued to have the blinding, disabling headaches that began in Korea. They weren't constant but came and went, gradually decreasing in frequency. I no longer have them, but that first year back, thinking I was losing my eyesight, I went to three different doctors. The last one told me that if the headaches continued I should see a neurologist. That was when I quit going to doctors. After all, they were probably going to tell me that it was my nerves. But I had just survived seven months of combat, hadn't I? Obviously there was nothing wrong with my nerves. (I recently read an article about trench mouth, which I developed in Korea, also being related to tension.)

There's something else—and it's for all the psychiatrists, psychologists, social workers, and others who try to help people solve emotional problems. I'm certain they're great at helping solve imaginary problems people have created in their own minds, but combat is not imaginary. It's real. The sights, the sounds, the smells, the hunger and thirst, the heat and cold are all real.

A friend who is a social worker—an excellent one, in my opinion—once told me that he was counseling a Vietnam veteran and that he told the vet he was going to have to forget some of those real things I just mentioned. That's impossible. You don't forget. You accept and learn to live with a reality that in a brief period completely altered your life. But you never forget. You just keep it under control until some circumstance—like a "M*A*S*H" episode on boredom—rips open old wounds. You bleed afresh as your mind carries you back to a world that you hope no one you love will ever understand.

I went to a party when I first came home. I was having a good time, laughing and joking, when a former classmate, a woman who had stayed in St. Louis and earned a doctorate in psychology, said, "Bill, I had hoped the army would help you mature, but you're the same as always." I just stood and looked at her and thought of the places I'd been and the things I'd seen and done. There was nothing I could say.

1

HOMEWARD BOUND

I no longer remember the exact date, only the suddenness of the orders. I was number two on the list to return home when troop shipments were stopped at the beginning of December. Now, in late December 1953 or early January 1954, I was told that there was room for 200 men from front-line units on a ship leaving Inch'on for the States. Orders were being typed. I was to hurry, pack my gear, and go—the ship was waiting. There was no time for farewells, but neither was there the need: my comrades from combat had all preceded me. Now it was my time to return. A truck was waiting to take me and several others south to the port at Inch'on.

There wasn't much to pack. Most of my personal gear had been lost or stolen during one or another of my moves. I had the uniform I wore, spare underwear and socks, and my field ration, which consisted of equipment for which I was responsible but which was not permanently mine, such as my parka, helmet, and rifle. I worried some about the rifle. In keeping with tradition, I took the worst-looking bolt action M-1, giving my lightweight M-2 carbine to someone who might need its fast firing capability. My concern was that some zealous quartermaster might not accept the rusted, useless rifle I was going to turn in and make me pay for a new one. But I thought I could handle that later if it became necessary. The immediate thing was to throw my gear together and go. Soon I was on a truck headed south.

When the truck arrived in Inch'on, the first order of the day was a shower. We entered a barnlike room with benches along the side and a counter, behind which Korean workers were busy sorting clothing. We stripped, turned in all our clothing, and shook everything inside our duffel bags onto the floor. (To my later sorrow, I also inadvertently turned in my wallet, which held a number of mementos I would never see again.) Then we went through the shower. I expect it was a delousing shower—which would have made sense, even though I didn't have lice, nor did I know anyone who did, but we probably had other things. A bad smell, if nothing else.

When we came out of the shower we received half of a regulation issue of clothing. Thus, instead of the two pairs of boots we were required to have as peacetime soldiers in the United States, we received one pair. The same was true of everything else: half of the required dress uniforms, half of the fatigue uniforms. If regulation issue was only one of something, we received that. An example would be dress shoes. We also received a field issue for the States, which included an overcoat and a field jacket. The clothing was new and we received our correct sizes. It was quite an experience—the first time in a year that I had any clothes other than what I was wearing. In a sense, the excess clothing we'd turned in on arrival in Korea was being returned to us. In the excitement of receiving new, clean clothes—clothes that fit—I didn't miss my wallet.

Soon we were told that a mistake had been made: the information that brought us to Inch'on was false. There was no room for the 200 of us from the front line on the ship that was getting ready to leave, and we would not be allowed to wait for the next departure date. Fortunately, however, there was room for us on board a ship leaving Pusan at the southern tip of the Korean peninsula—but we would have to hurry. We were put on a train heading south at about six in the evening.

The train was a twin to the one I rode when I first arrived in Korea. As before, there was no heat, even though it was winter. Nor was there glass in the window openings in the cars. Nor toilets, though holes in the floor served when necessary. Actually, we had little need of these as no one thought to put any water or other liquids on board for us to drink. There were C rations, but no knives or forks. My can opener did its work and, as on my first night in Korea almost thirteen months earlier, I cut my tongue licking beans and franks out of a C ration can.

As dawn arrived, we found ourselves riding through a peaceful Asian countryside. The terrain was a quilt pattern of small rice paddies separated by dikes built around the fields to hold the water the rice required. Irregularly shaped, the paddies rose in patterns of flatness, uneven steps in a staircase to the sky, until even the softened contours of the southern mountains were too steep to be cultivated. Periodically, we passed small clusters of homes made entirely of rice straw, thatched sides as well as thatched roofs, more permanent buildings having been destroyed by one army or another in the rage of war. The gleam of winter frost and ice overlay all.

It was early morning when we arrived in Taegu, the sun peeking above a rosy horizon. We were parked on a siding for a short time to permit a northbound train to pass. During this stop, a Korean boy came alongside the train selling cans of American beer stolen from one of the many shipments that never reached us at the front. After our twelve hours without liquid, he did a brisk business at five dollars a can. It illustrated perfectly the law of supply and demand: in the north, a Korean would work all day for one dollar; that morning, a dollar wouldn't buy you a can of beer. I would have spent the five dollars gladly if I hadn't lost my wallet.

It's important to note that this was not, to us, an uncomfortable train trip. For one reason, we were all front-line infantrymen. We had seen a lot worse. The true reason, however, was that we were homeward bound. When you're homeward bound, all is well, all is comfortable.

2

THE INITIATION

The two years minus seven days that constituted my military career were occasioned by President Harry Truman's decision to defend South Korea from the North Korean attack. The announcement of the Korean War was a shock. I had registered for the draft, as did all young men of my generation, but no one expected to go anywhere. World War II was over. The newspapers no longer provided daily updates of campaigns; no longer did every edition list the killed and the wounded. We were at peace. Young men's lives were no longer forfeit. We could plan our futures—and have them.

My friends and I went to school, worked evenings and nights to make money, and spent lots of time talking about girls. The more daring would go "downtown" to see adult-only shows—which were less revealing than many of today's prime-time television commercials. Girls' fathers and mothers mistrusted us, but the girls knew our innocence—or, more accurately, our incompetence.

The army didn't require innocence or incompetence. I and others like me had to be changed. Sixteen weeks of basic training after our induction into the army began that process, but only began it. After that came travel to Korea and then war itself—from which some of us managed to return.

We were different people when we got back, no longer the credulous youth whose only previous life experiences had been in the classroom or a first job. Instead, mixed among comrades we could trust, we found others interested only in their own safety or comfort. Some of our assigned leaders, commissioned and non-commissioned officers alike, were incompetent, some dishonest, and some both. Many of us encountered rampant corruption for the first time. We learned to trust by choice, not habit. We returned, still young but no longer innocent.

Throughout the process I wrote numerous letters. This chapter includes those that survive from my initiation. They report the beginning of this series of events that would so harden me that I could dispassionately view my own father's unexpected death. From fresh and eager to weary and resigned, it was a two-year spiral of change, ever downward.

In mid-1951, along with some of my friends, I took a medical examination for the military draft. I stood behind a football player from the University of Missouri and in front of a basketball player from Washington University in St. Louis. Both were splendid physical specimens, the kind of guys the girls would look at, seeing past me, as we walked down the street. These guys dwarfed me, a skinny six-footer. Both of them failed the physical while I passed with flying colors.

I knew that weeks and months of waiting to be drafted would be too much for me, so I enlisted in a two-year program designed to provide junior officers. I was given June 19, 1952, as the date to begin my military career.

That day a group of us were gathered in downtown St. Louis, sworn into the army, and told that from now on the army would be our mother and our father. We were told, "You can send your soul to God, but your ass belongs to the army." All we had to do was obey. It was also the first time we heard the oft-repeated phrase, "There are three ways to do things: the right way, the wrong way, and the army way. You will do them the army way." No questions were welcomed, no reasons given. We were to follow instructions to the letter, and to do so again and again and again— until the required procedure, whatever it happened to be, was so routine that no alternative existed in our minds.

Following the induction ceremony we were loaded onto a bus headed for parts unknown. Actually, the orders we carried told us the destination, but we didn't know how to read the two pages of abbreviations and acronyms, spiced with our names, which gave it. Children going to summer camp, we laughed at our ignorance, got to know one another, and lost track of where we were and where we were going.

Our destination was Camp Crowder. I still don't know if it was in Missouri or Arkansas. Neither would have claimed it as it was then. Rows of two-story wooden barracks with faded or peeling paint lined dusty streets of crushed limestone. The heat was oppressive and relentless. No wind, no breeze—nothing stirred the air to provide relief, though all the doors and windows stood open in vain hope. If an air conditioner existed on the post, it wasn't where we could see it. This was a gathering place for recruits, mustered there only to be sent elsewhere. Little attention was paid to looks or comfort.

Upon our arrival at Crowder we were issued uniforms, bedding, and a place to sleep. We were also given the traditional short haircut. As the barber yanked at my hair with worn shears, he criticized me for washing it the night before. He said that made it difficult to cut, so the pain resulting from his efforts was my own fault.

"Clean the barracks!" was the final order of the day, issued after our return from supper. Our efforts in this activity were not highly regarded. The sergeant in charge ridiculed our first attempt, perhaps deservedly so. Periodically he would reappear to examine our work and order us to continue or try something over again. With mop and bucket, scrub brush, and soap, we redid some jobs several times before finally gaining grudging approval and permission to get some sleep. I suspect the sergeant was ready for bed himself, since it was well past midnight.

The pattern for our time at Crowder was set. We were up late doing and redoing our jobs, often working eagerly but unnecessarily. Then it was off to bed and back up at six to begin another day of orientation, paperwork, and make-work. Many of us were recent college graduates with the work ethic and innocence of middle-class youth who had spent their lives in classrooms—places where thought and effort were sometimes rewarded. We believed our enthusiasm and our ideas would be appreciated. We were wrong. Disciplined obedience, a necessity for success in combat, was the goal. This was a truth we were still to learn. It is a goal that combat teaches soldiers to appreciate.

After two or three days we were permitted to go to a small post exchange (PX) to buy beer and cigarettes. Of course, the more adventuresome among us already knew the way. The cold beer was good; the relaxation and camaraderie were even better. Shared misery gives birth to fellowship.

Before long some of us were sent to Ft. Riley. According to a letter I wrote, we traveled by bus, but I have no memory of that trip. I do remember our arrival. Our first assigned duty was to clean the barracks. We knew that routine! Our new sergeant went into shock when he returned to find the floor flooded. "That floor was just refinished," he moaned. "Get the water up as fast as possible so it's not ruined. Use damp mops in the future!"

• • •

[Undated]

Dear Ethel:

I realize that I am a bit late on this, but I plead innocent on the grounds that when I'm not working or eating, I sleep. It is nothing anymore if we get a half hour or hour off to see ten or fifteen fellows stretched out on the wood floor—sound asleep. (We are not allowed in bunks during duty hours.)

Camp Crowder was a hell hole of the first order. We were kept going from 4:30 A.M. until midnight as long as we were there (except Sundays), which was twelve days. . . .

Monday we traveled all day by bus and arrived at Riley Monday night. Fort Riley is a big dump. The whole of the 10th Infantry is stationed here (that's what I am in) as well as elements of engineers, artillery, First Cavalry, etc. I imagine there's over 10 thousand men + a few WACs here. Quite a sizable place.

Since our work doesn't begin until next Monday—we'll be through 16 weeks later—we've done almost nothing this week. As a consequence, we're all well rested, fat, and happy. However, tomorrow is the last day of the leisure. Then comes 16 weeks of work that will go on from 14 to 18 hours a day, 6 to 7 days a week. Time will fly then, but not fast enough.

This time I'm in "E" Company which has a reputation for turning out the best food in the place. This they've lived up to so far. For instance, yesterday we had (at lunch) lemonade and grape juice, fried chicken, mashed potatoes, gravy, string beans, lima beans, salad, bread and butter, and ice cream with chocolate sauce. Of course we had to get up to get seconds. An inventory of all the meals would show the same variety and quantity, even breakfast.

Well, I'm back again—this letter being written in short jerks. Someone just told me there are slightly over 18,000 men here.

I won't get anywhere near St. Louis until November, but I might get down to see Joe sooner. We're allowed passes after 4 weeks of training, but are confined to a 250 mile radius of camp. Since I am just out of Junction City and not far from Manhattan, Kansas, I think I can go to see Joe legally. Well, you can send me letters, but don't expect too much from me—no packages please, I'm well fed. How's Johnny and John?

See you soon.

• • •

My memories of Ft. Riley consist of vignettes of people and activities, of personalities, and fatigue. Our workdays began early and ended late. Often we would be up until midnight or later on night exercises and then reawakened at five or six to shower and clean the barracks so as to be ready for the new day. If our efforts on any given day didn't satisfy, we were kept working until they did. Following particularly poor efforts, we'd get a wakeup call at three the next morning. We were assured that running through the streets in formation would help us remember to do better on this day than we had on the preceding day. Many nights we would simply lie on the floor so that the next morning we could steal some extra sleep during the time we would otherwise be making beds to the perfectionist standards of the cadre.

Cigarette breaks were ten minutes every hour. I often fell asleep during those breaks, to be reawakened with a kick. Once I didn't need the kick, because a cigarette I had lit burned my fingers and awoke me.

The army exerted its control twenty-four hours a day, seven days a week. We were housed in two-story wooden barracks. Each floor had two rows of double bunks on either side of a center aisle with eight or ten double bunks in each row. In front of the bunks were footlockers in which underwear, socks, and shaving gear were kept, folded in a prescribed manner and in a prescribed location. Behind each bunk was a rod on which we hung uniforms, also in a prescribed order.

On the first floor, in addition to the bunks, were eight toilets in two rows of four, facing each other. This was a great place for conversation and rumors, one of the few spots where we retained some individual freedom. On Sundays, our one day off, we would sit there in the morning and gossip, trading rumors, jokes, lies, and pornographic magazines. An adjacent room had a row of wash-stands on one wall and urinals on the wall opposite. Next to this was a room with four shower heads. Modesty and privacy were not considerations.

No civilian clothing, books, or alcoholic beverages were permit-ted in the barracks. If the army didn't issue it, we didn't have it. Each company had a supply room that issued the clothes and field gear, such as rifles and helmets, that we needed. Initially, we were embarrassed by the newness, the greenness of our fatigue uni-forms. It was painfully obvious to all that we were the new boys on the block. The embarrassment passed. With time the clothing faded. So did we.

A collection was taken and we purchased two automatic wash-ers so we could do our laundry in the barracks, instead of going to the launderette. I assume these were repurchased by those who followed us, the money going to someone other than us.

How thoughtful or considerate supply personnel were depended on the sergeant in charge, typically a regular army type. The ser-geant at Crowder tried his best to supply clothes that fit. He was the only supply sergeant I remember who was so considerate—that is, until I headed home from Korea. When I was issued my winter uniforms at Ft. Riley, I received an overcoat that would have held two of me. When I asked to exchange it, I was told to keep mov-ing. That weekend I discussed the situation with a recruit from New York who had a similar problem. He asked me if I had fifty cents. When I said I did, he said, "Come with me."

The two of us went to the supply room. There my friend looked at the man in charge and said, "Look, money talks. For a buck, let us change overcoats." The dollar was taken and we were permit-ted to find overcoats that fit. Our salaries were seventy-five dol-lars per month, so a dollar represented half a day of work.

Just as no one was permitted to have civilian clothing, no one was permitted to have a car on base. It was walk or take the shuttle bus if we had the time, energy, and money to go anywhere. This was rare but it happened. One Saturday night I attended a movie in Manhattan, Kansas. I paid my way in at seven and leaned back in my seat. When the theater closed at midnight the usher woke me up. I saw no part of any of the movies. Nor was I disturbed by the lights or by people moving about. The air conditioning and the dark worked their magic.

Basic training was meant to teach recruits—civilians—how to use the tools of war and how best to protect themselves while killing assigned enemies. It also had to prepare us for the hardship and dehumanization of war. There were people who enjoyed doing this; people we saw as vicious, sadistic types who found fulfillment when inflicting pain on others. Such people appeared to discover their reason for being as trainers of recruits. They had well-deserved reputations for self-serving, brutish behavior. Thankfully, this was not our lot in E Company.

Fate smiled on us when we were assigned our platoon sergeant and our company commander. Each had service in two wars, each had seen combat, and each exercised quiet leadership. Sergeant Maun was a tall, lean, soft-spoken southerner with a quiet sense of humor. A scar that puckered one corner of his mouth and his lower cheek served to emphasize an otherwise handsome face. I never heard him swear and never saw him ruffled. I can still hear him hurrying us along with, "Come on, you clowns, you future American heroes, move, move!" He left before our basic training was finished, to leave the army or for another assignment—I have no idea which. I was sorry to see him go. I was even sorrier once I came to know his replacement.

We also lost our captain before we were finished. He was obviously on good terms with Sergeant Maun, but it's difficult to know if the captain developed people with Maun's style of leadership or simply attracted such men to work for him. He seldom spoke to us, but when he did we listened. He talked of the need for combat discipline. He once said he never thought he'd have to walk behind American soldiers telling them that he didn't care if they had lost their rifles—if they turned back he would kill them. But in Korea, he said, he had done just that. He had become disenchanted with the professional army. I don't know if he transferred or left the service, but I do know he was an excellent officer. He was replaced by someone quite different: a short-tempered, brittle little man who turned out to have better qualities than were initially apparent to me.

We were constantly busy. There were day marches over long dusty trails through the hills, night marches, day exercises, night exercises, weapons classes, marksmanship classes, and individual combat classes. In between we cleaned the barracks, picked up litter, painted anything needing paint, and, in general, did whatever we were told. Life was a kaleidoscope of activity with limited time out for eating, personal hygiene, and sleep. It was harsh, but it worked. Physically and mentally we became tougher as the weeks passed.

Violence was the order of our lives. Bayonet practice consisted of three types of drills. One was charging straw dummies, thrusting and stabbing, withdrawing and using the steel-covered butt plate of the rifle to hit and crush. It was brutal. Another drill was more artistic: we were lined up in formation, moving and chanting en masse, bayonets glistening as we thrust and parried in unison. That drill gave a lasting impression of unified, coordinated force, irresistible force. It was impressive, an art form costumed in olive drab, but it was brutal as well. In a third drill we were paired against each other, thrusting and parrying. Bruises were common and carelessly placed hands could lead to broken fingers.

Thirst, fatigue, and unrelenting pressure were daily companions. At the time, much of it seemed unnecessary. While our bodies obeyed, our minds had time for critical digressions and evaluations. We saw little use in all that senseless discipline. But we were wrong—it was necessary training, as I was to discover in Korea. We made long marches on the Kansas plains in July. One quart of warm water carried in our canteen was to last the entire trip, regardless of the length of the walk or the heat of the day. We pushed ourselves to exhaustion and then were pushed a step beyond. Gradually we changed.

We didn't just receive brutality, we were also taught to employ brutality. In one lecture we were told, "You've all been taught not to kick a man when he's down, but when is a better time? He's less able to hurt you and you're more likely to win." In another we were informed, "If you get in a fight with a necktie on, take it off. Your opponent has complete control of you if he grabs your tie."

Violence became ingrained in us without our real awareness. I was on the rifle range one rainy day toward the end of basic training, lying in the mud to fire my rifle, my elbows and legs in pools

of muddy water collected in the hollows made by countless pre-
decessors. Rain beat on my helmet and soaked through my pon-
cho openings, running down my back and between the cheeks of
my ass. The range master stepped on my feet and told me to keep
them flat on the ground. I looked around and snarled, "Get off my
feet, you son of a bitch, or I'll kill you."

He walked on. Two months earlier, I wouldn't have said that, but
if I had, I wouldn't have meant it. Nor would he have believed it.

We changed as individuals and we changed in our relationships
and behavior with one another. A member of our barracks who
didn't shower routinely was scrubbed with the harsh bristle
brushes we used to clean the floors. After he returned from the
hospital, he showered daily. Another, whose behavior resulted in
our group being punished on multiple occasions, was thrown
down the stairs from the second to the first floor—several times.
When questioned regarding his injuries, everyone remembered
that he had stumbled and fallen down the stairs. We never saw him
again after he was taken to the hospital.

Not all of what we were taught turned out to be sensible. Too
few of the trainers were combat veterans. They simply taught what
they'd been told or had read. Sometimes things they said appeared
to make sense but were really stupid, as I was to learn. In one class
we were told, "If your rifle or machine gun freezes up in the cold
weather, simply piss on it. That warms it up enough to go back into
action."

Now, having worked in cold weather, I know the idiocy of that
advice. First, it would take a most unusual person to summon up
urine for that purpose when under attack. Your mind is elsewhere.
Second, if you're so sloppy as to permit your weapon's working
parts to freeze up, you might as well relax because you're going to
die.

Such instructors also lacked the background to supply us with
those little niceties that serve to keep you alive. Things such as
weakening the cotter pin on your grenades so they could be pulled
easily and the grenade activated quickly. Or putting the cartridges
in your ammunition clip so the rim of each is in front of the rim
of the one beneath it, making the ammunition less likely to jam.

Those sixteen weeks of basic training left a haze of remembrances and fragments of thought too chaotic to write about in

their entirety. We'd been changed, hardened, and prepared for the future, but not to the extent we thought. Approximately a week before graduation we received our orders. That pleasant, sunny Saturday morning, prior to giving us our weekend passes, our captain assembled us and slowly read our names, detailing our next assignments. No one really expected much of a problem. For weeks, only the goof-ups and troublemakers had been sent to Korea. We had a good record and many of us were college graduates with special skills. Maybe 15 or 20 to Korea and 200 to Germany or some other form of paradise.

For weeks that had been the pattern, so that was our expectation. Then our names and assignments were read. Almost all of us were headed for Korea. There'd been heavy fighting and a heavy loss of men. More bodies were needed and we were available. It was quite a shock. It's one thing to train for war, another to go. We all headed for town—Manhattan—to think it over.

That night I called my father from the American Legion Hall. I still owe the Legionnaires the bill. Later I wrote to my sister.

● ● ●

October 21, 1952

Dear Ethel:

I received your letter tonight and conveniently, for tonight is the first night I've had a chance to write an answer in several weeks. Of course I could have written Saturday night but we were celebrating. All of Company "E" went to Manhattan, mainly with the intent of having fun. About fifty of us adjourned to the American Legion Hall later in the evening and showed them just how tame their conventions are. They finally got rid of us about 12:00 by spreading the rumor that the M.P.s [military police] were coming and closing the place. The occasion? We received our orders. I will be home sometime next week for (10?) days—after which I will report to Fort Lawton—Washington for overseas combat duty. Lawton ships to F.E. Com (Far Eastern Command) which covers from Panama to Alaska. The majority, naturally, go to Korea. As the unofficial punishment for dropping O.C.S. [Officer Candidate School]. I and another fellow have been classed as riflemen and dropped from other possible jobs. There is a slim chance that I may get to Alaska but we won't know our final destination until about

Thanksgiving when we are on board ship and out on the open sea. I have a wonderful chance of spending Christmas in Japan and New Years on the front.

I told Dad, but as yet have not said anything to Mom about my destination. Of course I don't really know myself—and don't really give a damn. I do feel sorry for some of the fellows. The internally stronger—for the most part—are married and are downhearted at leaving a wife and children behind. Most of the bachelors are farm boys who are already lost so far from home and are left even more hopeless by this turn of events. Since, as you know, I am neither simpleminded nor married (the two seem to go together don't they?) I am in one of the best positions. Our main war over there at this time of the year will be with the cold and by the time spring breaks we will be experienced in staying alive. All in all, this is part of what I enlisted for—to do my fighting while I was free and unattached. As you know I always expect the worst—though it seldom comes, it's easier not to be disappointed when it arrives. I am glad that I'm not going to Stoneman in Calif., as many are, for that is strictly Korea. Many of those going to Lawton expect Alaska or Okinawa and the islands (Hawaii, Philippines, etc.).

Our training has taken an interesting turn lately. We've had "rules of warfare" and "methods of escape as prisoners of war." Some of the methods of escape were most interesting, the most proven being simple things such as just sitting still in a secluded spot during a rest and allowing the others to march away. Jump out of the right side of a train because 9/10 people are right handed and a right handed man would have to lean completely out of a window to shoot at you, etc.

I'm going to try to hitchhike down to see Joe this weekend—if we get off on time. I would like to see him before I pull out. Getting up to see you will depend on the amount of time I have. In 10 days I won't be able to make it, but if I get more—which I hope to do—I will try to drive up there some night, spend the day, and then come back the next evening. You learn to take long hours in the Army. Most of us get along very well these days on four to five hours sleep a night and that way I would not spend too much time away from home.

Our barracks is very cheerful tonight—4 more days of basic training to go; Wed., Thurs., Fri., and Sat. till noon. If we're for-

tunate enough to get off at noon I'll head for Ponca City, otherwise
I guess I'll have to depend on letters from Joe, which I never get.

Well, maybe I'll see you in a week or two—

• • •

The assumption in the letter that I was being punished for dropping officer's training—Officer Candidate School—was conjecture
on my part but possibly true. Originally, I signed up for OCS thinking I might want a career in the military, but my basic training
experiences convinced me that I didn't. When I attempted to re-
sign, I was told that I had to write a letter explaining why. This
irritated me, so I wrote a letter saying that from what I could see
the army was best for immature individuals who needed someone
to tell them what to do, and that I was not such a person and had
no interest in becoming one. I was dropped without further ado,
but when I attempted to sign up for schools as a veterinarian's assistant or a mental health assistant, programs for which my biol-
ogy and teacher education majors at college had prepared me, I was
refused without comment. A fellow soldier, also with college credentials, received similar treatment on dropping OCS. I decided
the refusals were punishment.

The party mentioned in this letter was quite an affair. We were
all in a state of shock. Basic training had toughened us physically
and hardened us mentally, but deep in the recesses of our minds
the boys at summer camp continued to exist. We weren't ready
emotionally to assimilate orders to a combat zone. We did what
so many young men in the military do in such circumstances: we
went to town to get drunk, not as a cohesive unit, just as a couple
hundred individuals, all struggling with the same idea, avoiding
thoughts of possible consequences.

I was extremely fortunate. My companion of the evening was
Dave Dillon, who laughingly described himself as a professional
car thief from Detroit (as a civilian, he worked for a company that
repossessed cars). A tall, slightly stooped man with wide, sloping
shoulders, Dave was intelligent and had a ready sense of humor.
A nonsmoker, he enjoyed harassing disliked cadre with a request
to chew gum, a prohibited activity, during smoke breaks—cadre
tended to be upset by any question beyond the expected. He was
also a nondrinker, so I suspect he went along to take care of me,

which turned out well for me because I drank way too much that night. I remember Dave taking me back in a taxi after the American Legion closed, and I think we stopped once or twice for me to be sick.

When I returned from Korea I tried to find Dave to thank him and repay him the cab fare. But he had been discharged and I wasn't able to locate him.

About midnight someone alerted our despised captain that his company was in trouble in town. He, in turn, woke up a personal friend (another captain), the first sergeant, and every person who had stayed home. The two captains, using their own automobiles, drove a few sober fellows into town. The drunks were collected and lined up on park benches, and our underrated captain and his friend spent the night ferrying the souse-ees the eight or so miles from town to the fort. When they arrived at the barracks, a new crew collected watches and wallets, to be placed in the company safe, and tucked the sinners into the nearest beds. It was quite an operation.

The next morning I awoke in the wrong barracks, minus wallet and watch. When we were feeling better, which for most of us wasn't until Sunday evening, we collected our possessions and worried about the consequences of our Saturday night adventure in the coming week.

That sixteenth week was quite an easy week, a true letdown from the preceding fifteen. The only true dissonance occurred when we were to be paid. While standing in line to receive our seventy-five dollars, we were told that we'd have to sign a release permitting the army to deduct from our pay the cost of rebluing the rifles we'd been using. We had worn them shiny with constant, required cleaning. A few signed, but most refused, saying we couldn't be ordered to sign our names to a document. That was an illegal order. Eventually the matter was dropped and we were paid.

When we assembled on our final Saturday morning of basic training, not one of us expected to receive a weekend pass. Instead, our captain, who had suddenly grown in stature, quietly mentioned that he would really like to get a full night's sleep this Saturday. Then he said we would all get passes into town and turned us loose.

I hitchhiked down to my brother Joe's house. It took from noon until about three in the morning to cover the 200 miles from Ft. Riley to Ponca City, Oklahoma. I went to sleep as soon as I got there, figuring that I could worry later about how to get back to the base. I sincerely appreciated my brother driving me back following a too-brief visit of a few hours. I slept all the way.

3

HEADED FOR THE FRONT

The chute to Korea included five distinct phases: gathering at a port of debarkation, the ocean trip to Japan, processing in Japan, the trip to the war zone, and, finally, joining a specific unit. Constantly on the move, always a stranger in a strange land, we rapidly made and forgot new friends. As with most chutes, there were few exits. The majority of us were headed for the large opening at the predesignated end: combat.

Immediately following basic training, those selected for Korea received thirty-day leaves—a last opportunity to spend time with family before taking our next step toward that unknown world: war. During this time I attempted to earn extra money by substitute teaching, a lucrative effort for a soldier who made only seventy-five dollars a month, since substitute teachers in St. Louis were being paid twenty-five dollars a day. But I quit after a disastrous day with a kindergarten class. The money wasn't worth it. I doubt that I've ever been so embarrassed or humiliated as I was by thirty active five-year-old darlings. I would recall that catastrophe under other circumstances.

On my final day at home, Dad took off from work and rode the bus with me to Union Station in downtown St. Louis. We sat at the end of a row of chairs as I waited to board the train, he slumped next to me in the last chair, wearing his worn, chocolate-brown jacket and his old felt hat pulled down over his forehead. I remember that his gray pants needed pressing. His face was tired and serious. He said not a word during the hour or so we sat there. Now, as a father, I understand the silence of a man sending a son to war. His thoughts must have cruised, as I'm certain mine would, over the things he had put off and the love he hadn't voiced as often as he would have liked during the years of working and parenting—all measured against the question, Would the opportunity again exist?

The train ride through the west, from St. Louis to Seattle, was delightful, primarily because I sat next to an attractive young blonde, a woman enlisted in the air force, with me talking most of the way. I was the type who normally didn't appreciate until the next day what a date might be suggesting when it was time to say good night, so the young lady may have traveled in a bit more safety than she'd expected—or, perhaps, desired. When night fell and the lights were turned out, she mentioned that the train was cold. I hadn't noticed, but I got my coat out of my duffel bag for her.

Ft. Lawton was a relic of the past. Ancient, one-story, creosoted, frame buildings heated with potbellied oil stoves served as our barracks. A door in the center provided the only means of entrance or exit from the long, narrow buildings. When we arrived, we were told that if a building caught fire we were not to attempt to reach the door or save any possessions; instead, we were to leap out the nearest window.

We were issued passes to town and ordered to stay off a certain street—I've forgotten the name—because all the lumberjacks and whores hung out there. We were told that the military police routinely patrolled that street and anyone caught would have his pass confiscated and be hauled back to the fort.

That turned out to be true. We were picked up by the MPs, our passes were taken away, and we were returned to the orderly room. Following their departure, we were issued new passes and told to watch out for the MPs. The orderly on duty advised us not to get caught again because he was tired of writing new passes.

While walking down this street on another night, a friend and I saw three men head down an alley. We sensed adventure and decided to see where they were going. They arrived at a tall, unpainted, wood-shingled building and climbed a long series of rickety outside steps, entering through a second-story door with a beer sign over it. When we went through the same door we found ourselves in a small, well-lit room with a bar, four bar stools, and a heavily made-up woman bartender—she must have applied her cosmetics with a spatula. As she leaned on the bar, long, unkempt black hair fell about her shoulders. No one else was in the room. A dirty brown curtain hung in a doorway at the rear. My friend and

I looked at each other and, in silent communication, decided there were other places to see in Seattle. I still wonder where those men went, but I'm also glad we didn't go through that curtained back door.

The people of Seattle were truly friendly. When four companions and I were wandering along—same street but on another night—a friendly native asked if we'd like to meet some girls. A short while later he deposited us in a room, collected a twenty-dollar finder's fee from each of my friends (remembering the lectures on VD, I lost my nerve), and told us to wait until we were called—which, after about fifteen minutes—we finally figured out wasn't going to happen. Following our complaint, a police sergeant roundly damned the friendly native for failure to satisfy, assured my friends there wasn't a chance in the world they would ever see a penny of their money again, and suggested greater care in the future.

Not all my time in Seattle was spent on forbidden streets. My former psychology professor, Dr. Ira Young, had provided me with the name and telephone number of one of his brothers who lived in the city. I telephoned and was invited to a party where I spent a very pleasant afternoon and evening. I also met an attractive student named Roberta with whom I corresponded for some time before losing touch following one of our moves in Korea.

The grayness of Seattle surprised me. Fog and light rain were constants. I was at Ft. Lawton for three days before I realized that the downhill walk from our barracks to the mess hall gave us a view of the harbor. The fog had been so thick that we hadn't been able to see the ocean.

On the fifth day we were transferred to a nearby navy base. We were still sliding along the chute. Now, fences, gates, and guards restricted our freedom. Gone was the casual supervision that permitted us to roam Seattle at will. No more evening passes so we could do as we wished. We were in the pipeline to Korea, and we were there to stay. On the plus side, the navy base was much cleaner and the food was much better.

I didn't write many letters from Seattle because there was too much to do. The next time I wrote, I was at sea.

• • •

November 29, 1952

Dear Ethel:

The sea is a marvelous thing. Any man who writes and says he describes it is a liar. It is so vast and changing that to describe the sea as a whole would be like describing the unknown qualities of eternity. Yesterday, in the heart of a storm, it was a remorseless enemy, throwing about the ship until the men inside of it cowed in their bunks to forego its wrath. Tables, chairs and men were hurled from side to side as it sent its waves lashing across the decks and the ship plunged and rolled in the ebbs and swells of an angry sea.

Tonight, however, all is different. The sea, like a spoiled child, still mutters defiantly after having thrown her tantrum, but is generally calm. Lacy clouds hang in the sky while a full moon spins its magic over the night. The calm has penetrated the ship and everywhere men are to be found talking, reading, writing, playing cards, roaming the decks, or just lying on the gun turrets watching the sea and sky.

Many a person has left a movie dreaming of the play in which we are now acting. I admit that there is a lot of misery connected with it, but as long as we come back alive, the values gained will be infinitely more valuable than the losses we've suffered. If you remember, Kipling said, "Pity not! The Army gave freedom to a timid slave, in which freedom he did find strength of body, soul, and mind." There is more to that than meets the eye.

I've been thinking today of that little article on democracy on board ship you had me read that was in the Sat. Eve. Post. We had a somewhat similar incident today, of course we only have 2800 men and about 200 officers. The PX was open from 8:30 to 10:30 for officers and from 10:30 to 11:30 for the men. We believe in sharing all things in proportion. Of course, there is always someone like the old boy in wrinkled khakis who wandered through the mess hall today checking on the quality and quantity of the food (incidentally, both have been excellent all along). The beat up condition of his clothes and his slovenly military bearing would have given an MP fits—but I noticed that when he turned his head a certain way you could see a Maple Leaf on his collar. Of course where we're headed now we are running into combat officers more and more. As a group they're the finest type of men to work under. They very definitely have a different set of values than the spit and polish brass you find in the states. Of such steel, I think, was MacArthur made.

Well, I guess I'll go to sleep. Tomorrow is always another day and I like to be ready for it. If this letter reaches you when I think it will, a belated Merry Christmas and a happy New Year. This will have to serve as a Christmas card and present. I don't know where I will be Christmas Eve, but I have a good idea that I won't be caroling, which I will miss.

December 11, 1952

It is hard to say who is ahead in letters at the present time. This is the third letter I've written to you while I've sent Mom two, a post card and a map. None of these have been mailed yet since we're still at sea, but they will be.

The last few days storms have slowed us down and driven us off course, but we should reach Yokohama by the fifteenth. The fact that we're five days late gives us, I think, a better chance of being held over for Christmas in Japan. However, ten days would be a long time to be held over, so we might still spend Christmas on the front although now I consider this improbable. We still have pretty much to do before we reach there. We've been at sea 16 days now and have about four more to go. It will be a relief to sit down to a meal again. (On board we eat all of our meals standing up.) If I get a chance to go into town in Japan the first thing I'm going to do is get a thick steak and some French fries. After that I'll tend to the serious business of seeing the town and drinking beer. They claim Japanese beer is better tasting than American beer and about 2800 men on board are going to try and find out. It will also be nice just to stand up without having to hold on to anything to keep from being thrown from side to side.

Unfortunately, before I do anything in Japan I will have to get some money. It is our understanding that we will get a partial pay of $20 when we reach Yokohama. This will be most welcome. I have to replace my pocket knife, which was stolen, replenish my tobacco supply, get shoe polish, and visit a laundry. This will probably take about $6.

I'm also planning on increasing my allotment home as soon as possible and taking up some of the educational courses through the

Army Education program. I won't take any scholastic courses but will probably concentrate on agricultural or mechanical subjects.

You know Ethel, if it weren't for the folks I think I would get the devil out of school teaching and take up conservation. With the GI Bill it would be comparatively easy to do, that and the back log of savings I'll have. By the time I get out of the Army I should have close to two thousand saved. Of course I know just how Mom and Dad would react to the idea of my leaving St. Louis or on my launching on an entirely new program at the age of twenty four. Anyway, as you can see, I'm still very undecided on what I'll do when I return to St. Louis. I might stick with the schools and work towards the idea of teaching at Harris. Anyway, I have a year and a half to make up my mind on that score. And the next year should be very interesting.

Well, say hello to John, Little John, and Fritz for me. I will write again when I next get tired of my own laziness.

• • •

We boarded ship, the USNS *Gen. C. C. Ballou,* in the misty half-light of early morning. Gray Ladies passed out hot coffee as we walked past them. I don't know who they were, volunteers from what organization, but they were wonderfully thoughtful and pleasant. Their quiet gray uniforms blended with the fog, creating a scene more impressionistic than real. I suspect most of them had sons about our age. They were to be our last taste of home for a long time. For some of us, it would be forever.

The ship was not like those featured in Hollywood war movies— unless it's a comedy. Run by the merchant marine, it was rusty and dirty with peeling paint. Clean steel showed only where feet and hands had worn away the filth. Our bunks were deep in the hold, down several flights of a narrow, winding steel stairway. We lived and slept in compartments that did not permit a tall man to walk upright comfortably. Bunks were made of canvas, held taut by steel rods, and were stacked four high, eighteen inches apart. You couldn't sit up in one; there was only room to lie down.

Fortunately, I had a top bunk. I wasn't pleased with that, at first, because I knew that I would bump my head on the steel overhead if I moved incautiously. However, I was to learn its value within a day or two. The aisles between bunks didn't permit two people to pass without turning sideways. Only at the ends of the aisles was there room for five or six men to gather and play poker or simply stand and watch.

Each bunk came equipped with a flat, orange-colored, rubber life preserver. On each was printed, "To inflate pull string on gas cartridge," but there were no gas cartridges. They were all missing. It occurred to me that if the North Koreans had a submarine, they could have eliminated entire regiments one torpedo at a time. The finest of swimmers wouldn't have lasted long in those white-foamed seas, and there were no other ships around. Years later, at a meeting of the Outpost Harry Survivors' Association, I recalled this experience to others. They reported that the same lack of preparedness had existed on other transports.

At the time of boarding, we were issued meal ration cards. These were punched as we entered the mess hall, which was two or three flights below the lower deck, prior to each meal. Someone must have feared that people would try to stow away on a ship headed for a war zone in order to get a free meal. I had completely forgotten this until I found my card the other day while looking for something else. Only four or five meals were punched. Storms interrupted this absurd procedure, and it was never resumed.

A day or two out of port we ran into a violent storm. If the ship was dirty before, words cannot describe the filth and stench during and after the storm. I was glad to be in a top bunk. Seasick men vomited from their bunks, the spew cascading onto those in lower bunks. If not sick before, those men rapidly added their contributions. I would walk along the aisle by placing a foot on the outer rail of the bunks on each side, in order to straddle the flooded deck. Meeting someone coming from the opposite direction always resulted in a sort of intricate dance.

If the sleeping quarters were bad, the toilets were revolting. Urine, feces, and vomit rolled back and forth over the steel floor with every movement of the ship. This soup of slime formed a pool about two inches deep, held in place by the steel rim that surrounded the room. The only way to get to a toilet was to wade through it. While we could urinate over the side of the ship, we had to hope for constipation.

Unaffected by seasickness, I spent all possible time on deck. The enlisted men's deck was regularly swept by waves during the

storms, but climbing up to the off-limits, deserted officers' deck,
I found both quiet and clean air. I enjoyed standing there, braced
against the wind and the roll of the ship. Holding on to steel cables,
I'd watch waves smash over the lower deck. Once I saw a passing
oil tanker; its bow would plunge into a wave, completely disappearing into the blue-black ocean. Then, with a slow roll and shud-
der the bow would reappear as the stern vanished. I wondered each
time the ship plunged if it would survive. Standing there alone, I
marveled at the strength of the storm's force and the smallness of
man.

The first storm continued into Thanksgiving. Of the 2800 enlisted men on board, only 7 of us, scattered about the room, ate
Thanksgiving dinner, which was a masterpiece. I thought it rather
fun, bracing against the bolted-down tables and holding onto the
tray to keep it from sliding away—all while standing and eating.
For once, we had all we wanted to eat. My appetite dimmed, however, when a man a few tables away threw up onto his tray, the
vomit overflowing onto the table. I looked the other way and
finished my dinner with less enthusiasm than I'd begun it.

For the most part I enjoyed the trip, though it wasn't designed
for comfort. After the storms, details of soldiers cleaned the worst
of the filth and normal life resumed. The PX reopened on the same
schedule as before: two hours a day for 200 officers and one hour
a day for 2800 enlisted men. I was never successful in getting
through the door.

Another problem was personal cleanliness, because fresh water
was scarce. Showers were turned on only two hours a day—but
what time of day was not widely publicized to the enlisted men.
There was no laundry, so we learned to run ropes through sleeves
or trouser legs and drag our clothes through the ocean to wash
them. When they dried they were wrinkled and there were white
streaks of salt running through them, but at least they were clean.

I can't recall a single movie or performance of the type that
Hollywood portrays as a routine occurrence on board troop ships,
though there may have been church services. I don't know. If held,
they weren't widely publicized either. Mostly there was daydreaming, gambling, bragging, and lying.

The purpose of basic training was to teach us military skills,
toughen us physically and mentally, and give us a "group obedi-

ence" type of mentality. The sea voyage served to continue this indoctrination into "group think," of necessity if not of choice. I loved the ocean, but life on ship was another step away from the world of my youth. Cattle on their way to market don't require comfortable quarters. Nor do infantrymen headed for combat.

I became acquainted with a private from the Carolinas, I believe North Carolina, named Charley Brown. He was even younger and more innocent of the world than I was. A thoroughly nice human being, he was a farm boy with a girlfriend back home. His ambition was to return home, marry, and farm. His friendship enriched my days at sea.

On the whole, life on board ship was pleasant. The food was good, my sinuses—a chronic problem in St. Louis—didn't bother me, and the ocean was beautiful. I was intrigued by a flock of slender, long-winged birds that followed us across the Pacific, swooping down to pluck garbage from the waves as it was thrown from the ship. I spent hours standing at the stern of the ship watching them. As my letters indicate, I was young and romantic, and I hid with bravado my concern about an uncertain future in an army I barely knew.

Still, not all nights or emotions were comfortable. Many a late evening was spent leaning over the rail looking at the water swirling and sparkling with reflected moonlight in the wake of the ship, thinking that if I simply slid over the rail into the sea I would probably be spared a lot of pain and encounter the same result I thought awaited me in Korea. I believed I knew the end of my story: I expected to die in combat. If I jumped off the ship, death would simply come a few months, or perhaps weeks, earlier.

Almost a month after leaving Seattle our storm-battered ship arrived in Yokohama harbor. It was a cold, dim, blustery evening. Standing on deck I watched a small boat pull the antisubmarine net open. As we moved into the harbor the dark, cigar-shaped silhouette of a surfaced submarine glided past us, out through the dusk. Watching it move seaward, barely visible above the waves, I wondered where its goal, what its purpose. It was part of the same excitement, the same adventure, that gripped me.

4

THE FAR EAST

Japan revealed a new army to me. I began to appreciate the lure of military life to certain types of men and the dictionary meaning of the word "soldier" when used as an intransitive verb. Soldiers in Japan had evolved a luxurious lifestyle in a highly bureaucratic system. Small fees collected from the masses moving through, a dollar or less per person, enabled permanent cadre to hire Japanese to do much of their work. Japanese cooked, cleaned, and maintained the barracks. Not for soldiers permanently stationed in Japan the cleaning, painting, and digging portrayed by comic books and Hollywood movies; they had time, excessive time, and energy for leisure. Prior to the start of the Korean conflict, minimum effort was placed on training, maximum on the pursuit of pleasure. They were so comfortable, in fact, that when the fighting began our pampered soldiers were neither prepared nor equipped for war, so they died unnecessarily—by the thousands.

Still, by 1952 the tasks of arming and shipping men for combat were being efficiently conducted. Shots were administered; helmets, rifles, and bayonets were distributed; and weapons were test fired. Soldiers were received, processed, and continued in the pipeline. It was a short, efficient step from the ship that brought us from the States to the ship that carried us to Korea.

The voyage to Korea resumed my descent from civilization. My new ship, the USNS *Gen. John Pope,* was larger and more crowded than the *Ballou,* and the food was much worse.

In Korea, the last stop on the way to the front was a replacement depot. Gone were the amenities of Japan. No bars selling cold beer and soda pop, no PX, no legions of cleanly attired civilians maintaining spotless workplaces and serving excellent food. Instead, there were rows of benches in drafty, poorly heated tents where we sat while green-clad army privates punched out orders on old typewriters with cold-stiffened fingers. We washed in steel helmets placed outdoors in below zero temperatures. Unlike a roller coaster that slows as it reaches its destination, our downward plunge became more rapid as we neared the end. Ever faster we left the comforts and pleasantries of civilization.

• • •

December 13, 1952

To Mrs. J. W. Van Cleve:

From her slightly surprised brother. Here we were, comfortably loafing along the Pacific figuring to disembark in Yokohama the next day when bang! The boom was lowered. We were told to prepare to disembark.

At 8:00 P.M. we assembled on deck, at 9:00 we sat in a train waiting for it to start its 3 hour journey to Camp Drake. On the way we received our mail—I got three letters from you. . . .

After we got off the train, a dinky little thing, we climbed on buses and arrived at Camp Drake twenty minutes later. We spent until about 3:00 A.M. processing papers, getting shots and being paid $20. After this we received coffee and donuts and had a chance to send a cablegram home. I was going to try to send you one but I barely had time to send one to Mom.

We will be here in Camp Drake two or three days. Unfortunately we won't have a chance to get off base in this time but from what we can see, it is very interesting. The trees are different and the people are different. But I'll get a chance to see more of it later on. . . .

• • •

The sudden debarkation surprised us. We arrived in the evening and expected to spend the night on board ship, departing in the morning. It would have been the civilized—the civilian—thing to do. Instead, we were marshaled on deck with all our equipment for a roll call. We stood there, in a gentle mixture of rain and sleet, for more than an hour before debarking. We simply waited, neither comfortable nor uncomfortable, qualities of little concern to those in power.

I remember the train because of its size. We laughed and joked about the small seats, which were a tight fit for two Americans. Along with our gear, we occupied all available space. Some men stretched out in the overhead baggage racks for additional room and rest. The novelty and sense of adventure were so great that no concern for the future was apparent in anyone. Our reality was unformed, shapeless. We were still children playing games.

I don't recall the "in-processing" described in this letter. Perhaps the times mentioned will serve as an excuse for forgetting. Why we so often moved at night remains a mystery to me, unless it was to conceal from the Japanese people the number of Americans moving through their country. There was no apparent attempt to keep the information from the enemy.

• • •

December 13, 1952

Ethel:

It's been a pretty busy day. We will be here at least one more day, probably more. From here we will probably ship to Inch'on. This is a six day trip so you see there will be another interruption of about a week before I send out many more letters.

Today, besides four hours of classes on the military situation, we were issued our brand new M-1 rifles with nice new bayonets. Only the best for the Army. Tomorrow we will sight in our rifles on the range—in other words practice shooting and sighting so we know we will hit what we shoot at. Afterwards we will get interviews on allotments home, wills, etc. After that we will turn in our old clothes and draw complete new winter outfits. Then we will be ready to go. I should be settled by Christmas but for some reason the Christmas spirit hasn't moved me much this year. . . .

The food here at Drake is marvelous. We are definitely getting the best of everything. We even have chairs in the dining room. The PX here is rather small and limited. I couldn't even buy a pocket knife to replace the one stolen from me on board ship. However, the beer hall is another matter. It is about a city block long and about 200 feet wide and so busy that, although lined with tables, most of the men have to stand while drinking. It is the gathering place where you go to look up old friends in an extremely friendly atmosphere.

Tonight I received a letter from you, one from Dad (rare!) and a Christmas card from the Howards. Tomorrow I am going to try to get some souvenirs if I have enough money and send them home. One for you and John, and one for mom. If I can't get them now I will on my R&R period in four months.

• • •

I recall few specifics of the military situation classes, but I know we were taught that the Koreans in the south were strongly anti-Communist and that, if captured, we could depend on the support of the old people who were sympathetic to Americans and were anti-Communist. At the time it sounded good; certainly it told us what the army wanted us to believe. However, experience taught us that not all Koreans in the south were friendly. Books such as *The Pusan Perimeter* by Edwin P. Hoyt (Stein and Day, 1985) cast even more doubt on those lectures. I suspect that if the truth in those classes had been an ax, George Washington could not have chopped down a cherry tree with it.

The beer bar for the enlisted was huge, still crowded and smoke-filled when I first arrived sometime after three in the morning, following completion of my paperwork. Both ends of the bar were obscured by the masses of men and the haze from their cigarettes. Everyone who had been on the ship appeared to have headed for what had to be the longest bar in the world—it seemed to begin and end in infinity. There, momentarily, both past and future were forgotten. Shipboard acquaintances had a beer or soda pop together, drinks we hadn't seen in almost a month. This, and the fact that we'd been en route and in processing for several hours without an opportunity for a drink of any kind, made for a brisk business. Dozens of Japanese bartenders worked frantically, but the crowd at the bar, with its friendly pushing and shoving for service, was still two and three deep. I was thirsty and drank two beers so quickly I got the hiccups, which ended my socializing and drove me back to my barracks, much to the amusement of Charley Brown.

• • •

December 14, 1952

Dear Mom:

Today we finished processing. I increased my allotment home to $65 a month. This will become effective at the January pay—

January 30. Don't worry if you didn't get my allotment for November yet—it should come through about the same time the December pay comes in. Incidentally, how do my finances stand now? I figure about $275 in bonds—is that right?

Tonight I bought a Japanese picture. It cost $7.50. It should be home in about a month because I sent it airmail. If I had sent it parcel post it would have taken about 3 months. I like it very much—it is made of silk and is a mountain scene. When it comes, if you happen to go downtown, I wish you would check and see what a similar picture would cost, because if it's worth it, I'll get a couple more for us and a couple for Ethel and if Joe wants one, one for him. When I come back on R&R, I plan on spending about $100 on such things, including chinaware.

To go back to finances a moment—when my income tax stuff comes in send it on to me. I'll fill it out and send it in from here. I should get money back this year.

Tonight I found a scale and weighed myself at 158 pounds, so you see I've gained about ten pounds since I left home. I knew I'd be gaining weight with this good food and lack of exercise.

Another thing I forgot—this picture will have to be framed. Take the money out of my allotment. First, if you like it, it's yours, if Ethel wants it and you don't care, she can have it, but I would rather that you just collect all of the stuff and when I come home we'll split it up between us. Nothing goes to Joe unless I specify it to him. I will send something home eventually for Joe and C.A., but I don't make much money and where I can spend on Ethel and write it off as thanks for her letters, I can't to Joe. C.A. has written me once in the Army, Joe never. . . .

I told you I would appreciate socks. . . . Please take this out of my allotment, these little items add up I know.

Well, it's getting pretty late and your son is tired (or lazy) so I guess I'll sign off on this. If you don't hear from me for about a week don't worry about it—it just means that I'm on board ship. Well, a fellow's going to mail these, so I'll finish right now. It will save me about a three block walk.

• • •

It's difficult to write a letter that won't worry a mother or father when you're spending your days getting ready to go into combat.

Consequently, you discuss matters of small concern in great detail. This also serves to distract your attention from your own uncontrollable future. Notice the temporary pique toward my brother, Joe, and his wife, Clara Ann. Mail was terribly important, and you weren't happy with family who didn't send it—and send it often. Who cares if your brother was working twelve hours a day as a young engineer—he still should have taken the time to write to me!

I sent a maximum allotment home as our necessities were free and luxuries were inexpensive. For example, cigarettes were ten cents a pack in Japan. After we entered combat they were free.

• • •

December 14, 1952

Dear Ethel:

I want to write this because I don't know how much longer I will get so much time to write letters. The difficulty is that I have nothing to write about. In my last few letters I have given a blow by blow description, but so far today, there have been no blows. This morning we did go out and fire our rifles in order to get our battle sights, but since then we have done absolutely nothing. It looks as if we will not finish processing until tomorrow. That will be Monday. In this camp everything operates on a 24 hour day and a seven day week—including barber shop, beer hall, construction work, etc.,

The barracks we are living in was once part of a military academy and then part of the Japanese Imperial Army. It is a very big building. The patio is almost a block long and about 150 feet wide.

Here at Drake you can still see a very few signs of the war with Japan. There are several condemned buildings which were treated rather poorly during bombing raids. While the debris has been cleaned away, the holes remain as mute testimony of the efficiency of our air force.

The Japanese are, in general, like all people with whom the Americans come in contact. A great many are friendly, some are hard working who will give a favor as readily as they will ask one, perhaps quicker, some rather obviously don't like us (and considering the conduct of many of our soldiers, I'm inclined to agree with them in part) and a great many regard us as suckers ripe for the plucking—which is also quite true.

Christmas draws closer. . . .

• • •

Not mentioned in my letters were my continuing opportunities to exit the pipeline by admitting my ability to type. Men who could type were in short supply, and at every stop there was a request for anyone who could type to step forward. Those who could normally exited the pipeline at that point. I considered it the better part of valor not to let the people at home know of these bypassed opportunities.

During orientation, we were informed that every four months we would receive a trip to Japan for five days of rest and relaxation, to enable us to better endure the rigors of Korea. Reality differed. I received my first and only R&R some eight months after my arrival. I had friends who served longer than four months and were killed before they got to take their R&R. In fact, it was a sore point for those of us up front. We were firmly convinced that soldiers living comparatively luxurious lives in the rear areas received these trips regularly, while we received them only if our presence was not immediately necessary.

• • •

December 15, 1952

Dear Ethel:

Here it is—Monday morning—and we are waiting around for inspections of the barracks and our orders. A few of our boys received their orders last night and left this morning at 5:00. About 100 more were just placed on orders. I am expecting mine sometime today or tomorrow. . . .

We just received instructions to fall out with a pencil and paper to receive our orders. I hope we don't leave too quickly, I have clothes in the laundry and they won't be open for a couple of hours yet. All of my handkerchiefs, most of my shorts, T-shirts, and towels are in there.

Getting back to the subject of Japan for a moment. Around here it is very flat. So much so that they had to dig down for their firing range so that the bullets wouldn't hit anything.

I am going to join the 3rd Division. It is at the present in the Punch bowl area around Old Baldy. I expect to leave tomorrow morning or late this evening, but it could very easily be this afternoon. We will sail to Inch'on and from there be routed to our various outfits. If it's later this evening, we'll probably get mail call before we leave. I expect to have time to write on board ship but, sister mine, after that don't expect too much in the way of mail from me. I'm a rifleman going to an infantry division that is on the line so—you know as much as I do about how much free time I'll have. . . .

December 16, 1952

We still haven't shipped out. We turned in all of our bedding and were supposed to leave yesterday but last night we got 2 blankets back to sleep under. It is now 7:00 in the morning and we just had a very good breakfast. Pancakes, eggs, bacon, cereal, and all the milk or coffee we could drink.

The principle occupation these days is pulling stupid little work details, cleaning up rifles, and dodging other work details. At night we are free to go to the show, the PX, the beer hall and other barracks. That isn't much freedom, but what there is of it is used to the utmost.

I imagine that when you get this Johnny will be about through raising his Christmas hell. As I remember, children can be rather messy around that time of the year.

I really have no idea of how long it takes mail to get to the States from here. If the airmail packages are any criterion for judgment, this letter will probably get there in time for Easter, or your birthday if it hustles. I have, however, a great faith in Army mail. I don't believe they lose more than 99 out of every hundred letters. . . .

December 17, 1952

We are told that we will leave this evening at 5:00. Perhaps this is a good thing for our boys are getting very wise. As you know we are restricted to the camp at all times. The camp has a fence around it and is patrolled by Japanese guards. Since we've been here the guard has been doubled. Every night crowds of men go down, wait for the guard to turn his back, climb the fence, and take off. About half of these are caught and returned to the company. Their main punishment is being caught. The rest enjoy themselves for the evening and then sneak back in. I haven't been playing this game myself because I can't reach the parts of the city I want to see and also because I am about broke.

Yesterday we received all of our winter clothing and field equipment. Carrying all of it I can hardly walk a city block. I also used some of my money to get another pocketknife and this paper. It seems that I ran out.

Today is another gray day. Yesterday it rained steadily all day and far into the night. Today it seems to be trying to repeat yesterday's performance. The streets are a quagmire of mud and the lawns where most people are walking now aren't much better. The grass is wearing out fast.

The radio, right now, is playing what is called "RA music." In other words, military calls. One of the country's shining lights brought a portable radio along with him and of course in our present location we get all of the Tokyo and Yokohama stations. As a result we get a lot of music but as I said yesterday, surprisingly little Christmas music. In fact, I haven't heard any at all.

On the side of mail, it takes 11 days for a letter to reach me here in Camp Drake. Incidentally, the first two days we got all kinds of mail, but since then we've only had about 20 letters a night come to our company, where close to 1000 men live. Someone is fouling up, not just casually, but by the numbers. The discussions about the matter are long and bitter. . . .

• • •

Poverty is the parent of virtue: my reason for not going over the fence was not enough money to buy anything when I got there!

"RA" was an insult. Soldiers whose serial numbers began with "RA" were "regular army," meaning they had joined voluntarily and often intended a career in the military. Serial numbers for draftees began with "US." Early in World War II there were violent fights between the two groups as the regular army men used their superior status and knowledge of army procedures to their own advantage during duty hours, the drafted soldiers (US) responding with off-duty violence. This forced changes in uniforms to avoid the easy recognition of RAs by US troops. Even though I was an RA, I was one of many during this time who had enlisted only for the period necessary to serve in the Korean War. In truth,

I shared the low opinion of the regular army that was held by the draftees.

I had forgotten about all the clothing mentioned in the letter. In combat, we had only the clothing on our backs. So somewhere we turned in all the clothing that was issued to us in Japan. It may have been at the replacement depot, or it may have been at the company supply. On consideration, giving it to us was a stroke of genius. How do you get replacement clothing of the right size to a combat area? You have the men going there carry it. That way you should have the right amount and the right sizes—at least in theory.

Mail was a continuing problem. We suspected that lazy, malignant RA types were sabotaging our one contact with a civilized and decent world. We also cursed family and friends who hadn't written. The sabotage idea was, of course, never true in the sense we felt it. I remain convinced, however, that bureaucratic incompetence and the indifference of many mail clerks in the rear areas contributed to our problems.

The lack of Christmas music might have been deliberate. Why awaken nostalgia in young men who have no opportunity of returning home in the near future? Why play music that has a theme of love, forgiveness, and peace to men going into combat?

• • •

December 18, 1952

Dear Ethel:

I am sailing on board the USNS Gen. John Pope. It is a very large ship—far bigger than the Ballou. We boarded last night and I was so fortunate as to draw K.P. [kitchen police] today. For once, KP has been a pleasure. Immediately after a terrible breakfast we found a whole pan of muffins in the kitchen, so each of us had four or five muffins. Later we swiped five chocolate cream pies that had been baked for the officers and, following the pies, we ran across some cake. Your ever watchful brother then discovered some hot sweet rolls and had himself three choice pork sandwiches. Since I've been on board I seem to have lost my appetite—I didn't eat any dinner.

I'm finally off K.P.—praise the Lord and let me sleep tomorrow. After KP I went up on deck for a while for a smoke before returning to write the rest of this letter. From the lights in the distance it is easy to tell that we are still following the shore but are we speeding along. The ship is not only twice as big as the Ballou, it is also twice as fast.

This afternoon I went up on deck for a couple of hours. After we got past the anti-sub net, we ran into the fishing boats. Close to the shore (That is to say just a few miles out) we passed dozens of ships that looked like the "Chinese junks" of old movies. Low, canoe-like boats with one large square sail.

As we got out further the sails disappeared and motors replaced them, but the low, canoe form, continued. At the present, we are in the sea of Japan.

I won't brag about seeing Tokyo until I get a chance to see more of it than you can from the window of a train. That will be when I get back to Japan on my rest and relaxation period in May.

Incidentally, don't tell Mom that I said I would be on the front. I told her that the 3rd is acting as a supporting division to a ROK [Republic of Korea] division. There are three American divisions actually engaged at the present time. They are the 2nd, 3rd, and the 25th infantry divisions. The 25th, which has been in a long time (the third American division in Korea), is due to go back to Japan as a unit sometime in the future. The outfit which has spent the next greatest amount of time in Korea is the 3rd.

The nice thing about this Korean business is the pay. Besides my base pay of $82, I get $8 a month overseas pay and $45 a month fox hole pay. As it is I'm having $65 a month sent home automatically and intend to save as much of the rest as I can (probably all of it) for a fling in Tokyo on my R&R. I can dispose of about $150 without leaving the PX in Camp Drake and then when you add on five days and nights of luxurious living. Sis, there's no doubt about it. I have to start saving my money. I want to have about $250 for that five days and I'm going to spend every cent of it. I'm going to spend about a hundred in the PX and then after I mail it, go live in the fanciest hotel in Tokyo, one with hot water and room service deluxe. I will eat the finest and most expensive food three or four meals a day and smoke good cigars. During the day I'll tour the town and at night I'll hit the nightclubs.

Of course you realize that only an idiot would do such a thing, but it's still fun to dream. If you're worried about a birthday present for me, I have a suggestion. Some nickel Muriel cigars would be nice. I don't like the big cigars, but I'm an all out addict of the nickel (small) Muriel—which can't be had for love or money over here. . . .

• • •

How innocent we were. Talking of what we would do, believing that we would receive those trips every four months, as promised. Concentrating on such simple, familiar things as money or food. With these, we occupied our minds. All the while we sharpened bayonets, checked, cleaned, and rechecked rifles, and never ever mentioned the immediate future. The atmosphere was somber, our futures clouded and threatening.

I was still traveling with Charley Brown. We had established a firm friendship and both of us were pleased with the knowledge that we were not only on the same ship but were also headed for the Third Division. We were on KP together on the day I wrote that letter. Our job was to keep four tubs, used to cook such items as oats and potatoes, clean—spotlessly and shiningly clean. While not cause for overwork, it wasn't as easy as the average housekeeper might imagine. We could stand up in each of those tubs—and we had to crawl inside them to scrub them properly.

I see my pay had been increased. It was an automatic promotion from rank E1 to E2 following basic training.

• • •

December 20, 1952

Dear Ethel:

Today we are in the Yellow sea. Tomorrow we should be at Inch'on, Korea. . . . It has been very windy, cloudy, and stormy looking all morning but now it is beginning to clear up and at the present moment the sun is out. While it is getting colder, it is still not very cold out. Since we're still on a fairly warm ocean this is easily explainable.

The lice who are running this ship put a Christmas tree up in the mess hall. Usually it's easy enough to forget how close it is to Christmas, but with that tree sitting there you remember it at every meal—three times a day. We'll only be on board this tub for another day and then this taste of Christmas will be over. I don't imagine we'll get much more this year.

I'll be glad when the first of the year starts—by that time I'll be finished with all of this moving around—for a few months at least. It shouldn't be rough while I'm over there. There won't be much fighting during the winter, then the rainy season in July and August, and then I'll be getting ready to pull out. So long as no one starts a spring offensive, all will be well.

I managed to buy a couple of candy bars from a reluctant friend so I'm not quite so hungry now. The eggs that we get for breakfast have been kept in storage about two years too long, and as a result the taste is sort of over powering. Maybe I'll be able to eat them someday, but I certainly can't yet . . .

It is now 5:00 P.M. and on the right we can see the snow covered mountains of Korea. Official word has come down that we will unload tomorrow beginning at 10:00 A.M. on to LSTs which will transport us to shore. There will be trucks waiting to transport us to our replacement companies. Our reception promises to be rather cool—it is 15 degrees below 0 in Inch'on at the present time. I'll take a hot shower tonight and make it a long one because I think it will be my last for about four months. . . .

December 21, 1952

We are now at Inch'on Harbor surrounded by a dozen ships as large as ourselves, but there are none of the small fishing craft that we saw in Japan and along the coasts of southern Korea. To the east and north are unbelievably craggy mountains, not in the slightest bit rounded as are the Missouri hills. They are completely barren and snow covered. The many islands that surround us are nothing but huge, jagged rocks tossed helter skelter in the sea and liberally covered with snow.

As far as the sea itself, it is easy to see how it got its name. It is a murky, muddy yellow, the water looks more like the Mississippi river water than like the ocean.

Ethel, I just learned that we have a fourteen hour train ride to the Third division. Unfortunately the train won't be heated, mainly because there are no windows in it. Too bad it isn't summer.

In the last two months I've crossed the northwestern states, seen Portland and Seattle, sailed the Pacific, been in Tokyo and Yokohama, sailed the Sea of Japan and the Yellow Sea and now I'm in Inch'on. Quite a trip.

• • •

The ship was crowded and dirty, the American equivalent of the cattle cars the Germans used to send their infantry to the front in World War II. The mood of the soldiers was serious: a great many men spent hours sharpening their bayonets and checking their rifles. There was little conversation about that. The food was poor. To be selected for KP was a distinct pleasure. It enabled me to steal food prepared for the officers' mess, which received much better food than the enlisted men's mess. I joke about it in the letter, but we resented the great discrepancy.

Debarkation at Inch'on was made an unnecessary hardship. Because of the lack of port facilities and the presence of approximately a mile of mud flats, we had to wait until high tide; then we unloaded from the ship onto landing craft that took us across the shallows to the shore. High tide was not until evening, but we were assembled on deck in the morning in subzero cold, the temperatures announced during the ship's newscast. The captain of the ship knew the tides, so he must have informed the commander of the troops of the wait. What was the logic? Why have us on deck in formation for more than eight hours other than for the convenience of the leadership?

Shortly after we boarded the train at Inch'on, men rushed through the cars warning us to make no noise and light no cigarettes. Even though our air force dominated the skies, an enemy aircraft was circling the area. It was assumed the Communists knew of our landing and were hunting us. This went on for some time. It certainly wasn't two hours, but it seemed like it as we waited in the bitter cold and the dark in our unheated train, whose windows had had all the glass blown or knocked out.

Cans of C rations were passed out as we waited. I received a cold can of wieners and beans. There were no spoons, so once we got the cans opened with our knives we ate as best we could. I cut my tongue trying to lick the last delicious bite out of the can. It was my first meal in about twelve hours.

I learned two things during that wait. First, a love of wieners and beans. Second, the belief that you don't really need a lot of airplanes or to control the sky to wreak havoc with schedules or lives. You only need one plane in the right place at the right time.

• • •

December 22, 1952

Ethel:

At present I am sitting in a tent in some base just northeast of Seoul. The tent is large, unlighted, and drafty, housing 18 men. Outside there is snow on the ground, a cold wind, a multitude of mountains, and incessant air traffic overhead. In the last half hour that I've been listening to it there has not been one moment when I could not hear one or more planes overhead. I think they are rather angry—their hive has been attacked two nights in a row— last night and the night before.

But let's go back to the beginning. I left you in the last chapter on the Yellow sea. We ate dinner yesterday at 9:30 A.M. We had already anchored and were waiting to disembark. After a slight period of waiting in line (formed at 10:00 A.M.) we began to disembark at 6:00 P.M. . . .

• • •

I'm not certain where the replacement depot was, but it may have been near what is now Uijongbu. It was late when we arrived, and, along with many others, I searched through the darkness for the urinals. In basic training we were taught that field urinals were pipes driven into the ground. All of us were relieved when we found a row of these. The next morning, when I walked out of my tent, I saw a long line of pipes, each with a helmet on top, and a large sign overhead that read, "This is not a urinal. It is a wash basin." I don't believe I washed my face or hands during the few days we were at the replacement depot.

In the early morning hours of that first night, we heard the pounding and grunting of the Korean guards beating someone. A period of silence was followed by rifle fire in a nearby village. Looking back on the incident, with the perspective of experience, I suspect an infiltrator had been caught who, following persuasion, had given the location of his friends. The veteran's joke about pliers being the Koreans' lie detectors reflected a reality we believed more than a true joke. We quickly learned to have no sympathy for the North Koreans. They brought a viciousness to war that was unmatched by the Chinese. War is always brutal, and civil wars are the worst. In Korea, it was a serious mistake to be captured by the other side.

• • •

December 23, 1952

Dear Ethel:

Am going to radio school. We'll be there 6 weeks—write from there.

December 24, 1952

As you can probably tell I've fallen into my first real break since I've been in the Army. To begin with I'm in the 15th which at present time is back of the lines on rest. So I'm about 10 miles back of the front. Second, I've been assigned to Head Quarters Co., which takes care of the Regimental HQ and never gets too close to the front and in the third place, in about two days, I leave here to go to the NCO [noncommissioned officer] academy for radio operators at the end of which I'll come back here.

There is only one hitch. Since I'm not on the front as a rifleman, I won't get as many points and I'll probably be here a year or a little more. But it has its compensations as you can see from the first paragraph.

Yesterday we had a very interesting time, if it wasn't highly enjoyable. We got on the train about 12:00 and spent 6 hours on it going to the railroad head where we got off at 6:00 P.M. There we sat waiting for trucks to move us to our various outfits. We waited until 8:30 when they finally arrived. Incidentally, it gets a little cool sitting around at night in Korea.

Then we loaded on the trucks and the fun began. The truck which brought me and 10 others to HQ was the last one and had several gaping holes in the floor. The truck was open, not closed. We took off at comparatively high speed over the roughest roads you could imagine through the mountains. We had 30 miles to go to get to the regiment. Within 30 minutes, one helmet was lost over the side of the truck. In another 30 minutes, a duffel bag was seen sliding off of the trailer and in replacing it we found that we had lost four duffel bags fully loaded with clothes, blankets, etc. We finally gave these up for lost and moved on. Finally, we were stopped by a sentry who asked the traditional: "Halt, who is there?" He got various answers such as "an airplane," "One truck and 10 Chinese spies," "A horse cart, you damned fool," etc. On asking, we found ourselves in H Company. Then we found out that our driver didn't know where we were to go, nor where HQ was. After finding and stopping at three more companies, we called up and found out that HQ didn't know we were coming and didn't know what to do with us. At 12:30, four hours after we started, we were shuttled to a service company to spend the night. This morning we got to HQ without any more trouble.

The land through which we passed is terribly torn by war. Every house is filled with shell and bullet holes. All men are in uniform and carrying loaded arms. Even the rice paddies have armed guards watching them.

Many of the old, substantial, stone and mud brick homes have been so devastated as to be untenable and most people now live in straw thatch huts. A few frame dwellings persist, but very few. Even the forest lands have been torn up by the seesaw fighting and about all that is left is the mountains themselves. . . .

To stay on the subject of Christmas for a second, several pine trees have been cut in the hills and been brought down and decorated in front of the various platoons. Tomorrow we will have services and a full turkey dinner.

• • •

In the morning, an officer made the usual plea for anyone who could type, which I again ignored. Soon after that we received our final destinations. I still have my orders for radio school. Only seven of us are listed on them: James F. Gay, Douglas H. Glascoe, Robert E. Maltby, John C. Weber, Charles P. Brown, Joe C. Freeman, and me. There must have been four others going elsewhere. That would account for my letter claiming eleven men in the truck.

I don't recall the second train ride from the replacement depot; in fact, I'd forgotten its existence until reading the letter. Nor did I recall the truck ride until reading the letter, when vague memories returned. But the wait between the train and the truck at the end of the rail line is engraved in my memory. We sat in the snow in subzero winter darkness, soldiers somewhere near the front, with rifles in hand but no ammunition, not another human or building in sight, waiting for someone, anyone, to give us direction.

For the most part we didn't know one another, Charley and I being the exceptions, so there was little talk. Just several isolated beings, each with his own thoughts, waiting, we knew not where, in an unknown land. Jim Gay got frostbite that night that was to cause him pain in the months to come.

The truck driver was in no hurry to come to where we were, but once he arrived he was in quite a hurry to get us where we were going and be rid of us. If we suffered a little bit as a consequence, that wasn't his problem.

When a soldier left Korea depended on the points he earned, not how long he was in the country. We earned four points each month for being in combat, three for being in a rear area—not that three-point areas were terribly safe. My friend John Weber, mentioned in the orders, was in the three-point area of regimental headquarters when he was wounded by enemy shell fire. We received two points in a safer area and one when way back in the rear. Thirty-six points meant a return to the United States. It was possible to go home in nine months if you had, and survived, nine straight months of combat.

Incidentally, don't fault us, or think us stupid, for not knowing exactly where we were. Pretend you're in a strange land, with every landmark blasted away and every street sign or village sign destroyed. If, by some miracle, any signs exist, they would be in an alphabet you couldn't read and a language you didn't understand. In addition, you'd travel only at night without lights, any lights. Under those circumstances, would you know your location? It's no criticism of infantrymen to say they often don't know their locations, just a recognition of reality. They have more important things to think about—such as staying alive and eating. I know.

We finally arrived at the Headquarters Company on Christmas Eve morning, all of us being assigned to the antitank platoon until we could be sent to our schools. Charley and Joe were taking a switchboard and message center course; the rest of us went to radio school.

Before leading us to the mess hall for our first meal at our new home, the platoon sergeant gave us a short pep talk. I stalled to get to the rear of the group following the speech and ran into Jim Gay. Jim looked at me and said, "That is one stupid son of a bitch!" From that moment on, with that common understanding, Jim and I were close friends, friends throughout our stay in Korea and into our return to the States. Friends still, should we meet again.

Later, when my parents had the St. Louis *Post-Dispatch* mailed to me, we were amused to read of the spirited American troops vigilantly guarding the front lines on Christmas Eve. So far as we could tell, Christmas was freely celebrated with alcohol. I remember saying that the only reason the Chinese couldn't have reached Seoul that day was because too many people would have offered them drinks along the way. Of course, I wasn't on the line, but neither was I too far back.

Arising the next morning, Christmas morning, I walked outside the bunker in time to see a shell explode in a cloud of smoke and debris about three hundred yards away. Perhaps we weren't as far behind the lines as I thought. At the time I was really impressed, but, as I later realized, the Chinese were just wishing us good morning and Merry Christmas. They weren't being serious. I would learn about serious later.

5

RADIO SCHOOL

Thirty-one of us were chosen to attend radio school from among the hundreds passing through the replacement depot. Why us? I don't know. We were to learn to operate radios in six weeks. We were told this took sixteen weeks in the States.

We'd been preparing to enter combat. Four months of progressively more difficult training, moving from place to place, always closer to where many would die—some slowly, some quickly—and others would be wounded. Pain and difficulty faced us at the very least. We knew this. We weren't fools. We were as emotionally prepared for such a future as possible, short of experience in combat itself. Then, suddenly, we few were selected for a six-week reprieve. It was common knowledge that radiomen lived safer lives. The result was a tremendous release from tension, a tension that had built up so gradually that we'd had little awareness of it.

We were glad to be studying to be radiomen and we worked hard to succeed at learning Morse code and learning to operate the radios. We spent much less time trying to be soldiers. This created a problem, but not for us. The letters will explain. There are a lot of them, since the radio hut was closed in the evening, leaving plenty of time to write. Daytime power shortages and equipment failures further increased our free time.

To appreciate the incidents reported, you need to know our situation. I didn't, and still don't, know where we were in Korea. Somewhere well behind the lines but north of the Thirty-eighth Parallel and on the shores of a large, manmade lake that was completely covered with ice. It was a school for noncommissioned officers where enthusiastic young enlisted men were drilling, learning to be leaders. Those men wanted to be good soldiers, to have a career in the army.

Those of us in radio school were young and enthusiastic, but not about the army. In fact, everyone in my tent was either a graduate of a military academy, a dropout from Officer Candidate School, or both. None of us had any interest in a military career or even in being proper, parade-ground soldiers. This posed the root problem for those who wished us to be like the NCO trainees.

Official awareness of our shortcomings as soldiers was intensified by our highly visible location within the camp. We were in two tents that stuck out like a sore thumb onto the parade field, right next to the NCO school's C Company and directly across a mud street from the mess hall.

• • •

December 29, 1952

Dear Ethel:

I guess I will practice my printing on you. From now on all of our work will be done in this type print, so I might as well build up some speed in it. As you can see I lost my pen somewhere in my travels.

Today, some of our men received mail for the first time. . . .

December 30, 1952

It doesn't look as if I'll ever get this letter mailed. No mail today because our APO [Army Post Office] moved, probably none tomorrow for the same reason. We won't get mail on New Year's Day, so it will be the first of the year before I get any mail.

School goes merrily along with eight hours of Morse code a day. It gets very boring.

This New Year's Eve promises to be very sober in contrast to Christmas Eve. Not only is no beer or liquor sold or allowed around this school, but we don't have any money to bribe our way back to our outfits where we can get some. No herring and no drinks, I'll probably go to bed about 8:30 and wake up in 1953. Days don't mean much over here—it's just another working day.

In this particular school we have a bunch of sharp boys. There are 31 of us. Mostly college and ex OCS (Officer Training School)

boys who strayed. The result is we have a lot of fun. We do our
work quickly, avoid a lot more even quicker, harass the officers of
the nearby NCO school with our sloppiness and cheat our way into
the front of the chow line as regularly as we can. Our ways are not
making us too popular with the rest of the school. Today a company commander told us that we were to eat after his company, not
ahead of them, and asked if there were any questions. Everyone
said they understood so he dismissed us. Immediately 31 men
bolted into their tents, grabbed their mess kits, and dashed for the
chow line. His Sergeant saw us and made us go back. So we immediately formed a platoon and started to march over. This time, the
Lieutenant stopped us. In one last desperate attempt, we went over
and called out his company—telling them to fall in behind us—
which they did. We immediately headed for the mess hall. Once
again the Lieutenant saw us and started over, but he evidently got
discouraged because about half way he turned around and went
back. Such is life. . . .

• • •

We radio students were not quite as selfish as it might seem.
There were only thirty-one of us, whereas there were several hundred in the NCO school. We had one hour, no more and prefer-
ably less, to leave our radios, eat, and return. If we were first in line,
we had no problem. Otherwise, the time spent standing in line
meant we lost practice time, which everyone considered important, or food, which *we* considered important. We found that by
leaving class a few minutes early, we could eat and be back at work
in about forty-five minutes. Otherwise, if we were at the end of the
line, we barely had time to eat. We worked at being first.

Not mentioned was the extreme cold. It was during this time
that I learned how to sleep when it was truly frigid outside. During the day I was always cold. It was comforting to crawl into my
Arctic bag completely dressed. This meant wearing woolen long
underwear (army issue), my woolen sweater, my woolen shirt and
pants, and my fatigue jacket. In the morning, however, as a result
of perspiring slightly during the night, I just about froze when I got
out of my sleeping bag. I soon learned to strip to my long underwear and socks and tuck my woolen shirt and pants inside the bag
with me so they would be warm and dry in the morning. I would

then slip the fatigues between the sleeping bag and the canvas of the cot to keep them dry. On colder nights I also plugged the hole in the bag with my woolen sweater, curled up in my sleep like a larva in a cocoon. This way I was as warm as I could be—which didn't mean that I wasn't still cold. On particularly bitter nights, I wore my sweater and used a towel to plug the air hole. Mind you, this was in a tent with the stoves going.

• • •

January 1, 1953

Dear Ethel:

Here in the tent the boys are whiling away their free time with the inevitable pinochle and rummy games. They go on during all free time and will probably last as long as the Army lasts.

I took quite a few pictures today but won't have a chance to get them developed until I get back to my outfit. . . . They have an unauthorized photography shop set up and develop pictures for nothing. Here we can buy film but can't get them developed. Up there we can get them developed, but can't buy film. . . .

January 3, 1953

At present I am seated in a class for Morse code and the blasted stuff is rattling off in my ear. Since this is the sixth hour of Morse code today I'm rather sick of the stuff. I thought you might be interested in some of the things that have been going on—extra curricular so to speak.

We have adopted a motto for our tent. "A good GI never gets taken." In line with this—as I previously mentioned—we are always first for chow. We also have an overabundant supply of oil for our tent. The main problem has been where to hide the extra can. We fill it with oil we steal from various sources after dark. The other morning when I inadvertently put my foot through a plank in the floor the answer was found. We cut out a couple of more planks, stole some lumber and built a trapdoor. We now have our oil under the tent. Also in the line of unauthorized tent renovation we borrowed a lighting fixture from an unoccupied officers' tent and cut it in on the electric line that runs through the tent. We have a string hitched on it so that we can pull it up out of sight during the day. As soon as we can pick up a light bulb, we'll have two lights instead of one. At the present time, we're working on the acquisition of a light bulb and a method for turning on the stove without getting up in the morning. We are also discussing methods of acquiring 45s and getting them home. Our tent, I might add, works as a unit with a precision which is a thing of beauty.

I am enjoying my stay here in Korea very much so far. I can easily see why men prefer duty overseas to duty in the States. We actually run ourselves. We've only seen our Lieutenant a couple of times. Once at the start, again a couple of hours later when he told us not to let anyone push us around and to take orders only from the Sergeant and himself (we never see the Sergeant), and today when he walked in the classroom. All he said today was, "Is it always this cold in here?" When we said, "Yes," he turned around and left. Now we have another stove. The Lieutenant in charge of C Company has given up in his try to reform the signal school. All he does now is snarl when he sees us. This morning he did tell the fire guard to wake us up at 5:00 but when we threw boots at the fire guard he left us in peace.

New Year's Day Jim Gay and I set off to climb the mountain to the west of us. It is the highest around here and has an intriguing point on it. After we started out, we found it to be farther away than we thought. In fact, between the camp and it there are two ridges and three valleys. We got to the top of the second ridge but had to come back because of lack of time. We are going to climb it next Sunday but we'll start out in the morning and pack a lunch. As it was, the second ridge was very interesting and we poked around up there for quite a while. The ridge told quite a story. There were many shallow G.I. fox holes dug there. The G.I.s were moving through fast as was evident from the poor holes. On the other hand there were quite a few Chinese bunkers down the ridge from them. These bunkers were beautifully dug in. In fact several times we'd be walking across the top of them without realizing it. They were usually about seven feet deep, dug through granite weathering. They had open gun pits with long covered tunnels leading into underground rooms.

As I mentioned before supper, the signal school never gets cheated. At supper our portions were rather meager. During the middle of chow—while we were relaxing over cigarettes—the lights went out. Immediately 32 men from the signal school busted back into the chow lines. They passed out candles for us to see by as we ate. Later, as we walked out, back to unlighted tents, there were many bitter complaints about the lack of food and light, but not from the signal school. We all had two official dinners and had all but two of the candles in our pockets.

We just had mail call and I got two letters. This is my first mail since Dec. 13. One letter was from a girl I wrote in Massachusetts and was mailed Dec. 1. It went from Mass. to Lawton to Pier 91, to San Francisco, to Yokohama to Third replacement Co. to HQ and HQ to NCO Academy here. I also received one from you mailed Dec. 8. Looks like my other relatives and so called friends have been taking a vacation—guess I will too, for about 18 months. . . .

• • •

This letter reveals our cheerful acceptance of necessary hardships coupled with continuing efforts to reduce them without over-concern for regulations. We had one light bulb per tent, not enough for a tent full of men trying to play cards, read, and write letters. This one bulb went off automatically at nine o'clock when electricity to the enlisted men's tents was turned off. A partial solution was to steal another light fixture and rewire the tent. This still left us in the dark, except for candles, after nine. Later, someone, I believe Jim Gay, wired our lights into the officers' lines, which gave us electricity all night.

The trapdoor was primarily my idea and the result of my work. It wasn't easy to build. Try cutting through one-inch pine flooring and building a trapdoor with pieces of flooring when your only tools are a bayonet, a rifle butt (metal), and nails salvaged from wooden boxes.

The letter illustrates the way in which we worked to make ourselves comfortable and stay well fed. The closer you were to actual combat, the poorer the food, the equipment, and the clothing. I came to believe it was because we were expendables. Why waste the best on such as us? We faulted the hierarchy for this. Few of the men with whom I served had any use for the "important" people in the military.

In the years since Korea I've spoken with men who served in the infantry in World War II and in Vietnam. They all felt the same way. Just as you don't waste time or money servicing and caring for paper towels, you don't worry about your infantrymen. Instead, you throw them away after you've used them.

Note the surprise of our lieutenant when he discovered how cold our classroom was. We'd been there more than a week—better than one sixth of the course—before he came to see where and under what conditions we were actually working. He was surprised when he found us wearing our parkas and gloves inside a classroom where we were supposed to be learning Morse code and writing messages. I found this lack of supervision common in the army. A plus to him, however, in that he fixed the problem. Later, I learned how seldom this happened. To this day the army has regular procedures for reviewing programs, normally followed by "Lessons Learned" reports. In the eleven years I conducted and evaluated research for the army as a civilian, I found many problems noted but only a few solved.

• • •

January 6, 1953

Dear Ethel:

When you reminded me about it in your last letter I checked back. So far I have received letters 1, 2, 5, 7, 9. As you can see this is a pretty fair average. In the last three days I have gotten letters from you, Mom, Charles Scollay, [my Masonic] lodge, Mary Lou Blackman, Peggy Homans and Janet Johns. What a wonderful change from the past month.

I wonder if you people have gotten all of the letters I have sent. I've been writing every other day at the least, sometimes every day. Naturally, this can't continue too long but I have sent quite a few. So far I have managed to get off a letter to everyone whose address I know.

Ethel, frankly speaking, I'm getting tired of the Morse code. Listening to it hour after hour, day after day . . . gets a little tiresome.

January 7, 1953

. . . This morning I came in, sat down, and passed 8 words a minute, so now I'm on 10.

I got two more letters from you last night but I forgot to check to see what numbers they were. They were mailed on the 10th and 11th (December).

We were hamming around taking pictures at noon today when two officers walked by. Now at that time I was sitting on the shoulders of another fellow. We both gave a precise salute (an unheard of thing) and the officers nearly dropped. Saluting is a very casual thing over here. . . .

• • •

In this letter, as in practically all of them, is the continuing concern about mail. Mail is an infantryman's lifeline, his thread to sanity. We wrote to everyone and anyone. I still remember fondly those who took the time to write back. By contrast, we were highly critical of those who didn't. We gave no one credit for having other things to do in life than write to us. The closer to the front we got, the worse our attitude, mostly because every mile closer reduced alternatives to mail. There were no books on the front line, no radio, no TV, no movies, and no visitors. Nor could we take walks in the mountains in our spare time. There was just each man, what he could carry on his back, and his daydreams. Mail was our life.

Mail processing was another matter. Undoubtedly some was lost—and that was understandable. Not understandable to the foot soldiers were the frequent and unnecessary delays. Mail clerks who had radios and watched movies after duty in USO clubs couldn't appreciate the importance of mail to us. I'm absolutely certain no clerk ever missed a coffee break to expedite a letter. Worse—because they should have been more responsible—were those officers who decided to close the mailroom for a day for inventory, or to clean up, or for Christmas, or for an inspection, or for a staff party, or for any other reason. Perhaps if they'd been forced to come farther north, where letters were important events, they would have been more considerate.

• • •

January 10, 1953

Dear John:

Since the last letter I received was from you, I suppose I had better send one in answer.

As for Eisenhower's election making any vast difference in our present status—well—outside of Truman's War, the most common term is the Endless War. Endless it seems and endless most of us believe it to be. We're waiting mainly to go home on rotation or for our tour of duty to end.

About the time you were thinking that there was about to be a change for the good—according to the date of your letter—I was receiving orders changing my status from rifleman to radioman. So you see, maybe old mental telepathy was at work.

Incidentally, tell Ethel that she can't get ahead of the Army. When I read Fritz's diet of horse meat, cottage cheese, pine needles, and a Christmas tree ornament to a couple of friends, one of them commented, "Sounds like what we had for lunch." If you were to feed a GI caviar the only audible comment would be, "Damn fish eggs."

We have had quite a thaw here recently. This terrible Korean winter is turning ice fields into lakes, roads into streams, and hard earth into mud flats. This morning most of us took off our sweaters. So now all we're wearing is skivvies, long johns and wool uniforms (shirt and pants).

Today we are having an inspection tour by some three-star General. He just arrived by helicopter with his understudies. All in all, we now have 11 Generals wandering the camp. If you ever want to see spit and polish you ought to see this. At the present, the band is marching up and down—in highly polished boots—the mud flats playing while they welcome (?) the Generals.

I'm not sure, but from the way our instructor's prancing around I'm afraid he's going to have puppies. He must think the General is going to kiss him personally on the cheek if we're all working. He should live so long.

Today is the tenth and we are supposed to get some money to tide us over to payday. I sort of have my doubts. I hope though that it does come through. I'm out of stationery and just about out of envelopes (2 left). Supplies of all sort are running low—except razor blades—and I figure I have enough of those to last until 1956. Mom sent me a package of tollhouse cookies. Those lasted about 2 1/2 minutes or one time around the tent. But they were very good. The outer cardboard box was hanging on the rest and the inner tin box had dents kicked in it, but the cookies, for some reason, weren't too badly broken up.

• • •

The military leadership spends a lot of time rushing from one place to another for quick, superficial inspections. The noncommissioned officers/radio school was an excellent location for such visits: far enough north of the Thirty-eighth Parallel to sound dangerous, far enough behind the front to be safe. I observed similar visits at other locations during the years I worked for the military as a civilian. We worker bees called them "dog and pony shows."

I can remember only one occasion when anything meaningful happened as a result of such a visit. A sergeant put his career on the line by saying "No sir" when a general asked if his soldiers were well trained.

Mostly the visits were simply glitter, showing off something designed only for appearance sake. If any careful analysis was actually done of what was happening, I never saw it, except on that one occasion. The sergeant was proven right. He was also transferred.

By the way, the "Fritz" mentioned in my letter was the family dog.

• • •

January 13, 1953

Dear Ethel:

. . . The most constant rumor over here is that Army time is being extended. Just before Truman left he extended the time of the Korean tour of duty and that caused no happiness. We saw in the paper where some Hollywood people were entertaining the front line troops at Taegu. They must have meant the front line long range bomber pilots because Taegu is a good 100 miles back of here and we're 8 miles from the front. . . .

We just got a radio. I am sitting here listening to "Life with Luigi." Morale has gone up 100% in our tent. You don't realize what a luxury one is. Since we got it set up at 6:00 everyone has been gathered around. I don't think anyone in the tent has missed a program.

It's rather cold in the tent tonight so it must be darned cold outside. We've kept it warm in here when it was as cold as 30 degrees below outside. So it must be cold because we're doing everything but burning down the tent and it's still cool in here. Pity the guys on patrol tonight. . . .

. . .

My parents sent me the St. Louis *Post-Dispatch* and several others received newspapers from home. Enthusiastic articles about how Hollywood stars and entertainers came to visit "front-line" troops always annoyed us. I don't know if we were more irritated at the newspapers we read for the misrepresentation of facts and the flat-out lies or at the reports that we were receiving things we never saw. USO shows were primarily for the rear area soldiers, who had no real need for entertainment considering the friendliness of Korean and Japanese girls. A few USO shows came as far north as the NCO school, but we never saw them when we were anywhere near the front. In our opinions, people in the rear areas were cared for while we were ignored.

The radio was important. I know of no way to make normal people understand how boring life can be in a situation such as we had. Beyond work, there was only talk and the mail. A radio was a wondrous acquisition.

The relentless cold and the distance we had to walk to get to a toilet affected more than our sleeping arrangements. Most of us severely restricted liquid intake after lunch. No coffee at supper, and no water after supper. It wasn't a perfect solution, but better a little thirst than crawling out of a warm sleeping bag for a long walk in subzero cold. Slowly the cold and the distance to our toilets had another effect. The snow and ice around our tent gradually turned yellow.

. . .

January 16, 1953

Dear Ethel:

Another day without any damned mail. This makes seven straight mail-less days and we are all getting slightly touchy about the matter. . . .

There is a nasty rumor going out that the camp is short of oil.

At any rate our oil supply has been cut down. But I guarantee you that if anyone in this camp has oil our tent will have it. We've gotten too adept at acquiring it to be caught short now. . . .

All of our warm weather has fled and the cold is back in full force. The other day I saw what looked like some wax on my hand but it wouldn't rub off. I finally realized that it was a burn that I must have gotten off the stove but since I was outside most of the time my hands had never warmed up enough for it to hurt. Actually, we get used to this pretty quickly and it's only when our hands get stiff that we realize the cold. . . .

This one fellow in our outfit was assigned to the 65th (Puerto Rican) and was highly incensed because he had to shave off his mustache when he got there. The Ricans, who are very proud of their mustaches, were ordered to shave them off after they flunked out on Kelly Hill. They won't be able to regrow them until they regain their honor as a unit in combat. At the rate they're going it looks as if they'll be a clean shaven bunch.

The same fellow is the one whose mother sent him a book of airmail stamps so that his letters would travel faster. Our free mail gets top priority over all regular stamped mail.

A helicopter is coming in. Probably another General. Visiting radio school must be a fad with them at the present time. Yesterday I made a quick trip to the Army version of an air conditioned out house. When I returned someone was pulling on the door from outside so I gave an extra hard yank and looked up into the faces of a Major and two Generals. Needless to say I sat down and got quietly to work.

While I was at the latrine, I fell into an interesting conversation on what would happen if one of these visiting stars—say Marilyn Monroe—had to use one of our comfortable wooden seats in our beautiful doorless, windowless, roofless outhouse on some day when the temperature was around zero.

With that interesting thought I leave you for the day. . . .

• • •

The cold was intense. I remember one lunch when I was warm enough to take my gloves off to eat. As I was standing there, I saw that I'd gotten some airplane glue on the palms of my hands. I idly scratched at it, trying to get it off. When it didn't come off as easily as it should have, I realized I was trying to scratch off scorched flesh. In the letter I say I thought it was wax, but I remember standing there and puzzling over airplane glue, wondering how and where I'd gotten it on my hands. I would have known where I'd picked up some wax.

The Sixty-fifth Infantry Regiment originated as a Puerto Rican National Guard unit. By the time I arrived in Korea, most of the original members had been rotated home; however, the unit was still heavily Puerto Rican despite the integration of many from the States and was now primarily a unit of draftees who had little use for the army. Adding to their problems was a preponderance of non-English-speaking enlisted men with non-Spanish-speaking officers. My derogatory comments concerning the Sixty-fifth Regiment were nothing extraordinary. We were harsh critics of one another.

The outhouse, which was in a safe area, was nothing more than a canvas wall around some open seats. It was also a place where we could relax and gossip, although the weather limited that. As you went north, where life was less safe, the canvas walls disappeared. This made it easier to leap for safety in case of artillery or mortar fire. On the road north, where mine fields limited freedom to leave the road, it was fairly common to pass an occupied wooden box sitting in the open, the occupant waving cheerful greetings at passing drivers.

• • •

January 19, 1953

Dear Ethel:

Received your letter last night along with two from home and one from J.J. As this was the first mail in twelve days, I was glad to see it. Sorry to hear about that case of flu. Over here we have very little illness—even the common cold is uncommon.

Actually we don't worry about civilians as we never see them. We are in a dead zone extending across Korea into which no unauthorized civilian may enter. Some men are hired and brought in as laborers—but they wear GI clothes, sleep in tents, and eat our food. It is an extremely effective way of combating guerrillas but vacates thousands of fertile acres.

Yesterday, being Sunday, we spent the morning indulging in our favorite sport, sleeping. In the early afternoon, Jim Gay and I took a walk across the lake. On the far side we found a concrete and steel overflow gate that had evidently once been used as a sniper's nest. What had happened to the sniper was very plain to see. . . .

Last night after the mail arrived, we all felt invigorated so with a new zeal we returned to our card games—devising strange and often slightly daft schemes for cheating our opponents. Our card games are slightly wild affairs enjoyed by spectators and players alike. . . .

• • •

As I think back, the lack of colds was really remarkable. We were rarely sick. We were cold and, later, wet, tired, and hungry, but we never got sick. Or perhaps it was the case that illness never stopped us.

I included the response to the mail because its arrival was always important. Morale simply shot up unless the news was bad, and even then it could be treated lightly. The mother of one of our number, Don Frechete, routinely sent clippings from his home-town paper that listed the dead and missing in Korea. Don, who was not only the best radioman among us but also had a marvel-ous sense of humor, would laughingly rant and rave up and down the tent, turning what could be depressing for a person facing com-bat into a funny event. I believe it was Don who had to shave his mustache because of assignment to the Sixty-fifth. Another of our tribe, John Tamas, who in civilian life was employed as a comedian, claimed that if he could be as funny on purpose as Don was by accident, he'd be world famous and wealthy.

The numerous letters during this period are generally lively; they detail the continuing and humorous battle with authority. But we all remembered that the day would come when we were headed to a world that was much less pleasant—and much more chancy.

• • •

January 27, 1953

Dear Ethel:

. . . As we've gone along we've done everything in our power to make this school a snap. First we weaned the cadre from the idea that we should get up for reveille at 6:00—now so long as we're in

school by 7:30 or thereabouts they don't care when we get up.
You've heard about the acquired oil, light bulbs, radio, water can,
cooking cans, etc., so I won't go into that. Our latest attack on stupid ideas has been retreat. As a general rule all students stand retreat at 5:15 to 5:30 P.M. A week or so ago we just stopped going and
no one has said a word since. To tell the truth, I think our joking
and talking used to create a little disturbance and I think that
they're relieved that we don't come out anymore.

Also, we finally received a full scale surrender from the officers
on the matter of when we eat. All along they've been insisting we
eat on schedule (Why should you men eat ahead of everyone else?)
and all along we've been going when we damn well felt like it—
usually first. The other day our Lieutenant told us he didn't care
when we ate but please go in formation. So now, at noon, we go in
formation (first), but at breakfast (dark outside) we go as individuals when it's convenient (usually about 7) and at night we also
wander over when we're ready.

The other day one of the cooks asked one of our guardhouse
lawyers if he wasn't in line twice and back came this answer. "Hell
no! You think it's a pleasure eating this whatcha callit? It's a necessity, a case of survival of the fittest—but to ask for punishment
twice in one meal—hell no!" The cook didn't say another word.

• • •

The incidents mentioned in this letter marked the end of our
struggles with the officers, though there was more to the retreat
problem than I described. Retreat was a solemn occasion each
evening. The troops stood at attention in formation while the flag
was lowered and then marched past an officers' reviewing stand.
Initially, we ignored retreat, but noise from our radio and our card
games floated out onto the parade field during the ceremony.
Worse still, the fellows in the other tent decided to clean their
stovepipes one evening during retreat. In full sight of all the soldiers standing at attention on the parade field, they climbed onto
the tent, took down the stovepipes, and beat the ash and cinders
out of them.

The army couldn't afford to have twenty or so enlisted men so
blatantly ignoring duties required of others; consequently, we were
told to show up for retreat in the future. We received this order

after those who had been in the field wire school had graduated and gone back to their units, so all of us remaining were radiomen and had that OCS/military school background.

When first ordered, we decided to show the others how good we could be. We drilled in private, on the weekend, practicing some of the nonstandard steps one sees in special drill units. I don't know how we looked from the reviewing stand, but we wanted to look like we knew what we were doing and we thought we'd succeeded. We certainly made an impression, because after the second day we were told that we could no longer march as a unit. We would be scattered within C Company. We didn't like that, and we resolved to make everyone involved regret the decision.

After marching with C Company, we were laughing among ourselves about the things we did as we passed in review. I, for example, tried tapping the helmet of the soldier behind me with my rifle barrel. Our initial pleasure was brief. C Company was informed that its efforts (that is to say our efforts) were so horrible that there would be extra drill. As a result, the men in C Company attacked our tent, trying to get in so they could humble us. We were defending ourselves with our rifle butts when their lieutenant intervened and sent them back.

Later he came to talk to us. We were told that the officers had agreed that if we kept our radio off, stayed in our tents, and lowered our voices during retreat, no one would miss us. I still remember his parting words: "We have decided you guys aren't really bad, you're just like a pack of dogs that has run loose too long, and it's too late to put you on a leash. But if you have any friends coming to this school, tell them it's going to be different for them."

While I still enjoy the memory of those trivial victories, both we and the officers overlooked something. There are two kinds of discipline. There is parade ground discipline, when you do *as* you're told, *when* you're told. That was the discipline of the charge of the Light Brigade and of the British at Bunker Hill as they marched to what they must have seen as certain, stupid death.

The other type of discipline is an internal voice that can't be ignored. We had that. Our only continuing leadership came from a Private First Class Boulanger, who held the same rank as some of us. We seldom saw our lieutenant and never saw our sergeant, yet we were always in class on time and doing our work—faster and more efficiently than radio students in the States. This was a credit to PFC Boulanger, who provided excellent leadership, but we deserved some credit also. We became radio operators largely through our own "undisciplined" efforts. Perhaps we weren't so undisciplined except in that rather primitive sense mentioned above.

Baron von Steuben, the great revolutionary war general, wrote that in Europe you said to a soldier "Do that" and he did it, but in America you said to a soldier "Do that and here's why" and then he did it. The baron would have understood us. The lieutenant didn't.

• • •

January 29, 1953

Dear Ethel:

. . . We've had quite a bit of snow the last couple of days and it's blowing cold again. Actually we're very comfortable and the snow just adds scenic value. Last night, especially, with a full moon and clear sky and everything covered by snow, it was very beautiful out.

. . . I got some mail today at noon. Charley Brown up at HQ and HQ wrote saying he was getting my films developed and would hold them for me. . . .

I guess I've told you I received a package from Mom yesterday, mailed Dec. 12. From the looks of it they must have thrown it over here. Fortunately it was hard candy—a little broken—yes, rock candy broken, but not badly so. May I suggest that a good type of inner paper for wadding is toilet paper. While not worth sending by itself it does have a twofold advantage. . . .

We have acquired a South Korean in our tent. As a thief, he's almost as good as us. So far he has provided a table, a couple of chairs and a bottle of Jap beer for us. We, in turn, buy his cigarettes at the PX for him which I gather he sells on the black market. I don't think he smokes three cartoons a day. He also does our wash at reduced prices. Very nice.

• • •

Our numbers had been reduced when Charley Brown, Joe Freeman, and others in the wireman school graduated and returned to their units. Charley and I kept in touch, and he was able to get my legally acquired film illegally developed. Actually, the photography situation was interesting and exhibits a bit of the army's use—and misuse—of manpower. The regiment was entitled to a regimental photographer who took pictures of important events such as the colonel receiving visitors. This occupied very little of his time, so he used the facilities provided for processing official photographs to develop our photographs—as a favor and, I suppose, as a relief from boredom.

Note the suggestion that toilet paper was preferable to crumpled-up newspaper for padding in packages. Everything must be useful when you carry all your possessions with you.

The letter also reports my first experience with a KATUSA soldier—that is, a Korean Attached to the United States Army. When the North Koreans first attacked, they were well armed with tanks and airplanes. The United States had refused to supply South Korea with the equipment necessary to defend itself against such weapons. Consequently, the South Korean Army, despite the valor of many, was rapidly destroyed as a fighting force. When American troops arrived—professional soldiers stationed in Japan and Okinawa—they discovered their equipment was inadequate, and their units were similarly pulverized. As better trained and equipped Americans, primarily draftees, arrived, a policy of attaching individual Koreans to each squad was developed. Each of the squads to which I was attached had a KATUSA. Every KATUSA I knew was a welcome and valuable member of his squad.

As the letter indicates, the KATUSA program benefited both the Korean and American soldiers in ways not planned by the generals who developed the policy. We had no concern about the black market at that time. While the U.S. government paid the Korean government for these soldiers at the same rate paid to American soldiers of equivalent rank, the KATUSAs themselves were paid at the rate for Korean soldiers—barely sufficient for cigarette money. Consequently, the KATUSAs did all kinds of things to get enough money to help support their families and, for that matter, to improve their own standard of living. Our willingness to assist them in this made KATUSA positions highly desirable to Korean soldiers.

The black market went beyond enlisted Americans and KATUSA soldiers. For example, we couldn't legally acquire American beer—or, for that matter, any alcoholic beverages. We resented this. We could die, but we couldn't drink. Officers, however, who in theory needed to have their senses about them at all times, had ready access to alcoholic beverages. We believed some made modest fortunes selling liquor to enlisted soldiers. A bottle of scotch, for example, cost an enlisted man twenty dollars, but the officer selling it paid approximately two dollars for it in a tax-free PX in the rear area. Along the front, helicopter pilots were the main distributors. I was never involved in this, partly because I had no opportunity to meet helicopter pilots, but I was informed of the situation by others who liked an occasional drink.

• • •

February 1, 1953

Dear Ethel:

I expect this letter will reach you in time for one of those special occasions known as a birthday.

Some people, narrow minded and usually deficient mentally, don't like birthdays—thinking of them as indicators of undesirable old age. . . .

Birthdays take away from the aged the sole possession of retrospection. Even the nine year old is permitted to say proudly, "Why, when I was eight . . ." Thus for one day, without fear of censure, we are permitted to speak of the days which are past. Of course some were sad and hard but always these fade into pleasant dreams of childhood and the years of schooling.

Thus each birthday permits us to claim the richness of life which is rightfully ours. Even so there are yet greater joys to be found in a birthday. On this personal day we can express audibly our hopes of the years to come. Enjoying in advance the fullness of life which we will gain with each coming birthday.

So—sister mine—I can very sincerely wish you a happy birthday and express that oft repeated hope that you will see many more of them.

February 4, 1953

Today has been quite a day 1) I got paid, 2) went to the PX, 3) no longer need to worry about too much money. Candy, cookies, chocolate milk, envelopes, etc. Wrote letters, took a shower, got mail, sent mail, worked (but not too hard).

In fact, I spent most of my free time listening to Radio Moscow where I found out many interesting things.

1. Thousands in US are freezing to death because of a severe clothing shortage.

2. All children in New England under 12 work in the fields from dawn to dark.

3. 14,000 American officers were killed in Korea last month.

4. American soldiers are mistreated (with this I heartily agree).

A very interesting program. The longer I'm here the less tolerant I become of American communists. . . .

• • •

We spent hours listening to Radio Moscow, primarily because of the good music. The propaganda was interesting at first, but after a while it became irritating in its gross misrepresentation of the United States. I suppose Koreans or troops from Turkey or Greece could have believed it, but there was no way anyone from the States could. The assertions were flagrantly false. This changed my personal attitude toward American Communists. Until I listened to Radio Moscow, I reasoned that they could be misguided. I knew there were many problems in the United States, and I thought they were just trying to take the wrong road to improve things. However, there was no way an American could believe the propaganda from Moscow. It was too untrue; it went beyond the distortion of facts to the creation of its own reality. Thus, I decided that U.S. Communists were simply knaves trying to sell out our country for their own—their personal—advantage. It's a belief I still hold.

• • •

February 7, 1953

Dear Ethel:

. . . today is my last day here at school—tomorrow I'll be back at my own outfit—which won't be a bad thought. It will be nice to be on the move for a while and then it will be still nicer to settle down with a regular outfit for a while. . . .

6

THE COMMUNICATIONS
PLATOON

The communications platoon of the Regimental Headquarters
Company of the Fifteenth Infantry Regiment eagerly awaited our
arrival. There was a serious shortage of radio operators. We were
packed and ready to go early Sunday morning.

• • •

February 8, 1953

Dear Ethel:

Today I was supposed to be back with my outfit but they never
came to pick us up. As a result the five of us from HQ plus Tamas
from the artillery are still loafing around the tent here at signal
school, playing cards and shooting the breeze. I am sure that by
tomorrow morning they will be down to pick us up. . . .

February 10, 1953

Here I am, killing another day loafing around the signal school
waiting to be picked up by head and head [regimental headquar-
ters]. We were supposed to be picked up Sunday morning and here
it is Tuesday noon and I'm still here. But that's all right, I'm doing
no work. . . . The showers open in about 15 minutes and I will drift
down there provided our trucks don't get here by that time, and
five will get you ten they don't. . . .

• • •

Every few years the army adopts a new "official" motto to inspire
the troops. Most of these mottoes are soon—and best—forgotten.
The unofficial one that all enlisted men and women would recognize is "Hurry up and wait." Those were words to live by in World

War II, Korea, and Vietnam, and they remain true in the "volunteer" or professional army of today. I'll bet it was even true at Valley Forge. Three days of waiting is not at all long in the military.

I mention showers. The army established showers at specific locations in the rear areas. Each site consisted of three joined tents on a wooden platform. Water pipes with shower heads extended the length of the center tent. You entered the first tent and stripped, took your shower in the second, and were handed clean clothing in the third. Then you went back and retrieved any personal possessions, such as a belt or a rifle, from the first tent. The system had several problems, some unavoidable.

First, the showers were in the rear. If you lived there you could get showers regularly, even though they were open only at specific, often sporadic, times. When the shower point was closed for inspection, or to be moved, or because something broke down, or for a holiday or staff morale party, it was no real problem for rear area soldiers. But as you moved north, your shower problems increased. It might be a half-day trip if—and that's a big "if"—you could arrange transportation. If the shower was closed when you arrived, you went back and stayed dirty until another trip could be arranged, which might be in a week or a month.

A trivial problem was that no attempt was made to size clothing. Whether it did or didn't, one size was made to fit all. Most of us quickly abstained from turning in our dirty clothing. In the rear, the Korean soldiers attached to each unit, eager to earn money, would wash and press your clothes for perhaps fifty cents a uniform. The farther north you got, the less possible this became. Up front, very dirty clothing was worn for long periods of time. Better dirty pants that fit than clean pants that didn't.

A third problem was theft. On my first trip to the showers, I trotted around to retrieve my belt and boots only to discover that my belt was missing. Since my newly issued, clean trousers were several inches too big around the waist, the loss of my belt was serious. I looked around and saw where someone else had left his belt and boots. It was an easy decision: better him than me. When putting on this newly acquired belt, I saw my name stenciled inside.

Those of us farther north took very few showers. When we were successful in getting to the shower point and finding it open, we left a guard with our personal and field equipment (belts and wallets, rifles, helmets) while we washed, then we protected the guard's equipment while he showered. Shower trips were rare, however, as the nearest shower point was far south of regimental headquarters, near division headquarters. I averaged less than one shower a month after moving north—and this was the rule, not the exception. Interestingly, the difficulty in bathing and getting appropriate clothing aroused little comment among the enlisted. We had become different people from those who took showers every evening in basic training.

In warm weather, we washed in the creeks and streams. They were always open and transportation and theft were not problems. In the fall and spring we preferred pools in the small creeks for bathing, as the water there tended to be warmer. Summer days found the streams and rivers crowded with jeeps, trucks, and nude men. First you washed your clothes and hung them up to dry; then you washed yourself, and finally your vehicle. The last was essential as it was against regulations to wash or swim in the creeks and rivers. We could always say that we were only washing our vehicles, which was permitted.

• • •

February 18, 1953

Dear Ethel:

Received your letter of Feb. 5 today. For some reason it took quite a while traveling. Yes, in regard to your statement, they did sort of overwork us at radio school. After six weeks there I am now unable to buckle my belt.

Life in all was very difficult. Yes, Jim Gay is still with me—that is he is at head and head, here, however, he is chief electrician while I'm a radio operator. This separates us some, but I still see him a couple times a day. That is if I bother getting up for meals. You understand I never make breakfast but usually I get in the other two meals. . . .

One of the men that just wandered in was singing a slightly original verse to a popular hillbilly song—it went like this:

> "Hear the patter of little feet
> It's the U.S. Marines in full retreat
> They're movin' on." . . .

• • •

Arrival at my unit took some adjustment. It was a full week be-fore I wrote to anyone. Headquarters proper was in a valley while we, because of radio requirements, were on top of the highest north-facing mountain, one much like those in the Appalachians. The medic had established his aid station about a fourth of the way up, our two sleeping tents were about three fourths of the way to the top, and the radio truck was just below the brow of the hill, the antennae rising above it to improve communication with forward units.

When I arrived I needed two rest stops to climb to my tent and a third to reach the radio truck. In a week or two I climbed to the tent without stopping. Then I received a box of cigars. Soon I was back to two stops on the way to my tent, so I quit smoking cigars.

Our location was the real reason for routinely missing breakfast. Who wants to wake up, dress, and walk a mile downhill in the dark and subzero cold for bad food? Especially when you have to climb back up immediately afterward. Often, only two of us ate break-fast. The operator starting a shift, already up and dressed, would bring back a tray of food, cold or frozen on arrival, for the guy going off duty.

We actually had less than two tents as living quarters, because the tent I lived in had frozen to the ground before it could be fully raised. So about eight of us crowded into half a tent with the ex-pectation that when spring came it could be put up the rest of the way. We had dirt floors, which made for a much warmer tent than those at the radio school with their wooden floors and open space below. Also, with a dirt floor there was no place for rats to hide. I learned to appreciate dirt floors.

We hung our metal mess gear on the tent sides, and for one or two weeks I slept very little because the gear jumped, rattled, and banged all night from the concussions of the firing of nearby ar-tillery and the less-frequent explosions of incoming artillery. Later, I became accustomed to this racket and slept soundly through the night.

The radio truck was just that, a three-quarter-ton truck, about the size of a large pick-up truck, with a wooden shelter on it. Ra-dios—the AN/GRC 46As (which we nicknamed "angry forty-six-a")—and batteries were mounted at the cab end of the shelter and two benches along the sides provided seats. A door at the rear provided entry. You couldn't stand up inside, and two people made for a crowd (though three people could squeeze in). There you'd sit for your three-hour shift, watching a generally silent radio except for the hourly checks with other stations.

Doug "Duke" Glascoe, Bob Maltby, John Weber, and I were still together. Jim Gay, as chief electrician, lived in the valley, so I routinely saw him at meals. It was good to be able to see Charley Brown and Joe Freeman again, though the opportunity for casual visits was reduced. I remember the others in the communications platoon as a group of fine men and excellent radio operators, but I've forgotten most of their names.

Contrary to the colonel mentioned in the prologue, I never saw courage as a problem anywhere in Korea. I encountered open fear or cowardice only twice. More common was a reckless disregard of danger. One of our men, John Morrison, a fine operator, achieved fame during a mass attack. When it appeared that a retreat might be necessary, he was ordered to get his gear together and be ready to fall back. Instead, he grabbed his camera and ran forward, shouting, "I have to get pictures of this. No one back home will ever believe that I faced a mass attack."

Initially, we beginners were partnered with experienced operators such as John. But as the others learned to trust us, we began working individual shifts. Now that the unit was fully staffed, we worked one three-hour shift every twenty-four hours, though sometimes a second or third person crowded into the radio truck, just listening. This left a lot of time, too much really, for card playing, writing letters, and just plain daydreaming. As usual, we complained about the mail, the food, and just about anything except ourselves.

• • •

February 21, 1953

Hi Ethel:

Surprise! Your package arrived today! The one with the choc. cookies and the canned food. As the boys would say, number 1. . . . I ate a can of peanuts, tomato soup, and the spice bread immediately with the able aid of friends. The rest, except for those choc. fudge cookies, I stowed away. The cookies I hid. They are for one man alone—me. . . .

February 24, 1953

Ethel—Good Morning!

This morning ushers in a new era in the life and fortunes of Bill Dannenmaier. Our mail has been plugged up for four days now and we were getting pretty well disgusted with the whole mess—but no more! We decided to get so much mail that they would have to send it through.

At the present time, 23 minutes after twelve, morning of the 24th of February there are better than twenty letters lying in the mail box to newspapers and girl's colleges throughout the country.

You are fortunate, Ethel, that you don't have to read those letters. You would cry for a week without stopping at the thought of us poor boys—working our legs off every day and never getting mail. Some were real gems of composition and others are a bit fishy—for example where one fellow made a mistake in writing our names and crossed it out with the explanation that he had been killed in action that morning. I must admit that we laughed ourselves sick writing those letters. Some of the places we sent them were the Chicago Tribune, Seattle Post, Santa Barbara Jr. College (girls), Washington Herald, St. Luke's Student Nurses Home—Cleveland, New York Times, Monticello, etc. We even sent one to the Globe Democrat but I kept that toned down because I have to live in St. Louis.

All in all we enjoyed ourselves thoroughly, and are now eagerly anticipating the results. I don't know what they'll be like but if any of our stuff is printed I guarantee we get mail from it. We even thought of writing the Daily Worker but rejected it because what we had to say to them is not legal through the mail.

I sent Mom a letter giving her the general idea and saying to watch the Globe for developments. When I left the tent to go on duty the boys were all still up and writing letters. I just told them to be careful not to promise anything. . . .

• • •

Give a group of young men something to complain about, such as lack of mail, and time to think and they will discover an answer—in this case both legal and ingenious.

Surplus time also led to interesting debates and arguments over trivialities. We once spent a full week arguing about, and trying to remember, how to solve a square root problem. It was important only because it occupied time. When we finally remembered the procedure, we had forgotten the reason for wanting to know.

On another occasion, two of our men on temporary assignment at the Greek battalion, where we provided English-speaking operators, got into an argument as to whose turn it was to walk down the mountain, wait for the oil truck, and carry five gallons of heating oil back up. The pair who relieved them at the end of the week found the two bundled in their sleeping bags in an ice cold bunker, neither willing to surrender, get the oil, and exchange pride for comfort.

• • •

February 25, 1953

Dear Ethel:

Your letters—28 & 29—were the first letters I have received in five days. They were extremely welcome. . . . Speaking of money, I believe I shall get combat pay over here of $45 a month in addition to my regular wages. At least, I will get it occasionally beginning possibly this month. If we spend six days a month in a combat area we get the $45 and if we spend 21 days there we get 4 points. While I live in a three point area we go up forward to police up wire every so often. I've been up there 5 times over five days myself so if the people in the orderly room wish to finagle a bit they can give me credit for six days. . . .

• • •

The army tried to maintain extensive telephone contact with all of its units and outposts. This meant laying miles, literally, of telephone (known as "commo") wire along roads, through valleys, and over mountains.

The enemy would cut this wire whenever possible. One trick was to drive a pin through it into the ground to short it out, wait for someone to come along hunting for the break, and shoot him.

Most of the wire, however, was simply broken by being blown up by the sporadic yet continuing artillery fire. The safest and fastest way to replace such breaks was to forget the old wire and lay new wire. As a result, we had a very messy battlefield, with miles of multiple strands of broken wire. Dwight Eisenhower had been elected president and had appointed a new secretary of defense. Rumor had it that he was coming for a visit, so Command was suddenly interested in a neat battlefield. At night, in the dead of winter, we walked the roads to pick up the surplus wire. We had to go at night because the enemy had a clear view of the area and would have found us easy targets during the day. For the same reason, we worked without lights, hunting the wire in the snow.

That went on for five nights. On the fifth night we felt the cold was more dangerous than the enemy. We built a fire in a small ravine, trying to get warm. Soon the first sergeant arrived with word that the company commander said to put out the damned fire before we were killed. Our mood had become dangerously ugly and we told him that the company commander would have to tell us that in person. The sergeant left but soon returned with hot coffee and a bottle of bourbon. He reported that the company commander had decided that as soon as we had the fire out we could have a drink of each and then return to our tent. Later we learned that our footprints showed we had wandered into a mine field and had just missed a mine that had surfaced through the snow. It could have been a very expensive cleanup for us, but I believe no one at home would have known why. What officer is going to admit that several men were killed because he wanted the front line to look prettier?

We didn't receive combat pay that month.

• • •

March 1, 1953

Dear Ethel:

. . . Tonight is beautiful out. There is a full moon which softens the harshness of this Korean landscape into a soft blending of grays and blacks. There is a thick fog in the valleys and the hills jut out of it—black islands in a pearl gray sea. Then, on the higher mountains about us, there is a second layer of fog laying a broad white stripe across the upper—visible—third. All in all, it is very impressive. . . .

March 4, 1953

I'm not at all surprised to hear that the war isn't very real to you. Actually it isn't very real to us and we seldom think of it or speak of it and don't forget that while we are, at present, about three miles behind the lines we can hear and see the fire fights that develop on Kelly, Papasan, and Richmond Hts.—directly to our front. We have also all spent time in the actual combat area. The only real things are the mud, our tents, and radios. Thus we are actually much worse off than you are in not realizing that there is a war on.

. . . This morning we were working on the mess hall and, when I left, a can of cocoa left with me. That means we'll enjoy hot choc. for another week or so. A can of cheese also happened to roll out in the bushes where it will probably be until tomorrow morning at which time it'll come to pay our tent a visit. Now all we need is crackers—but those can usually be had for the asking. . . .

• • •

A soldier's attention is necessarily narrow, "directed." My business was radios and little else concerned me. If I were with the Greek battalion, for example, and the enemy attacked, they were not my problem unless they attacked my bunker and I had to defend myself. Otherwise, I worked the radio. Each of us, cogs in the huge machine of war, had a job to do, and each of us did it. Later, as a scout, I would joke that only cowards made good scouts. A scout wasn't supposed to fight, he was supposed to locate the enemy and communicate that to people responsible for the fighting. Scouts who lost that perspective were useless to the Command. I would watch with only mild interest as helicopters carried out the wounded from other areas—it wasn't me and it wasn't in my area of concern. Of course, I was always interested in food and warmth, but those were personal, not business interests.

I made a lot of hot chocolate in Korea. It took forty-five minutes to mix chocolate, milk powder, sugar, and water and bring it to a boil in my canteen cup on our tent stove. That was a valuable forty-five minutes. Working only three hours gave me twenty-one hours to waste, unless I had mail or went to a meal. A cup of hot chocolate relieved the boredom for forty-five minutes. It was also tasty.

• • •

March 6, 1953

Dear Ethel:

How do you like my new paper? I stopped in the P.X. yesterday to buy some envelopes and, since they didn't have any to sell, they gave me some of this. There are three distinct supplies of stationery over here, the first is the P.X. and then we have two emergency supplies—this and the Red Cross.

Rumor now says that we are going to stay here all of March and possibly all of April. The story is that the 65th which relieved the Seventh fouled up again so that instead of getting twenty days in reserve and then coming up to relieve us the 7th was thrown back onto the line to replace the 65th. Strange how when I first came over I heard you spent forty days on the lines and twenty in reserve. . . .

Next week I think I may get to go up to the Greeks. Every week we send a couple of radio operators up there and it is a rather eagerly sought job. First, while there's no danger, you get combat pay. Second, up there you get all of the beer you can drink—rather a novel thing for us. And then, to top it off, there are no details to be pulled. So you can see it's rather an ideal life for a week.

Well, my calls are all out and I have three of the five stations reporting in. It takes quite a bit of work at this hour in the morning because from about 3:00 A.M. to about 9:00 the various stations have "breakdowns" which force them to spend their time sleeping instead of answering radio calls. . . .

• • •

The Fifteenth and Seventh Infantry Regiments seemed to spend an inordinate amount of time on-line, while the Sixty-fifth (these three composed the Third Infantry Division) was always training.

We all enjoyed being assigned to the Greek battalion. First, they gave us all we could eat, which was a rare treat. Among other things, they made delicious fresh bread, and we could have all we wanted. Their cooks would laugh at us when we first arrived because we would each take an entire loaf at meals. Our C rations may have been nutritionally correct, but they left us hungry. Second, the Greek Command permitted enlisted men to drink beer or cognac, which we could buy from them. It was good business for the Greeks, since the United States supplied them with American beer which they sold to us at three dollars a case. Third, when we were with the Greeks we got combat pay.

There was one problem that I should mention. The Greeks were used to slit trenches to relieve themselves, which were nothing like our sit-down toilets, boxes though they were. Consequently, they stood on the boxes and aimed at the hole, with little accuracy. We hoped for constipation.

About this time, a Greek patrol was trapped by a Chinese patrol and had to fight its way back. One of the men who was wounded managed to kill the man who wounded him and bring back his head. The nurses at the hospital got upset, especially since this Greek soldier wouldn't give up his "prize." We had to patch the Greek commander back to the hospital by radio so that he could order his soldier to obey the nurses. We considered it an amusing incident, laughing about the determination of the Greek and the reactions of the hospital staff.

Later, when attached to the Greeks as a scout, I mentioned the incident to one of their officers. He laughed about it too. He told me that during the Greek civil war loyalists were paid according to the number of Communists they killed. In the mountains they accepted heads as evidence. As a young officer, he had moved to the front at night. Looking around for a pillow, he found some sacks of what he thought were cabbages and used one to get a good night's sleep. In the morning he found that he'd been sleeping on a sack of heads.

• • •

March 11, 1953

Dear Ethel:

As per usual the mail is all plugged up. This time, however, they have done a better job. We are not only getting none in, but we are sending none out. Mainly this is because at the present time I am at the Greeks and the people who are supposed to bring us mail and take ours out—ain't. Anyway in a couple of days I'll be headed back to Head and Head—richer by a couple of cartons of cigarettes and combat pay ($45). The latter I'll receive in my April pay.

In your last letter you mentioned that you had some snow on March 1. Yesterday, I was all prepared to sit down and brag to you of the wonderful weather over here when it began to rain. That was at 1200 noon, a very steady downpour. By five o'clock the roof had started to leak. By 9:00 I was ready to go outside to dry off. Every-thing was wet—there was even a pool of water boiling on the stove. About four the next morning—this morning—the rain changed to sleet and by six the sleet changed to snow, however inside our bunker it was still raining as hard as ever. About one thirty this afternoon it stopped, leaving a six inch layer of snow covering everything. Now, at four thirty, I am sitting here in the middle of the room. All around me is a steady drip-drip except on my right where the water hits the stove and goes "sizzle."

Actually we are having a lot of fun and would be enjoying our-selves completely if the undertow didn't make it so dangerous. I might add that the only completely dry section of the roof, i.e. the only section that doesn't leak, is directly over my bunk. . . .

• • •

There was a bit more to this week than stated in the letter. There was a lot of action one night and the Chinese didn't want us talk-ing to headquarters. They jammed our radio frequencies com-pletely, but we had to keep trying to send our message. Our radio was powered by a hand-pumped generator. This wore a person out fairly quickly, so we rotated. One of us turned the crank on the generator, a second tapped out Morse code, and the third rested. We began that evening and didn't get the message through and acknowledged until the next morning, long after the attack that occasioned the need for the message had failed.

We were all exhausted, but someone had to stay alert. As I was the type who could stay awake indefinitely, I volunteered for the first shift. While the others slept, I crawled into my sleeping bag with rifle at hand, lying in a position that enabled me to see out the bunker's aperture. When all was quiet, I felt something at my feet. I looked back to see a large rat sitting on top of my bag, on the mound made by my feet, looking at me. As quietly as I could, I maneuvered my rifle around and aimed it carefully to be certain I had a kill; but then common sense took hold. It occurred to me that, considering the night we'd just had, if the other two awoke to a rifle shot in the bunker I might have two friends dead of heart attacks. So I waved the rifle at the rat until he ran back into his hole in the wall. We laughed about it later.

• • •

March 14, 1953

Dear Ethel:

. . . I promised to let you know how our letters to the newspaper came out. So far we've heard from one—The Press Scimitar printed our letter and we got about fifteen letters each from around Tennessee and Mississippi. We did not expect to start hearing results until about the sixteenth so you see this one came in early.

Most of the letters so far have been from high school girls (99 9/10% illiterate) who think it thrilling to write a soldier. However, we did get some very nice letters from slightly older groups. They were all very interesting reading—providing laughs if nothing else. Most of us carefully edited them and wrote in return to those who put forth an interesting letter. We have become the talk and envy of the company and, at present time, are looking forward to more results. We've had to write like the devil the last couple of days keeping up with it all. . . .

• • •

The requests for pen pals turned out to be a rewarding activity and I, for one, kept up several new correspondences for the next few months. Later, when my personal gear was stolen during a sudden move, I lost all the addresses and had to wait for letters to come in to reestablish contact. Unfortunately, I lost track of most of the people I had been writing to at that time.

It was in late February or early March that one of our military bureaucrats down south, in temperate, sea-level Seoul, decided that the weather was sufficiently warm and we no longer needed heating oil. He should have lived up north, in the mountains. We would have frozen if some second army bureaucrat hadn't decided we needed bunkers. These were prefabricated kits, with timbers twenty inches wide and ten inches thick. The bunkers were shipped unassembled from the States. One complete set was lying outside our stone-cold tent.

We warmed ourselves with what was probably some of the most expensive firewood ever delivered. Not as good as the cheaper heating oil, but it was better than nothing.

If the officer who decided we didn't need heating oil had visited us, he would have been a rarity. I remember only one such visit. A new, unknown lieutenant stuck his head in the door one day. When asked if he was lost, he replied that he was looking for the communications platoon. When told that he'd found us, he said he was our new lieutenant and wanted to meet us. He said he'd heard good things about us.

At that time we'd been having an argument about keeping the place clean. No one was willing to give in and housekeep the place. Consequently, it was a mess, with a huge stack of empty C ration and beer cans surrounding the tent pole. We had to stay in our bunks when in the tent as there was no room to move around (remember, half of our tent was still frozen to the ground).

Our sergeant, who was sitting on a back bunk playing cards, said, "I guess you want to meet the boys," and he stood up and sidestepped around the pile of empty cans to the door. Then the sergeant and the lieutenant sidled about the inside of the tent, each of us staying in our bunks as we were introduced. After meeting us, the lieutenant made his way back to the door, opened it as if to leave, and then turned and said, "By the way, sergeant, it's a little messy in here. Why don't you have the guys clean it up?" With that he slipped out. When we finished laughing at his understatement, we went to work and cleaned house. I've forgotten his name, but I remember that he was a really good lieutenant and the only West Point graduate under whom I served. I didn't see him again before I transferred.

• • •

March 17, 1953

Dear Ethel:

Received your letters of the 3rd & 4th today. Also, got some pictures back from the developer. If you want to see all of them, you'll have to see Mom as I am sending her the negatives. However, enclosed you will find a couple of snapshots.

Jim Gay and I both went to the same radio school—only he had previous experience as an electrician and radio repairman—so they made him an electrician here.

What do we do when we are jammed by the Chinese? That is the reason the three of us up at the Greeks were awake and working for twenty four hours last week. You just keep trying until you can send it. That one night it took us seven hours to send one ten word message. You can't quit—dammit!

Morrison just got back from R&R (five days in Japan). He spent about $350. About $100 on high living and about two hundred on gifts. It's very easy to do. Most people spend between two hundred and three hundred dollars in those five days. That may sound high but when you realize that is about ten months of fun packed in five twenty-four hour days it settles down to an average of from twenty to thirty a month. Gifts drive the price sky high. . . .

• • •

Today, $350 doesn't sound like a lot of money, but when privates were paid $75 a month and beginning schoolteachers made $1,200 a year, $350 was a large amount.

• • •

March 17, 1953

Dear Folks:

I received Mom's letter today. . . . Now Mom I've told you to see Dr. Rendleman and then the Red Cross to see if I could get home for a while. That might help cure Pop's nervousness. The least they can say is no. . . . At any rate, regardless of how things go I shall be home in a year or so. Then you'll be seeing too much of me again.

At the present time I have a cup of cocoa getting hot—along with a can of sausages. It's getting harder and harder for us to get canned milk, but we get enough and that plus powdered milk takes care of us. Tonight we are having extra special chocolate. Morrison brought back a can of Nestle's sweetened chocolate—which is much better than the Army stuff we've been drinking. . . .

• • •

This is one of the few surviving letters to my parents. It illustrates what unnecessary pressures can be brought to bear at an impossible time. I had no knowledge of the reality of the situation at home or the severity of my father's illness, but even if I had, there was nothing I could have done about it. It bothered me, as is shown in the reference to earlier advice and in a later letter to my sister, where I asked her to look into the situation. I also received regular reports about an aunt who died a slow and painful death from cancer, accompanied by urgent requests to come home and help. All I could do was worry and try to divert my mother's chain of thought with comments concerning my living conditions in Korea.

Soldiers in combat don't need letters of woe or, for that matter, clippings of friends who have been killed or wounded. I have no idea how many others received such letters. Don Frechette had the talent to turn such things into humor for all, but I didn't. I never shared these problems with my tent mates and they didn't share theirs with me.

• • •

March 23, 1953

Dear Ethel:

. . . Just a little mail came in yesterday, washed out roads being at fault. I received one letter from Santa Barbara Jr. College (for girls) and one from York, South Carolina. Both of them, surprisingly enough, were both readable and intelligent. What is the world coming to? . . .

When I last heard Dad was still home sick. I suggest you have a long and serious talk with Dr. Rendleman when you reach St. Louis. . . .

• • •

Note the date, remember that the previous letter refers to past correspondence, assume seven days each way for mail, and you can see that I'd spent a month worrying about my father. The military had and still has a procedure for family emergencies, and arbitration powers in such cases have been assigned to the Red Cross. If it had been determined that a genuine emergency existed, I would have been able to obtain a home leave. This would have extended the amount of time I spent in Korea upon my return, not gotten me out of any duty.

My father died on his way to work a few months after my return, so he really was ill. But the extent of his poor health was not recognized prior to his death.

• • •

Dear Ethel:

. . . The roads continue to be all fouled up as a result of the thaws. Also, the bridge down the road from here was knocked out by Chinese shelling last night. Thus our mail continues to be fouled up.

Events over here are shaping up—last week we had a "skunk hunt." This is when the whole area is searched and all civilians not having proper credentials are rounded up. I understand they rounded up about two hundred infiltrators. Then in the last couple weeks there has been some very sharp fighting over here. Last night, it was especially rough in this sector. For a while everyone thought the Chinese were opening their spring offensive, but it fell through. . . .

• • •

I intended to censor all my letters, as I believe most of us did, forestalling any thought that we could possibly be in harm's way. The problem was that some danger had become normal and we permitted references to it to slip into our letters home, since it wasn't "really" dangerous.

We had mixed feelings about the people who infiltrated the area. It's impossible for someone who wasn't there to imagine the devastation. The war had so completely destroyed the country that the Koreans had no way to make a living. Some of these infiltrators were simply people trying to get back to their homes, to see if anything remained. Others were struggling to scratch out illicit livings by doing our wash, or sewing, or prostitution, or anything that would permit them and their families to survive.

One elderly man lived at our headquarters. He worked in the supply room in exchange for food and a place to sleep. None of us knew his name, we simply called him "Papasan." We liked him. He had a heart attack and somehow received treatment at the hospital—illegally, I suppose. He returned when he recovered. We were all the family he had and he was the family we'd left behind.

Some of the infiltrators were guerrillas who sniped at isolated soldiers or were spotters for the Communist artillery. The safest thing for all, though harsh, was the official policy of keeping civilians south of the Thirty-eighth Parallel.

• • •

April 1, 1953

Dear Ethel:

I can't let April Fools' Day pass without at least writing a letter on it. It's impossible though to crack the usual jokes over here or in a letter.

One of the message center boys told me that the truce teams had at least agreed on the disposal of prisoners. But now I don't know if it was the April first facts or the real thing. Naturally, I'm hoping that it was the real thing. I believe that is supposed to be the only big issue holding them up. . . .

Today ends the second day of our three day alert and it looks as if nothing much is going to happen. Our intelligence had received word that the Chinese were to try a breakthrough here at the juncture of the Americans and the Greeks. Naturally, we were all alerted to be prepared to pull out at a minutes notice. In the meantime, the artillery has kept the Chinese positions opposite us well plastered. The big brass used the foreknowledge to line up extra tanks and artillery in this sector as well as bringing in a few thousand reserve troops. Tonight is the last night it is expected. If the Chinese try it they will get a devil of a shock when they run into all the power that has been concentrated in this sector. . . .

• • •

The three standard rumor mill topics were withdrawal from the line, peace talks, and the Communist threat, in that order. To receive four or three points, your unit had to be in position for twenty-one days. Always, about mid-month, rumors would fly that we were going to be pulled off the line so the high command could give us fewer points and keep us in Korea longer, thereby saving money. The recurrence of that rumor should have sent a message to our leaders concerning our faith in them, if they cared.

The other major topics of gossip were potential attacks, atrocities by the North Koreans, and how we returned their "favors."

• • •

April 7, 1953

Dear Ethel:

I'll be damned! So Johnny is going to have that little sister or brother. Well, congratulations all around—but I have an idea small

John has a devil of a surprise coming. Looks as if we can't keep big John in the poor house one way we'll just tackle it from another angle.

Well, back to letter writing, one of our stations called in on FM (voice radio) saying he was lost on CW (code). So I had to call him back in. In such a case we send out a series of V's which he tunes on. A "V" is dot, dot, dot, dash and it comes out in a steady dit dit dit dah, dit dit dit dah, dit dit dit dah, pause dit dit dit dah etc. We will send about three series of three each and then wait for an answer—if none comes we try again. The fellow who was lost was 9aa [Ninth Anti-Aircraft] and he came in after my second call.

At such times as the above is when the Chinese love to hop in on us with all their jamming. They know we are having troubles and are willing to lend a helping hand. Sometimes they will even send out a series of their own but we can usually tell the difference without much trouble. . . .

• • •

I have included this letter because it gives insight into our routine work. As often happened, it was written during time on station, in between calls. We normally worked on four different frequencies; primary and backup code frequencies and primary and backup voice frequencies. These were all changed at least once a week. Sometimes one of our subordinate stations would "get lost," that is, lose our signals because of a unit move or for some other reason. Then we would have to send out signals until he could tune his radio to ours.

Occasionally, the Chinese would send signals in an attempt to confuse us, but this was seldom a real problem. Code operators quickly learn one another's "touch." The way a person sends code is almost as distinctive as his voice, and there were many operators we knew by their touch, though we never met them in person.

We also had radios tuned to frequencies that permitted us to communicate with airplanes and with division headquarters. These were changed as routinely as the others.

• • •

April 8, 1953

Dear Ethel:

. . . Rumor says we will be here until the end of the month—and that is a happy thought. At three points a month and combat pay, I'd spend the rest of my time in Korea here.

Having just had to receive a message it is my opinion that if the Army ever has to depend on radio for its communications it will just be out of luck. The average radio operator seems to know nothing about radio procedure or—for that matter—about sending or receiving. . . .

Incidentally, one of our dogs—Lady—just had a litter. She has been keeping them in the wiremen's tent. Naturally, all of our hardened wiremen have been stealing the choicest foods out of the mess hall to feed her. The other day the cooks caught them at it and there was almost a free-for-all over the matter. Finally it was agreed that the wiremen would ask from now on, but that they would be provided with the extra food. . . .

• • •

I saw no inconsistency at the time between drawing combat pay for being in a danger zone and simultaneously drawing three points for being in a safe zone.

It was my experience as a radio operator that led to my current skepticism that the communications systems on which our military depends so heavily would be effective in a war in which both sides really wanted to fight. In Korea, there was no questioning the superiority of our equipment, especially our communications equipment, yet the Communists knew our every move in advance and could jam our systems whenever they chose.

• • •

April 14, 1953

Dear Folks:

Once again, I find myself up at the Greeks. As I have previously said, this is all right with me, in fact, the more the merrier. I feel pretty certain now that I shall get three points and combat pay for the month of April. . . .

This time my companions here at the Greeks are Weber and Matos. Weber I came over with and he is a hard worker. Matos, a new replacement (Puerto Rican), is also showing himself to be a hard worker. As a result I think there will be no dissension up here this time. . . .

April 19, 1953

Dear Ethel:

I suddenly realized today that I had not written you recently. Don't feel too badly, however, as I ran out of stationery and finally got messenger service to bring me up some from the Red Cross. Since I haven't been receiving much mail recently it doesn't especially bother me that I was unable to write for a while. . . .

• • •

Both of these letters must have been written while I was with the Greek battalion. Both have the same general lack of news followed by discussions of the weather and family matters. In the second letter I argued for the name Julia Ann instead of Julia Anne for Johnny's expected sister.

It was during this second trip to the Greek battalion that I first saw the difference between their discipline and ours. Large pots of hot soup, with the usual fresh bread, had been brought forward for lunch. We were in line waiting to fill our cups with soup, and one of the Greek soldiers was standing next to a friend talking, rather than staying the required five to ten yards apart. The Greek colonel walked up and, without saying a word, took a rifle from one of the men in the line, slammed the offending soldier in the head, returned the rifle, and walked away as the soldier lay on the ground. The Greeks lost far fewer men killed through carelessness than we did.

• • •

April 23, 1953

Dear Ethel:

As you can tell, I am getting very lazy when it comes to writing. This is partly due to the fact that I have nothing to write about and partly due to the fact that recently I've been kept busy doing other things.

There always seems to be firewood to chop or water to carry or

the tent to clean up or something else. Most of the men up here—
or should I say overgrown boys—seem to think they are entitled
to loaf while others do their work. Maybe they are right, but personally I'm getting mighty damned sick of it and have been explaining the facts of life to them recently—however it seems to do
no good.

At any rate, it makes my days pass quicker although it knocks
the devil out of my writing time. If it continues I shall move up to
the other tent. The hell with 'em!. . . .

I have some pictures being developed at present and shall send
you some copies when I get them back from the photographer. At
present, he is a little sore at me because we were supposed to go
to the showers together the other day and I forgot him and went
with Matos & Jim Gay. Jim and I continue to be the best of friends,
probably because we are so alike in so many ways. . . .

• • •

I enjoy the mention of firewood in this letter. Evidently, some
of our expensive, cured, prefabricated bunker material remained.
There was no other wood in our area, all of it having been used up
long before by one side or the other.

There was more to my frustration than is mentioned in the letter. It's true that some of our experienced operators did little in the
way of housekeeping, but it's also true that anyone getting ready
to leave a situation begins seeing and commenting on all of its
negative elements. At the time I wrote this letter, I had already been
interviewed for a position with the scouts and had accepted it.

I have two more short letters that I believe were written from
the communications platoon: one to my parents, the other to my
sister. Each is short and limited to comments on the weather and
family matters. The lack of information about work makes me
wonder if I had already moved to the scouts by this time.

The letters written from the radio platoon are marked by a
gradual decrease in information. Our lives were tedious, excitement being limited to family-type arguments as to whose turn it
was to do some small task. The enthusiasm of writing to various
newspapers gradually subsided, and no new idea took its place. Life
was primarily a matter of waiting, accompanied by brief interludes
of work. Less time was devoted to keeping warm than at radio

school, but it was still a problem at times, especially after Command decided we no longer needed oil.

Card games were common in both tents, men coming off duty taking the places of those going on. These were nickel-and-dime games of poker, pinochle, and red dog. We couldn't afford higher stakes. On warm days we weren't above playing children's games outside. I still have a photograph of Maltby sailing a homemade boat on a puddle we created with a small dam.

The only visit by an officer that I remember was the one described earlier. We had excellent NCO leadership, but that was it. I wish I remembered the names of more of the people I served with, but the only other person I really remember that I haven't already mentioned is Welton "Red" Hood, also from the St. Louis area. Red was not only excellent on the radio, but his farm background had taught him how to repair much of our machinery. If he hadn't been there, our radio would have been silent far more than it was.

Spring found me bored and ready for something new.

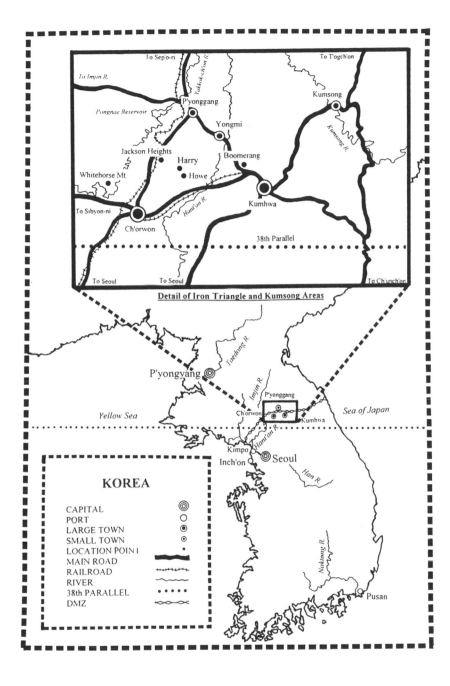

Detail of Iron Triangle and Kumsong Areas

KOREA

CAPITAL	
PORT	
LARGE TOWN	
SMALL TOWN	
LOCATION POINT	
MAIN ROAD	
RAILROAD	
RIVER	
38th PARALLEL	
DMZ	

Ethel Dannenmaier Van Cleve, the "Dear Ethel" to whom the author wrote and the one from whom he got such amusing letters, detailing her experiences as the young mother of an active four-year-old.

The interior courtyard of the barracks in Japan where we awaited assignment to Korea, December 1952.

The view south from the bunker we dug overlooking
Chinese positions on the eastern edge of the Ch'orwon plain. The mud road was our main supply road.
Note the complete lack of buildings or villages—war
had destroyed everything.

This truck is on the main supply route to the central front. There was a
speed limit, but as the road was under enemy observation, the limit was
universally ignored. Note the lack of villages or buildings in the once
densely populated area.

Papasan, the only name we knew him by, lived in the supply tent at regimental headquarters. A dentist who had lost his family to the Chinese Communists, he was loved and respected by the enlisted men with whom he worked.

The author, at regimental headquarters, with a captured Chinese burp gun. These fired extremely rapidly, so that if you got hit once you typically got hit several times. Fortunately, burp guns had less power than our rifles and carbines and didn't normally penetrate our flak vests.

The author's close friend Jim Gay, looking out over the Imjim River. The pontoon bridge visible downstream is the one referred to in a letter complaining that the Communists had blown up a bridge and caused another disruption in mail service.

The author outside the radio shack at the Greek Expeditionary Forces battalion headquarters, when war was still an exciting game. Note the camouflage and the sandbags. While not too close to the front line, this place was within easy range of Communist artillery and frequently under fire.

Stan O'Connor, leader of the First Squad, Scouts, Fifteenth Infantry Regiment, standing in front of a tank that overlooked the eastern slope of Outpost Harry. It was from this tank that Monk launched a shell into an enemy position about eight hundred yards away, causing a large explosion.

One of the many gardens within the walls of Buddhist temples that the author saw while on R&R in Kyoto, Japan.

The author outside the tent where he initially taught reading to men who reported less than a fifth-grade education and English to Puerto Rican soldiers.

Jim Gay looks at his cot and personal possessions left out in a cold fall drizzle after his tent was taken for use by the four-woman Red Cross team that delivered coffee to the enlisted men.

Downtown Seoul in 1953, during the author's weekend visit, following four waves of war that leveled large areas of the city, leaving
most of the remaining buildings uninhabitable. The shacks pictured
here were built of scavenged metal and wood.

Another view of downtown Seoul in 1953. When the author showed this
photograph to elderly Koreans in 1987, they commented, "Those men were
wealthy—they had shoes."

7

INTELLIGENCE AND RECONNAISSANCE

Fortune smiled on me during my transition to the scouts. I was assigned to the first squad, the squad Audie Murphy, the most decorated soldier in World War II, occupied. No heavy fighting was occurring in our area during my transition. Still better, my squad was sleeping at headquarters while digging a new observation bunker. That gave me a week to orient myself with little peril. My introduction to new comrades, new duties, and my first patrols were all on a relaxed basis.

Being a scout was less dangerous than I expected. Our job was to find the enemy, watch, and report. To do this, you had to stay alive. Occasionally, we led fight patrols whose purpose was to stir up enemy action, but these were uncommon. Our usual patrols were three-man information-gathering ventures conducted after dark. Also, I was a radio scout. My primary responsibility was the radio, not fighting. On patrol, I had to be close enough to the patrol leader to move alongside him so he could use my radio or else I'd transfer his messages for him, depending on the situation. On three-man patrols I was typically second as my squad leader, Sergeant O'Connor, would be first. On larger patrols I had to keep within sight of the patrol leader, who would often assume a position behind one or two point men in the middle of the patrol.

In the Fifteenth Infantry Regiment the scouts lived on the front line without break as long as the regiment was in combat. In 1952 American military doctrine required three fighting units plus a support unit at each level of command. Thus, there were three fighting battalions and one support or artillery battalion in a regiment, just as there were three fighting regiments and one support regiment in a division. The idea was to have two groups fighting and one as backup—resting—with the heavy weapons or artillery in a support position. This should have meant two scout squads on line and one resting, as each line battalion would have a scout squad patrolling its area. Our situation was different. The Fifteenth, in addition to its three American infantry battalions, had a Greek battalion assigned to it, so there were three battalions on line, with the fourth resting. That meant continuous line time for the three scout squads.

Our scout squads were scattered on the tops of the mountains, which offered the best observation of enemy positions. Sometimes we were on, sometimes slightly behind, and occasionally in front of the front line, which, in the Ch'orwon area, was a long series of bunkers connected with trenches and fronted with barbed wire and mine fields. Tanks guarded gaps in the line, typically at spots where dirt trails, the highways of the ox carts of the past, left our area and ran north through no-man's-land into Communist territory.

Our squad often worked with the Greeks, whom I came to know and respect. Tall, strong, brown-haired, green-eyed fighting men— I can still see them moving onto the line, a rifle slung over one shoulder, a long-handled shovel or pick over the other, and often a loaf of bread sticking out of one jacket pocket and a bottle of cognac out of the other.

One of the Greek officers, all of whom spoke English, told us that most of their enlisted men had been in prison serving long sentences. Some had fought for the Communists during their own civil war. They were being given an opportunity to earn their freedom and regain their citizenship.

A letter of commendation from the commander of the Greek Expeditionary Force is one of the two military awards I received of which I am proud. The other is the Combat Infantryman's Badge.

When I wrote to my family, I was deliberately casual in my announcement of my new job.

• • •

April 29, 1953

Dear Folks:

I received Mom's letter today telling of the books and of Aunt Tillie's funeral. I read the part about the food aloud and was almost chased out of the tent. No thanks on the offer of the corncob and tobacco. I can get all of the corncob pipes I want from the Red Cross and tobacco can be acquired through the PX.

I have a little news for you which I might as well tell you now. I have transferred out of the Commo Platoon and am now a radio operator for the I&R [Intelligence and Reconnaissance] Platoon. There is no real difference for I still live in the same general area— actually it is just a change in leadership. I have an idea I am going to like this new setup much more than the old one—although there will be a little more work.

. . . as to the other news. It began to rain yesterday morning and hasn't stopped since. My new bunker is completely waterproof which makes me very happy. It is a large four room job situated about a hundred yards from the mess hall. This is an improvement over Commo which was about a half mile up hill from the mess hall.

• • •

This letter introduced my parents to the fact that I had joined the scouts. I was proud of the move. All the scouts in our regiment were volunteers. All except for the three radio scouts were also ex-paratroopers. It was a fraternity of purpose and duty, and new members had to be accepted after volunteering. The squad had a week to decide if the proposed member was acceptable. I knew of guys who volunteered but were rejected by the squads. When accepted, we were told that if we lost our nerve all we had to do was ask and we'd be transferred to a safe position in the company. That promise was kept in the case of one fellow who lost his enthusiasm after he was wounded.

There was a slipup in the letter. To reassure my parents, I said I was almost chased from the tent, but then I forgot and mentioned the bunker. Submerged in the reality of Korea, I had forgotten that the people at home didn't understand the nuances of our living arrangements. Anyone who lived in a tent was assumed to be in a reasonably safe area. I thought I was reassuring them that I was in a safe area, but my message probably went straight over their heads.

I also left out a few things. Our platoon headquarters was at regimental headquarters. It was in a comfortable, dirt-floor bunker dug partially into the side of a hill and located reasonably close to the mess hall. But we didn't live there. We just slept there while digging in on a new location up front. As soon as our new bunker was finished, which took about one week, we began living on the line. We visited our bunker in the rear when reporting back from a patrol. If we had no patrol to report, a messenger and a "shotgun" guard drove back to get the mail, C rations, or other necessities. During these visits we were also able to pick up gossip, which, like the kudzu vine, grew by the minute.

• • •

April 30, 1953

Dear Folks:

Another day much like the others except that it was payday and the last day of April. By the time you receive this letter we will be well into May. One more month down on the list. Sounds good doesn't it?

. . . Today it cleared up and dried off so we had a very nice day. Warm and sunny. It was really a very nice day.

I spent today doing nothing just like back in the Commo Platoon so you see there isn't too much difference in the jobs. They tell me it will get easier once we get organized, but I don't see how.

Did I tell you my present squad leader was a senior at Ohio State when he did the same thing I did and signed up for two years? You would be surprised at how many 2 year enlistees there are in the Army. As a group, they are usually college men who signed up after graduating or else they interrupted their studies for it. Thus they are usually a pretty intelligent lot.

Well, I just interrupted this letter to go get paid. Seventy four dollars. . . .

• • •

Most of the scouts had attended college. As a group they really were intelligent as well as enthusiastic, never shirking either work or danger. They had an "it's all a game" mentality that I didn't encounter again in the military until I had occasion to work with some fighter pilots years later.

Our squad leader was Stan O'Connor. The night I moved into the scout bunker he was seated on his bunk, a candle burning by his feet, using a pocketknife to pick pieces of shrapnel out of his leg. First he located the tiny black bumps that indicated metal under the skin, and then he slit open the skin and squeezed out the bits of steel that had worked their way to the surface. When I walked in, he simply pointed to an empty bunk in the corner and said it was mine. That was Stan—never any fuss. He just anticipated what was needed and did it. He was a quiet, soft-spoken man of average height, nearsighted, stoop-shouldered, and duck-footed—no one would ever pick him for a movie role as a scout, but I believe Colonel Akers, our regimental commander, trusted him more than any of the rest of us to do a difficult job—and the colonel was right. Stan was dedicated, thoughtful, and fearless, qualities that confirmed leadership in an uncommon group.

I've always thought of Stan O'Connor as the bravest man I ever knew, but that might be unfair to many others, men like Jack, a silent, unsmiling Japanese American who was meticulously clean and neat. I remember him carefully trimming a pencil-thin mustache with a two-edged razor blade each day and washing whenever possible. Once, in a fight, Jack was hit about six times with slugs from a rapid-firing Chinese burp gun. Fortunately, all the slugs hit his ammunition pouches in the belt around his waist, so he wasn't wounded, just heavily bruised. He never said a word about this or reported for medical treatment; he just took off the belt, examined the damage to it and to his stomach, and went on as silently as before.

Ray Barker was a talkative, laughing southerner from Tennessee who became my good friend. A ready volunteer for any mission and the only man who felt free to tease Jack, Barker constantly joked about his own lack of courage.

Kim Shi Han, our KATUSA, was a gentle scholar who showed excitement only once—when a patrol, making a wrong turn, went too far behind enemy lines.

There were others, of course. As a group, all the scouts with whom I worked knew their responsibilities and fulfilled them with little fuss.

• • •

May 1, 1953

Dear Ethel:

As you can see another month is down and out. You can bet that next April I will be in the States. That is certainly a good thought.

I don't believe that I've told you yet that I've changed jobs. I transferred from Commo Platoon to I&R Platoon as radio operator. In this platoon I'll get four points while on line and rotate on 36 points. About that there is no doubt.

Today, I've done nothing all day long. . . .

For some reason I didn't finish this letter the other day. Evidently something came up that took me away from it. . . . Today was the first time I noticed it lying there unfinished.

I've been kept much busier in this new job and on the whole am happy about it. Time passes much faster. But—believe me—I'm still not being overworked. In fact, today I spent about five hours sleeping. Since I have one of the usual head colds I didn't mind the extra rest at all. . . .

• • •

My squad dug in on a new location overlooking the Ch'orwon valley. We were on its eastern edge, with mountains to our right and the Ch'orwon plain in front and to the west. The slightly elevated roadbed of a railroad ran north along the edge of the mountains, the rails and wooden ties having been long since removed by troops of one army or another. About five hundred yards in front of the base of our hill was a small grove of trees—saplings, really. The Chinese positions ran perhaps three hundred yards northeast of them. The grove was well known as a hunting ground for both United Nations and Chinese patrols.

Behind us was a low ridge and desolate countryside, with a dirt road immediately behind the ridge and parallel to the line. Our main supply road, also dirt, ran southward from the parallel. Farther back we could see the guard post on the trail leading to the Greek battalion Headquarters Company and the only large tree in the area. Both of these, the guard post and the tree, were blown up in the next week or two. I saw the tree explode, and I still believe some Chinese gunner looked at it and thought, What the hell, why leave one standing?

As usual, our position was at the top of the highest hill in our area. It gave us great oversight. It was also a long way up to carry water and food.

For the construction of our new bunker the army supplied timbers similar to those we'd used for firewood a month earlier in the communications platoon. These were delivered to the bottom of the mountain and we were supposed to carry them up. We also received a roll of chicken wire but no nails or staples. We had a hand saw, a hammer head without a handle, and picks and shovels for digging. We also had a pair of rusty pliers.

Our first task after we finished digging was to acquire some nails since our own quartermaster had none. Barker and I drove to the Sixty-fifth Infantry Regiment's quartermaster and almost got a case of nails before the sergeant spotted the emblems on our jeep. Our southern accents and blond hair probably aroused his suspicions, the Sixty-fifth being primarily a Puerto Rican unit. He told us to go to our own regiment, that he wasn't there to take care of the Fifteenth. Fortunately, on our way back, we found a spot where some engineers had been working and had left half a keg of nails when they quit for the night. There was no guard.

A second problem was the construction itself. Poor at the job, we were incompetent, not lazy. You should try cutting planks that are eight or ten inches thick and twenty inches wide with a hand saw—a dull one at that. The work went slowly. Following someone's lucky inspiration, Jack, Barker, and I acquired a truck and drove south until we located a Korean village where we managed to round up seven Korean men. At first they refused to get on the truck, but Jack said something in Japanese and they obeyed without further argument. When Barker asked what he'd said, Jack replied, "I told them I would cut their throats if they didn't get on." Barker and I were silent as reality intruded. We both believed Jack meant what he'd said.

That morning, under our direction, the building continued—slowly. At lunch, we surprised our "volunteers" by sharing our C rations and giving them all the C-ration cigarettes (which were really stale) and the leftover cans of corned beef hash, which we hated. When we started back to work that afternoon, the oldest of the seven Koreans, a white-haired elder, climbed to where one of our men was trying to drive in a nail with our broken hammer, took away the hammer, and proceeded to drive in the nail quickly and efficiently. Then he took charge. Soon, all of us—Koreans and scouts—were obeying his orders, given in a combination of Korean and hand signals. That evening, we gave each of the Koreans an American dollar (which was illegal) for their efforts and returned them to their village. The next day when we returned to the village, the same seven men were waiting by the road. Food, cigarettes, and a dollar meant a lot. Those men worked with us until the job was done.

I had one more encounter with that Korean elder. After the truce, the army rounded up all Koreans living north of the Thirty-eighth Parallel, confiscated contraband, which included U.S. money, and sent them south. My squad participated. Captured men stood in a large circle, their pockets inside out and their possessions lying on a cloth in front of them. I spotted the elder, his small roll of money and the rusty pliers and broken hammer—which we'd given him—at his feet. Showing no recognition, I walked over and silently used my foot to push the money and tools under the blanket on which he had laid out his other (legal) possessions. I stayed there until the inspector was safely past. Neither of us betrayed recognition. I've often wondered if he recognized me. I've also wondered what happened to all the money collected from those Koreans who had earned it in good faith by helping Americans but had no one to hide it for them.

The finished bunker had two rooms, one on the U.S. side of the mountaintop for sleeping and the other an observation room overlooking the Chinese lines. A narrow tunnel, perhaps fifty feet long, connected the rooms. Three feet of sandbags, rocks, and dirt were on top of the planks forming the roof. Bunks were made by cutting saplings for poles. We used commo wire to lace them together and tied chicken wire over them to serve as mattresses. The bunks were three deep and more comfortable than you might think; there were nine of them in the room, which couldn't have been more than nine feet by nine feet. From a center post hung a Coleman lantern for light, and we cooked on a one-burner Coleman stove we had somehow acquired. We were to lose both stove and light in a subsequent move, but we enjoyed them while we had them.

The observation room was smaller, with space for only two or three men standing shoulder to shoulder.

For some reason, during the week or two that we worked on that observation post, the Chinese didn't bother sending a single shot our way—not an artillery shell, not a mortar. During the same period we could easily observe Outpost Harry, which topped a hill to the east, where it was worth your life to be seen in the open, and the scout observation post that supported Harry, where men moved very cautiously.

I had my first patrol during this time. I remember it well, from the stark terror at the start to the sound of a bullet going past my head somewhere out in no-man's-land.

One morning Barker and I were informed that we were going out with O'Connor at dark on an information-gathering patrol. We were supposed to go out a certain distance, look for signs of enemy activity, and then radio in for further instructions. In preparation, we checked our weapons, grenades, and ammunition; then we rested. At the time, I had a bad cold and a deep cough, not a good situation for a man on patrol. I went to the medic at headquarters who gave me a pint of codeine cough syrup and told me that the next time he would stop me from going out. That was serious, since I was the radioman and an essential part of a patrol.

That night, in moonless dark, the three of us followed the trail down the back of the mountain to the squad jeep and drove to our jump-off point. The drive may have been the most dangerous part of the night, and not just because of Stan's nearsighted driving. The road was dirt, lined with mine fields on each side, and barely wide enough for two jeeps to pass each other. Our major fear was encountering tanks as they, like us, drove without lights and at full speed. An encounter would have been fatal.

When we reached the jump-off point, Stan parked the jeep and we headed for no-man's-land, staying ten or fifteen feet apart. I fought panic. My throat was dry, I had trouble breathing, and I needed to urinate. I was afraid Stan or Barker would hear my heart pounding and know how terrified I was. As we walked around the tank that served as a roadblock, Stan whispered to load up, take our rifles off safety, and be cautious going through the barbed wire, which was strung in front of the silent, dark trenches with their invisible, ever-watching infantry who were the front line.

All my problems disappeared once I touched the barbed wire. It was time to do my job. An enhanced alertness replaced the fear. We moved out along an old road, staying as far apart as we could and still see each other, skirting the Chinese positions to the east. Somewhere along the way I kicked a piece of metal, probably left

as a warning device. I was rewarded with a sniper's bullet crack-
ing past my head, which gave us a fair notion of his location. Not
too much farther along we reached our objective. Stan motioned
me forward so he could radio in our location and observations and
receive instructions. There were none, other than to return.

That patrol was the first and last time I experienced terror in
Korea. I've never been more alert and alive than when on patrol,
and it was true of that first patrol, once I touched the barbed wire.
For me, patrol action was a high to end all highs.

• • •

May 7, 1953

Dear Folks:

As I predicted in yesterday's letter my cold is almost completely
gone. As a result, I am feeling much better. I took a couple aspirins
last night and pretty well sweated it out.

I got a very nice letter from Ethel today plus an equally nice one
from Bert (Seattle). I also received a church paper from Mt. Tabor
along with a schoshee [very small] note from Rev. He certainly has
no idea of how to take care of his flock. At any rate, I was very surprised to receive it.

I have been very busy lately helping to build a bunker during the
day and working on my radio at night. The days have been passing very quickly. . . .

• • •

Patrol action and contact with the enemy had increased in our
area. On the morning I wrote the above letter, we'd just completed
a difficult, squad-sized patrol—bad enough that our lieutenant gave
us a bottle of whiskey when we returned to help us relax. We went
to regimental headquarters to report in, pick up the mail, and eat
breakfast before returning to our outpost to get some sleep. While
waiting for the mess hall to open, we drank our whiskey and read
the mail. Exhausted, my nose again rubbed in the filth and reality
of my life, I received a church bulletin, in the margin of which the
pastor had written something like, "Bill, I'm too busy to write."

The bulletin itself reported that Christmas packages had been
sent to seven church members who were in the military. But they'd
forgotten me, the only one in combat. It was the wrong morning

to get such a note. Upset and angry at the disinterest of a man I'd trusted, I wrote an angry reply—and never heard from him again. A young woman I knew from church wrote to say that the pastor had shown her my letter. She said her husband had been in the artillery, that my life wasn't so bad, and that I shouldn't write such things to the minister. I wrote back, saying what I thought of her opinion and of an artilleryman's right to speak of the infantry. She didn't reply either.

There are tremendous differences in the lives of artillerymen and infantrymen when in combat. The artillery lives behind the front line, whereas the infantry is the front line. Artillery rides, infantry walks. When I, as a scout radioman, walked, I wore a three-pound steel helmet and a nine-pound bulletproof vest. I carried a twenty-pound radio on my back and a seven- or eight-pound rifle in my hand. I also carried grenades and extra ammunition. Scouts often carried eight grenades: two concussion grenades for taking prisoners, two white phosphorous grenades for emergencies (the Chinese feared them because the bits of phosphorous would burn through uniforms and flesh; they also provided a smokescreen for a fast retreat), and four fragmentation grenades. Concussion grenades were carried in the left pocket, as you always had time if you wanted to use one, and white phosphorous grenades in the right pocket; the shrapnel grenades were hung on our uniform straps to make them quick to reach, and we loosened the pins so they'd be easy to pull. I also had a bayonet, a hunting knife, a canteen of water, a canteen cup, and a spoon. We weren't pretty, just functional.

As long as we were on line—and for scouts that was most of the time—we had to be alert. We slept lightly and ate lightly. Our lives depended on remembering that there were people out there who were being paid to kill us. Worse yet, there were some people who wanted to.

Artillerymen drove from one place to another, had vehicles to carry goodies with them, and relaxed in their bunkers between firing missions, secure in the knowledge that enemy soldiers were miles away with the infantry in between. To relax in that manner could be fatal to infantrymen—and was for too many.

This is not to say that I didn't appreciate the artillery, just that they couldn't speak for the infantry. We were lower on the "animal tree" than they.

• • •

Dear Folks:

It is now early afternoon and I have spent most of the day either sleeping or eating sandwiches of toast, fried eggs, and fried onions. It may not sound so hot but actually it is very tasty.

Today has turned into a very pleasant sunny day in contrast with the last two. Things are beginning to dry out and the world in general is looking up. During these last two days I've noticed the large number of fresh green plants on the hills. We've had all kinds of flowers for the last month but the leaves are first coming out now. . . .

Mom I'm sorry I forgot to write you a birthday letter—but what with changing platoons and taking up my new duties it slipped right past me first thing I knew. I first realized that I had bypassed it on the 9th and then went back to work again and forgot about it until today. Such is your son's memory. . . .

• • •

We moved frequently and had barely the energy and space for necessary gear. When we were on the move, there was no room for such luxuries as toothbrushes and razors, much less the pinup pictures and magazines portrayed in Hollywood movies, and no time to accumulate them when we stopped. Our patrols were normally at night. As a result, most of our days were spent waiting, doing nothing while remaining alert for the occasional artillery round or mortar fire or for any potential attack. One man was always on watch, often with a second or third man keeping him company, but shifts were short, given that each twenty-four hours was divided among eight or nine men. Our lives were filled with emptiness.

Interestingly, the scouts didn't gamble to pass the time when I was with them. Perhaps the job, with its immediate and potential dangers, intensified by the knowledge that we could escape by asking out, satisfied all our gambling needs.

Attention to the details of mundane activities helped fill the hours of waiting. Activities such as making hot chocolate and frying eggs became highly ritualized. We had a frying pan and our one-burner stove. At the time the above letter was written, we'd

acquired a case of eggs, a bag of onions, and fresh bread. We must
have been with the Greek battalion, because, while we could have
stolen the other items, we received fresh bread only from the
Greeks.

• • •

May 13, 1953

Dear Folks:

. . . One of the boys—Mangile—just left about an hour ago on
his way home. He was overseas 17 months. He spent nine months
in Japan before coming to Korea where he has spent eight more
before getting the necessary 36 points. You asked about my points.
At the end of this month I shall have sixteen. Not very many but a
good start. . . .

• • •

We had a strong belief, which was not true, that we actually had
to be shot at five days in the month to collect combat pay. April was
so peaceful that we rolled some grenades down the hill, reporting
them as incoming enemy artillery, so we could collect combat pay.
This must have confused the watching enemy!

Also interesting was how our behavior and reputations could
influence—erroneously—the decisions of our commanders. One
of our men routinely reported enemy sightings that none of the
rest of us saw. He would then call in the artillery to a designated
spot and report success. No one but him ever saw those enemies,
even if standing by his side. Ironically, after he left we were criticized for failing to report enemy movements.

My reputation for joking also caused a problem. Once I observed
seven enemy tanks moving between a range of hills 1,200 yards to
our front, but when I reported it I was told that my jokes were getting old, to forget it. I ranted and raved, and swore over the phone
as I counted the tanks in their leisurely movement between the hills,
but all to no avail. No one at headquarters believed me.

One of our people, I believe it was Mangile, earned his reputation at an earlier outpost. The squad was in position to observe
enemy soldiers as they came to get water for the day. He would
sneak out at dawn wearing a soft cap and from a forward location
shoot holes in enemy water cans. He'd return and laugh about how

thirsty they'd be that day. He quit this game after a sniper put a
bullet through his cap, singeing his hair.

• • •

May 14, 1953

Dear Folks:

I feel a lot better today. For the last two or three days we've had
a slight shortage of water. Plenty to drink—but not enough to
wash. This morning we got in all we needed and now—for the first
time in three days—I have a clean face and hands. It feels very nice.

Tomorrow or so I shall try to make it down to the shower—also
I will pass by the doughnut shop and try to bum some doughnuts
off the bakers there. That is one of those things we are supposed
to be getting—but that is limited to officers.

We now have a frying pan here so occasionally we can fry our
own eggs with toast. There is a new fellow in the outfit—Frank
Grasiano—who fries his eggs with onions, and believe it or not
they taste pretty good that way, especially if the onions are cut up
small. I still average about a cup of hot chocolate a day. Sometimes
more, sometimes less.

Everything has been pretty quiet over here recently. The Chinese
are getting nicer every day. They will now stop firing when our
medics go out to pick up the wounded—and you couldn't ask much
more. Of course it is still a war—but the peace rumors seem to be
getting stronger every day. . . .

• • •

In truth, patrol action had picked up considerably, often accompanied by contact with enemy patrols and short fights. There were
raids and counterraids all along the front. Enemy artillery fire had
increased dramatically, as had our counterfire. Large enemy patrols
were sighted in the areas of Jackson Heights, Old Charley, and
Outpost Harry.

The increased action may have been why our water wasn't arriving regularly. The nine of us were allocated five gallons of water a
day for drinking and washing—which was adequate if we received
it. I still have vivid memories of heating water in a helmet. Then
we would all sit in a circle, and we'd pass the helmet around and
each of us would wash his face, next each would wash his hands,

and finally his socks. If you were last, by the time the water reached you to wash your socks it was a thick, soupy brown, such that you questioned the value of washing the socks. Still, you washed them because clean socks were more important for comfort than clean anything else. We rotated positions, so a different person was last each time we had sufficient water for the ritual. It wasn't a bad system, if the water arrived. Unfortunately, often it didn't. We heard lots of explanations—jeep problems, water point problems, and the like. At the time, the explanations irritated us. Now, looking back, I suspect many of the drivers were in no hurry to drive into what they considered to be a high-risk area. Not all soldiers are heroes.

Getting a shower was more a joke than a reality. It was rarely more than once a month that we had an opportunity to go back as far as the shower point. This is another example of my forgetting that my parents wouldn't realize showers and bakeries were in safe areas. I never saw the doughnut shop, or a doughnut, until well after the truce.

Contrary to what you see in Hollywood movies, not all opposing soldiers killed each other whenever they got the chance. I know of at least four instances in which opportunities to kill were passed up. In one amusing case, not involving me, Stan O'Connor had run out of gas and, walking along the road, encountered three Asian mortar men who had built a fire. They had hot water and Stan had packs of coffee, so the four of them drank coffee together and, according to Stan, shared their mutual dislike of war. The next day he encountered the same three men in a prisoner-of-war camp. It turns out that they were Chinese soldiers.

We didn't consider the Chinese to be the vicious animals that we considered the North Koreans. When one reads of the atrocities, it was typically North Koreans at work. But units differed. At the time, we must have been facing a unit that erred on the kindly side of bloodthirsty. Still, no U.S. scouts or translators who were captured in Korea ever returned.

• • •

May 19, 1953

Dear Ethel:

Today begins my twelfth month in the Army. Eleven down and thirteen to go. That is not as good as it could be, but it is better than it was. I am, as you can see, an enthusiastic defender of Army life—for other people. I, myself, could do without it.

When I receive my leave I am going to visit all branches of the family. First, I'm going home though, and eat some of Mom's strawberry shortcake, after that I shall come up and see you about some of that cherry nutcake, and then I shall go see Joe and eat some of CA's pecan pies. The longer I'm over here the more my family devotion increases.

If I don't get out of the Army until late June, as I expect, I shall probably take the summer off. I have two plans of action in mind. I may float down the Mississippi to New Orleans. My companions in such a trip would be Jim Gay (who is quite willing to do anything but work his first summer home) and Rich Stieren, a fellow from Affton who is now at Head and Head.

The alternate is to take a tour of the west. We would go west on the northern route and return from California up the southern route. It wouldn't be too expensive since we could sleep out, wash along the way, and cook at least two meals a day for ourselves. We could also look up friends along the way for a good meal now and then. Main expenses would be gas, oil and "seeing" some of the towns we went through.

Whether or not I do it really doesn't make much difference—it is still a lovely plan. I am definitely planning on driving to Cleveland to see Jim Gay—I assure you that is one place I'll go and I'll probably come back through Cincinnati. But the rest is still in the idle dream stage. It actually hinges on the folks' health and the availability of a good companion. Jim would be good—we have not been good friends for five hard months for nothing, another acceptable partner would be Charley Moench or Don Zytowski. . . .

• • •

Not only our letters but also much of our conversation reflected our daydreaming. It was another way of passing the time. I remember one guy in the communications platoon who collected college catalogs. He selected either the University of Miami or the University of Florida and planned an entire four-year curriculum for himself that included not a single meaningful course. As I recall, he could get college credit for fly-fishing, swimming, and golfing. None of us took these plans seriously, but they were fun.

Charley Moench and Don Zytowski were, and are, friends of long standing. Charley and I went through high school, college, and graduate school together. Don and I went through college and graduate school together and were both employed at Washington University for several years. Charley and Don wrote to me regularly while I was in Korea, Don serving in Germany and Charley in the United States.

Charley Brown was not on my list of companions because I learned that he'd been killed in action. I'd gotten back to regimental headquarters one day and went to see Jim Gay. As regimental electrician he was always easy to locate. Sitting in his tent, he told me Charley had been killed while laying wire. Death had been quick and painless. I remember thinking about it a while and then saying that of the three of us probably Charley had been the best human being, with me second and Jim last; it seemed wrong for him to be killed first. Jim agreed.

That was the last time I spoke about Charley's death until now. One of the things you learn in combat is to live in the present, dream of the future, and write off the past. People simply disappeared unless, as in Charley's case, they were members of a special friendship group. That doesn't mean I haven't thought of him. I have. Often. To me, he'll always be the shy, gentle, blue-eyed, blond boy from the Carolinas who wanted to marry his girl and be a farmer.

• • •

May 19, 1953

Dear Folks:

Another warm sunny day. While it is still cold at night, it gets very warm during the day. In fact, down right hot. Fortunately, I am now living in a bunker instead of a tent. The bunker with its several layers of sand bags tends to stay cool—but the men living in tents roast during the day. . . .

I have heard no word of when I shall go on R&R. However, I expect to within the next month or two. I shall probably go in July. They used to put the names of those about to go on the bulletin board—however they have now stopped that practice so it's hard to know just when you are going. Jim Gay and I will probably go together although there is a chance that we won't. Guess I'll just have to wait and see.

• • •

Life in a bunker was surprisingly pleasant. The bunks were comfortable and the dirt floor was cool in hot weather and warm in cold weather. We also felt quite safe, though this bunker was blown up within three weeks.

The letter contains more hopeful comments about my R&R. By this time, those of us on the line were convinced that only favored people in rear areas and officers got their "rest and relaxation." Now I suspect Command had evidence of a coming attack by the Chinese and simply suspended R&R for enlisted men so that all possible bodies would be available. If so, it was a wise decision. We were to need all possible men.

Other troops were brought up from a rear area to dig a new line of trenches in the hills behind us, a second line in case we were forced to retreat. I never knew what regiment they were from, but they had an incredibly innocent lieutenant in charge. He had the men stack their weapons and march off with picks and shovels, leaving their possessions unguarded. We'd been on line continuously since January and our equipment was in sad shape. We went down and traded rusted and worn-out weapons for new ones. When they returned and discovered the loss, the lieutenant came charging up the hill and accosted Stan O'Connor. The exchange went something like this:

"Who's in charge here?"

" I am, sir, Sergeant O'Connor."

"Sergeant, your men stole weapons from my men while they were working."

"Lieutenant, if you'll furnish me with the forms showing the serial numbers of those weapons, I shall see to it that any with those numbers are returned immediately."

That ended the conversation. The lieutenant had no such evidence. None of us had paperwork identifying what weapons belonged to which soldiers. I suppose some existed somewhere, but I have no idea where. I do know it was common practice for anyone rotating home who had a good weapon to exchange it for the worst one in the squad. This practice alone would have destroyed the morale of the best military recordkeepers, if they'd been aware of it. At any rate, we obtained some nice new weapons. Too bad they hadn't left their nice new uniforms behind too.

• • •

May 21, 1953

Dear Ethel:

. . . The newest rumor is that we'll be here on line until at least the fourth of July. Jim Gay said that he heard we would be here until about the fifteenth of July. So you see we are not expecting any immediate move.

Mail hasn't come in yet so I don't really know much to talk about. With I&R I get mail about once every day—in the evening—so I'll have another hour or so to wait to see if I have any today. I can generally kill from a half an hour to an hour reading letters—i.e. if I get any. When I get newspapers, I can also waste a lot of time reading want ads and such—naturally, I always read the funnies first.

We have our radio fixed up now—as of last night—and have been catching up on the news, music, and baseball games. At present, we are getting a broadcast of a ball game—Dizzy Dean announcing. Takes me right back to St. Louis. I can kill a lot of time thinking about the things I shall do when I get home. . . .

• • •

Note that the rumor had the move on the fifteenth. A move on the fifteenth of any month would have denied to both us and the unit relieving us the four rotation points awarded to front-line soldiers since a unit was required to be on line twenty-one days for the men to receive four points. A move in mid-month would have kept all of us in Korea longer and reduced logistical problems and costs. My assumption that such timing was deliberate reflected my growing belief that to those in charge we were pawns to be manipulated for their gain.

The acquisition of a second radio, an AN/GRC 46A, like the ones we had in the communications platoon, permitted me once again to tune in Radio Moscow, which had excellent music, as well as American broadcasting. We weren't really supposed to be doing this, but we did, retuning to our assigned networks when necessary. The "angry forty-six-a" was a heavy, powerful radio that could send messages over long distances. I carried a much smaller, lighter radio on patrols.

When it was working, the radio helped considerably in fighting boredom, the monotony of the sameness, the emptiness, of our days. Another way to add a little excitement to the day and help pass the time was to ride shotgun on mail runs, a necessary practice at the time because of guerrilla attacks on jeeps traveling alone. I went on these as often as I could. The trips enabled me to get a hot meal at regimental headquarters and to visit Jim Gay.

On one of these trips I had another encounter with the medic. Our scout squad all cooked in the same pan and ate out of our aluminum canteen cups. Because we also cooked in the cups, they were dented and blackened—but carbon is sanitary, so we didn't worry. We ate with a spoon that we clipped to our belts and slid into our back pockets to keep from losing or from rattling when we were on patrol. At headquarters, they ate off trays using knives and forks and had water barrels in which they washed their utensils.

On this trip, the medic was inspecting everyone's mess gear to make certain it was sanitary. As he walked down the line of men, examining their trays, he sent soldiers who had bits of grease or food on their trays to wash them. I hid my cup and spoon (my only mess gear) behind me. He came to a full stop in front of me and waited. I had no choice but to show it to him. He looked at it, then looked at me with my dirty, unshaven face, helmet, flak vest, and rifle, all of which identified me as a visitor from the line, shook his head, and moved on. He knew I was doing the best I could.

An interesting event occurred one morning when I was on watch. Barker was keeping me company, just to avoid boredom, when we saw two men emerge from a bunker on Outpost Harry, which was on a lower knob of a mountain held by the Chinese. They walked straight up the mountain in the predawn light to the Chinese lines, disappearing briefly from sight. Then all hell broke loose with the smoke of exploding grenades and the rattle of American carbines. (Chinese burp guns were much faster than ours, sounding like a fast electric typewriter.) Suddenly the two reappeared, running down the hill as fast as they could. Later, we heard that they'd been up all night drinking and, about dawn, agreed it was a shame the Chinese could sit up there picking off their men and they couldn't do anything about it. Consequently, they loaded up with all the grenades they could carry, walked up the mountain, and, catching the guards asleep, killed everyone in sight before running back to safety.

Later this scene was repeated somewhat to the east of Outpost Harry but at the command level. The second occasion began with an artillery barrage, white phosphorous blanketing the top of the hill in smoke, while the infantry moved up to attack. I watched several men fall. One of our squads participated. I remember one of the men, I believe it was Baker, complaining bitterly because he couldn't get a replacement for his bayonet. He'd driven it through a man and into the doorpost of a bunker with such force that it had snapped off, leaving the man dangling.

We never knew the purpose of the attack, as no attempt was made to hold the hill. We believed at the time that it was a show put on for visiting dignitaries.

• • •

May 23, 1953

Dear Ethel:

I'm sitting here sipping hot cocoa and writing this letter to you. As you can tell from the lack of news we are still in the same place we have been in since last January. Our battalions have been moving around a bit but the regiment is still sitting in the same place. . . .

I expect that in July I shall go on R&R. At present, I have a hundred and thirty dollars saved towards it. Thus, I'll have that two hundred and whatever money I have in my pocket at the time I go. That should be enough. If I stay in Head and Head, I shall go with Jim Gay. I intend to use up about ten rolls of film in those five days and I should have some nice pictures out of it.

I have also been thinking that I might buy a good camera if I have enough money. It all depends on how my time works out. It is very hard to plan on doing anything definite in Japan while on R&R— too easy to get side tracked. . . .

• • •

On a stationary line, you're confined to your bunker and the trenches except when on patrol. Your only reading material consists of mail, if you receive it. Your job is to wait and stay alert, constantly alert, but this becomes a routine part of existence. There's little difference in hours or days. You occupy your time with trivia. You pass the time by daydreaming, making hot cocoa, frying eggs and onions, or writing letters about mundane matters to those who care about you. Recently, a friend, Leonard Lassor, who managed to earn three Purple Hearts as a medic during his year in Korea, said he believed that boredom was what led so many of us to volunteer so often: we were simply avoiding the monotony of our lives.

Surprisingly, despite moments of reality such as the death of a friend, many of us were still playing games, treating the situations in which we found ourselves as challenges to be overcome. We laughed a lot, sometimes about things most people would consider brutal or disgusting. We also played games to pass the time. A popular one was throwing bayonets. From easy targets, pine ammunition boxes at twenty to thirty feet, we graduated to games of dare, such as who could come closest to someone's foot. We'd joke about explaining to a medic how you managed to drop a bayonet through your boot and foot. The truth would have meant court martial. We laughed a lot over various explanations.

In some ways we led an extremely easy life; in others, an extremely difficult one. Our real enemies, in our minds, were the bureaucratic officers in the rear who interfered with our egocentric, pleasure-directed activities.

Our patrols during this period were of three basic types: small information-gathering patrols, normally of three men; patrols when the entire squad went out; and those in which we led infantry patrols trying to stir up a fight. My favorite rapidly became the three-man information-gathering patrol, mostly because it was the safest. This may not make sense immediately, so let me explain. The first rule of combat is to stay alive, but you must also take calculated risks. If you can get a whole bunch of men with one try—say, with a grenade—you may take it, counting on confusion to escape retribution. However, if you see three heavily armed men, widely spaced, and know that at your best you can only get one, which leaves two others to come at you, you're likely to leave them alone. Thus, three of us, keeping as far apart as we could, were probably safer than nine or thirty all bunched up. At least that was my figuring, and it seemed to hold true. Although we were shot at occasionally on those three-man patrols, we never had as much trouble as we did on patrols that included more people.

I don't remember most of the patrols, just aspects of them, such as being terribly thirsty and out of water on one but too exhausted from carrying the radio to go down to a creek for a drink. I do remember the routine, however. We slept in the morning, received our instructions and prepared equipment in the afternoon, and then, after dark, we were jeeped to a jump-off point. Once there, we'd load our rifles, being careful to take them off safety, leave the road, slip past any roadblock tanks or other positions, work our way through the barbed wire and any mine fields, and be off hunting.

8

THE CASTLE ON THE HILL

Toward the end of May, my squad moved from our quiet bunker overlooking the Ch'orwon valley and the west slope of Outpost Harry to one on the next mountain to the east. I concealed the move in the letters I wrote, having already described that position as dangerous. It was a higher hill, darn it, and a considerably more lively one, behind and slightly to the east of Outpost Harry, with the Sixty-fifth Infantry Regiment occupying the land to the right.

The bunker we moved into was magnificent. It was composed of a large sleeping room with a long, narrow observation room that had four apertures, each about two feet wide and a foot high. A shelf ran the length of the wall beneath those openings and, in addition to writing tablets, ash trays, and similar items, held a large periscope-like telebinoculars that permitted us to watch the enemy positions without exposing ourselves to sniper fire. I was to spend many an hour sitting at that table, lit cigarette in hand, watching the Chinese lines for signs of activity.

The bunker walls, including the one separating the sleeping room from the observation room, consisted of those large, preshaped timbers from the States that I spoke of earlier. Grasiano, experienced in construction, guessed it must have cost U.S. taxpayers well over a hundred thousand dollars for just those timbers. The roof was made of pine logs cut from the remnants of the Korean forest, the logs being covered with tarpaulins and then with the usual three feet of sandbags and rocks. Our wood plank door opened into a trench about six feet deep. This led westward and downward, perhaps fifty yards, and then phased into a rutted mud trail leading down the mountain. The land around the bunker and trenches was torn and devoid of trees or brush, testimony to the continuing, if sporadic, incoming mortar and artillery fire.

Officially, we were at Observation Post Howe, but in my mind I always thought of it as "the Castle on the Hill." Despite the luxury, not all was perfect. The bunks were a step down from our previous chicken-wire comfort. These were the more traditional ones of interwoven communications wire. Poorly made, they sagged badly. It was rather like sleeping in a hammock, our rifles slung on two wires next to us. Light, provided by a single lantern and a few candles, reflected poorly off the packed mud floor, leaving the interior room in perpetual gloom.

For the first time in my experience we had company. In addition to the scouts, this bunker housed a forward observer for the artillery, along with his aides and other occasional guests. For example, it was the custom of the commander of the Greek battalion, Colonel Koumanakos, to sleep on the front line when his troops were on line. He and his staff would come forward to the outpost at night, returning to their battalion headquarters to work during the day. This resolve of the high-ranking Greek officers to expose themselves to the same dangers as their men impressed me at the time and still impresses me. Our squad had not seen its own officer up front in the two months I had been on the line. So far as we knew, neither had our other squads seen him. To see the lieutenant, someone had to drive back to regimental headquarters. If our lieutenant needed to communicate with us, he used the telephone, if it was working, or the radio.

Our closest neighbor on the mountain, about fifty yards to the west and overlooking the valley, was a tank with a 90-mm gun. The tank commander was a really nice guy, a sergeant I knew only as "Monk." We also had a Chinese interpreter, Poy, on our hill. He spent most of his time searching Chinese radio frequencies and attempting to intercept messages. His other duties included broadcasting propaganda. A native of Detroit, he told me that when he was drafted and they found out he spoke fluent Chinese, he was immediately sent to the front, without basic training. His efforts would save many American lives.

All these people on the hill meant we had to change some of our habits. When we had been alone on our previous hill, we always knew where everyone was; now, there were too many people to keep track of. While no formal guard—in the "Halt, who goes there?" sense—was posted, precautions were taken. For one thing, there was no visiting at night. If you wanted to chat with Poy or Monk and the tankers, you did so during the day. Also, if you needed to go outside to urinate, you sang out your intention, the usual being, "I've got to go piss." A visitor, perhaps more cultivated than the rest of us, slipped out one night without the customary warning and we didn't know he was out there. When he opened the door and reentered, he turned sheet-white as he faced men with rifles trained on him, fingers on triggers.

We knew we were in a considerably more dangerous area, so when we were outside we moved quickly and stayed out of sight. Despite our caution, there was occasional mortar and artillery fire. As usual, our outhouse was a wooden box over a hole—a hole that was much fuller than was comfortable. No one was willing to dig a new one, however. We kept hoping the Chinese, who liked that area as a mortar target, would empty it for us.

It was our suspicion then, and it's still my opinion, that we were placed in the positions on and around Outpost Harry because Command believed the Sixty-fifth, which had been there, would run if attacked, while we would fight. This opinion is supported by the Fifteenth Infantry Regiment's 1953 yearbook. It says evidence of an enemy attack resulted in a decision to replace the Sixty-fifth with the more experienced Fifteenth Infantry. The same idea more nicely said. Command must have had some doubts about us too because they had other units digging in behind us. In the end, the men of the Fifteenth would fight and many would die, but we held our ground. As the letters I wrote clearly indicate, we had no inkling of the looming battle.

● ● ●

May 28, 1953

Dear Eth:

Received three letters from you today. Sounds as if you were having your troubles with the small one. Must be a girl—no boy could be that "ornery."

My new job will get me home for Christmas—no word of this to the folks—and possibly out of the Army next April or late

March. According to my calculations, I will be leaving here before the fourth week of November—and figure about twenty days to get home. This is, however—at this stage—strictly conjecture except for the fact that I will be home for Christmas and that is fairly certain.

Well, this letter just got a little fouled up. I got into a political argument and sat on it. At any rate I figured you would rather receive a crumpled letter than no letter at all, so you'll get it.

I have spent the afternoon talking with Jim Gay and his new partner (Rich Stieren). It has been a most pleasant way to spend a day I must admit. Outside of the fact that I was supposed to help in re-roofing our bunker my conscience would be quite clear.

· · ·

I have no memory of the exact day we moved; however, the five-day gap between this letter and the one that preceded it makes me believe our squad left the outpost we'd built and moved to Howe at this time. While five days were more than we needed to move, the move itself would have disrupted my letter-writing schedule. I remember, however, the goof-off time arguing politics with Jim and his new partner while I should have been helping to reroof the headquarters' bunker. Since I didn't live there, I didn't see it as my responsibility. One nice thing about being a radioman was that I always needed to consult other technical people.

· · ·

May 30, 1953

Dear Folks,

Mom's trip to Peoria sounded pretty nice and I imagine it helped Ethel along quite a bit. I agree that she ought to go up more often for the next six or seven months, and will be glad to help out in every possible way. I think little Johnny will need quite a bit of help in his new set up as an older brother.

. . . I am still operating a radio—in the same company—but in a different platoon and am living closer to the mess hall. No more danger, just pleasanter surroundings.

Incidentally, I have discovered what that pleasant odor was that I mentioned about a week ago. The hills have turned white with black locust shrubs, the type we had in the backyard at 66th street.

Tomorrow is payday and the end of May. That seals up my sixteen points and the next day begins the month in which I'll cross the halfway point, both of Army life and of Korea. The 19th will be half of my Army life and the twentieth should be half of my Korean career. . . .

· · ·

While I have edited out sections—such as the first paragraph—in other letters, I thought this one might be worth including to demonstrate the surrealistic thought that characterized so much of our correspondence. Basically, my mother acted as if there were no ocean or war between us. All the slight worries of home—the difficulties of making trips, the need for painting the house or the fence—were presented to me as if for solutions.

I wasn't alone in this. We all received such letters. There we were, several thousand miles from home, living in a world in which a hot meal other than fried, stolen eggs or heated C rations was a major event, the reception of five gallons of water for nine men for drinking and washing was a concern, and the threat of death was a more prominent reality than the promise of life, and we were expected to solve problems over which we had absolutely no control. Still, we had to reply. Note that I'm not talking about letters like those my sister sent in which she detailed incidents of everyday life, such as when young Johnny made eggs stand on end by crunching a dozen of them on the floor or made a path of graham crackers through the house and then happily trotted over it. These letters not only amused us but helped us maintain our sense of another reality while putting no pressure on us.

The remainder of the letter was the normal trivia whose underlying message was that I was alive and well and they had nothing to worry about.

· · ·

May 30, 1953

Dear Ethel:

Today was quite a day. We had a command inspection, which means personal equipment, rifles, bunks, and bunkers were cleaned and later inspected. It kept us all very busy. . . .

• • •

This was an understatement. The inspection was a matter of genuine concern. While we had very little personal gear, we had acquired a lot of gear we weren't supposed to have. The army issues one weapon per soldier. Soldiers aren't supposed to have more than is specified by the people writing the doctrine. We had considerably more. In addition to the nice new rifles that had fallen into our hands from the unit digging in behind us, we had some weapons we'd picked up on the battlefield. We had our own light machine gun, a weapon a scout squad was not supposed to have; and one fellow had a Thompson submachine gun. These had to be hidden in such a way that they could be retrieved undamaged following the inspection. Also, older or unwanted models, our legitimate equipment, had been left to rust. The idea of an inspector discovering the horrible condition of equipment for which we were financially responsible or, worse, taking away excellent equipment we weren't supposed to have, worried us. What didn't worry us was the prospect of the inspector reporting that our quarters were dirty. Who was going to discover dirt in a two-room, candle-lit, underground cave with a mud floor?

I don't remember the actual inspection. It may have occurred, but I doubt it. We were a long way from headquarters and very close to enemy gunners who would have wanted no finer target than an inspection team. We'd have cheered them on as long as they aimed at the inspectors and not us.

• • •

June 1, 1953

Dear Ethel:

Today is another day on foreign soil—and a much more beautiful day than yesterday. Our tent is all set up, and we have moved in—lock, stock, and barrel. In the tent we have sunlight, fresh air, and much more room—quite a difference from the bunker.

The other day some fellow made the time worn comment that the Koreans are now much better off than before we came. "Their fields have been plowed, their trees have been pruned, and their homes have been air-conditioned."

Our artillery is also leveling their hills for them. The hill formerly known as 360 is now 344. Another popular joke is that our artillery has changed Jane Russell hill into Margaret O'Brien hill. The people who formerly lived here wouldn't know the place. . . .

• • •

The first paragraph of this letter reflects my growing failure of communication with those who weren't in a combat situation. Again I attempted to be reassuring by indicating that I was living in a tent, which meant safety. I forgot that such a statement had no meaning to my sister.

Tents were not always safe places. Enemy activity had picked up by this time. Patrolling action was heavier and incoming artillery fire was more frequent. Incoming artillery rounds in the regimental sector had increased from a reported average of 275 per day to 670 per day. Also, a lot of artillery was being directed over us at our Headquarters Company in the rear, where many of the men lived in tents. For the most part we were amused, our attitude being that those living the high life in the rear area deserved a little excitement. I was distressed, however, to hear about my friend John Weber, who'd been one of the small group sitting in the snow while we waited for a truck the night before Christmas Eve. John was wounded back at headquarters while operating the radio. About the same time, a piece of shrapnel slashed through Jim Gay's tent immediately above his head as he was lying on his bunk. He complained to me that now the tent leaked on him when it rained, so he'd have to repair it.

We lost Red Curry in the second squad. He was leaning on his carbine talking to another guy when a mortar shell landed between them. When they picked up Red he was still alive but bleeding from his nose and ears. All the wood had been blown off his rifle and the barrel had been bent into a bow shape. Red was shipped off to the hospital and none of us expected to see him again, which we regretted. A nonswearing, nondrinking, roly-poly redhead who would have made a great Santa Claus some day, Red was completely dependable, quick to help or volunteer. I can't remember the other man's name or what happened to him. I have vague recollections of a tall, good-looking guy, but my memory stops there.

I suppose he took the shrapnel while Red took the concussion when the shell exploded.

The increased Chinese activity occurred all along the line. Every night we could see the distant lightning flashes and the low rumble of artillery from battles in other sectors. In the morning, helicopters would stream back and forth. We could see the wounded strapped to the stretchers on each side of the dragonfly-like machines as they rushed back to the hospitals. But this continued to be a matter of idle observation. It wasn't us, therefore it wasn't our problem.

The second paragraph of the letter relates to the devastation for which we were all responsible. We took no "war pictures" of shattered homes and torn-up streets because there were no remnants to photograph. The combined talents and efforts of the American, Chinese, North Korean, and South Korean armies had completely leveled the countryside near Ch'orwon, once a heavily populated area. The only sign that anyone had ever lived in this fertile plain was the elevated roadbed of what had been a railroad. Of course, as I mentioned earlier, the rails, ties, and anything related to trains had long since disappeared.

You could drive for miles through the countryside, which we did, without seeing a standing wall, much less a building, although I have memories of a single, two-story stone wall standing somewhere in the rear. At the time, someone told me it had been a power plant. Even the trees were gone. Anything over a couple of inches in diameter had a use: firewood, bunker walls, bedposts, anything—but always something. Pictures taken in that area reveal a landscape of plains and mountains, with little vegetation and no trace of human habitation. We joked about having to go back to Seoul to take pictures of the roofless, windowless buildings and the drunks lying in the streets to simulate war pictures.

• • •

June 4, 1953

Dear Ethel:

This morning we received our beer and coke ration. I turned down the beer in favor of coke. Of my original eight bottles I am now drinking my sixth. I have an idea the other two won't last until supper. To go with them I've been eating shoestring potato chips. I'm now on my third can of them. It's a vicious cycle. The potato chips make me thirsty and the cokes make me hungry.

Today has been a "gray" day all day. In fact, so far in June, we have had several such days. It looks as if it is slowly building up to a big rain one of these days. Perhaps it is just that we are approaching the rainy season.

Nothing came of the scare last night—as per usual. In fact Poy, our Chinese-American interpreter, told me that things were even quieter than usual. . . .

• • •

The first paragraph is pure fabrication. We weren't receiving beer and soda pop rations at this time. It was our understanding that the Woman's Christian Temperance Union had blocked the delivery of beer to enlisted men, although officers continued to receive it as well as other alcoholic beverages. We did, however, get beer through the Greeks. Soda pop was another matter— difficult but not impossible to obtain. Once, and I suspect it was here, I was visiting Jim Gay and saw that he'd acquired a case of shoestring potatoes—after all, anyone who wants electricity is kind to the regimental electrician. Meanwhile, I'd discovered a cache of a case of cola in a cold spring while walking behind the officers' quarters. The two of us, surreptitiously and systematically, drank the entire case while eating Jim's potatoes. We were careful to refill each bottle with cold coffee and replace it, so whatever officer had hidden it wouldn't be completely disappointed.

Our interpreter, Poy, was an extremely likable man who'd spent an inordinate amount of time in danger and accepted it with surprising equanimity. The only evidence of any tension in him was that he was never without a loaded .45-caliber pistol. Like the scouts, he had no intention of being captured. He spent almost all of his waking time on the radio or loudspeaker, either intercepting Chinese communications or broadcasting propaganda. A typical propaganda message went like this (after he translated it into Chinese):

> Brave Chinese soldiers. Look about you . . . look about you. Blood . . . Blood . . . Chinese Blood . . . Each day the sandy earth will soak up more and more Chinese blood.

We will come for you. We will come into your trenches. Fire will kill you . . . artillery will kill you . . . bayonets will kill you . . . grenades will kill you.

Our guns will fire more and more. Every foot of your battle lines will be destroyed . . . every foot of ground destroyed.

You can still live . . . you can live. One chance remains . . . One way to escape death. We will help you. Only the UN can help you. Join your many friends who live with us . . . live with us.

Speaking as a former professor of psychology, I can tell you that this was not a very promising sort of psychological warfare, if it can be dignified with that term, and I'm not certain that it had any effect. At the time, Command wanted prisoners so badly that we were told anyone getting one would receive an extra R&R in Japan. One Chinese soldier tried to surrender, but an overeager machine gunner cut him down. He died before they could get any information from him, so no one received an R&R for him.

• • •

June 6, 1953

Dear Ethel:

After six months of carrying an M-1, I finally got my hands on a carbine—four pounds lighter. This is certainly a day for rejoicing.

One of the boys is going home in a couple more weeks and was talking about home. He comes out with the statement, "Just think—the candle holders won't be made out of old beer cans." We took time and explained to him that they now have electric lights back in the States.

The chow tonight was very good. We had a new and exciting drink—lukewarm—called ice cream. Things are getting better all the time.

A Lieutenant just walked in and said that peace rumors are flying all over the place. That would be nice if peace would come in another month or so. At the end of this month, I'll be in the upper half of people to rotate so I shouldn't have too long a wait before going home if peace comes. Of course, it is probably just another rumor but it is certainly a nice one—and one I would like to see come true.

• • •

The M-2 carbines were not only much lighter than the M-1 rifles but much faster, being fully automatic, which meant you only had to hold the trigger to fire numerous rounds—and, if I recall correctly, they were capable of firing at the rate of 450 bullets per minute. Of course, you couldn't fire that many bullets that quickly since the magazines held only fifteen rounds. While not as accurate as the slower-firing, bolt-action M-1s, on our nightly patrols, where darkness turned targets into guesswork, the faster-firing, lighter carbines were highly prized.

In addition to my experiences as an infantryman in Korea, I've spoken to infantrymen from World War II and Vietnam. All of us had the same belief—that our lives were so completely different from those of civilians or of military personnel in other branches (e.g., artillery or transportation) that there was no real basis of communication between us. Our existence became so primitive, over such a period of time, that we forgot about things such as electric lights. The mistake about candleholders was an honest one, the speaker having forgotten about electric lights in his months of underground living and shared candles. Later, I was to experience the same disorientation. I once spent a week or two worrying that I was losing my sense of balance because I was falling so much, then I remembered sidewalks and streetlights and stopped worrying.

● ● ●

June 7, 1953

Dear Folks:

I notice that mom wants to know the name or number of the hills nearest me. That is almost impossible to supply as the only hills that are named are the ones on the fighting line a couple miles in front of me. The ones we live on are unnamed. Those up in front however are Jackson Hts., Old Charley, Silver Star, Camel Back, Iron Horse, etc. We live in the back of what used to be called the "Iron Triangle" of Kumswha, Ch'orwon, and Pyongyong (sp?).

Don't worry about the looks of the place. Next year when I'm home I'll paint it up and get all the details ironed out. I'll just take a month or so when I first get back to get all of that done.

As to the mail coming in jumps—well, I get it the same way. Nothing for a few days—then two or three in one day. I imagine it is just held up here and there in the many ports it travels through along the way.

As to when I get home—well, that's easy—next February. There is no way to hurry it up and there aren't too many ways to slow it down. As it is, I'd rather be in the Army in Korea than in the Army in the States so, as long as I have to be in the Army, I am content. . . .

• • •

The reported lack of knowledge of my location was misinformation. Scouts obviously had to know where they were. One of the difficult elements in a move was learning new locations, thus it would be 1,000 yards to hill X, 800 to Y, and 1,500 to W. When we reported movement, or requested fire support, we had to be able to specify locations. If we saw something halfway between ourselves and hill X, we could say 500 yards. I remember Stan O'Connor grilling us on distances and directions after each move. We were expected to know them by heart—and to know them quickly.

The stated preference for Korea was not misinformation. I suspect many of us who were scouts would have been called hyperactive were we schoolchildren today. Each liked action and each liked being able to do his own thing in his own way. In certain respects you can have no greater freedom than when you live on an outpost in combat. There is no nonsense such as fastening a button or saluting or eating on schedule. Officialdom comes nowhere near you. The only concerns are reality concerns. As a scout, as long as I did my job I had enormous freedom. By volunteering to ride shotgun I could make frequent trips to the rear area, visiting friends and getting hot, or at least warm, meals as well as enjoying the excitement of protecting the driver (and myself) from the increasingly active guerrillas in the area. Ordinary infantrymen had no such freedom of movement.

• • •

June 7, 1953

Dear Ethel:

Another rainy day. We have been getting quite a bit of rain the last few days. As yet, however, it hasn't bothered me in the slightest because I've been staying inside.

The last couple of days I've done almost nothing but lay on my bunk and sleep or loaf. You can't imagine how hard it is to write a letter when you do absolutely nothing. At any rate I've been doing it for six months now and shall try to do it for another six.

Yesterday, I got a couple letters from home. Mom seems to be rather anxious for you and Johnny to go down and visit so that Johnny will be accustomed to the house. It sounds like a pretty good idea if you can make the trip.

By the time you receive this letter, I shall be half finished with Korea. By the time I put in that much more time I shall be on my way home. This last half should go faster for I have R&R coming up in a month—and that will be eight fast days. After that it will just be a matter of killing time until I'm on my way home. About five months of killing time. . . .

• • •

Boredom continued to be our major foe. Shifts were only three hours out of twenty-four. There were no books, no magazines, no toothbrushes, no razors—only talk. Occasionally, we received free candy bars, usually a lot of jellied candies, Chuckles, and a few packs of caramels. When this happened there was a rush to get the caramels. We also received all the free cigarettes we wanted. Lots of arguments, discussions, stories, and rumors; retreats into silence and daydreaming; or simply lying in your bunk with a mind made blank—these were the ways we passed time, other than smoking or fighting for the occasional candy. We still had to be alert, of course, and under that quiet was tension. Even our sleep was light. No one wanted to be bayoneted in his sleeping bag because he'd been sleeping too soundly.

There were moments when the monotony would lift. Some were routine, as when I noted the glint of binoculars on an opposing hill. While I watched, I radioed artillery and gave the location. Soon an explosion eliminated the glitter. A neat bit that followed army doctrine.

Other moments illustrated the army's peculiar paranoia. I spotted what appeared to be a machine-gun position overlooking Outpost Harry, off to the right. When I radioed the location, I was told this wasn't in our territory, it was in the Sixty-fifth Regiment's territory. Even though it commanded our territory, we couldn't fire on it. The Sixty-fifth couldn't fire on it either, because its location on a western slope prevented the gunners of the Sixty-fifth from seeing it.

We went down and talked to Monk about the problem. Once the location was pointed out, he could see the position clearly, even though it was out of the territory he was supposed to cover. He suggested a solution. He was permitted to fire a few practice rounds each day, and if he took the block out of his 90-mm gun, he could sight directly down the barrel, guaranteeing a clean hit at about 800 yards. He would then put one round in the opening, which appeared to be about a foot high and three feet wide, and report it as a miss, so he wouldn't get in trouble for firing out of his sector. The idea made army sense.

I think it was more than a machine-gun nest. Monk put a high-explosive shell through the opening and a secondary explosion blew the top of the mountain off. He must have hit an underground ammunitions depot. A good day for us, a bad one for Monk. He had to report a bad shot, a shell that went astray.

We should have been aware that something was brewing, because there was too much enemy activity. Our telephone lines were being routinely cut or blown up. Once the telephone was out for several days before two linemen arrived to announce that it was once again working. I telephoned headquarters and said, "Hello, headquarters, this is—" and the line went dead. It had been cut again. Two days of dangerous work for the linemen, laying new line from headquarters to an outpost, and only four words got through. The increased activity meant more work for me too since I had to spend more time on the radio.

Artillery fire was also picking up. We were under an enemy barrage one time when I radioed headquarters and got our lieutenant, who had never visited us. The conversation went something like this:

> "Lieutenant, they're hitting us with heavy artillery, probably 150s."
> "Dannenmaier, they don't have 150s in this area."
> "Maybe not lieutenant, but they're hitting us with them."
> "Go out and measure the diameter of the holes."
> "Lieutenant, you've got to be crazy. We're under a barrage. I'm not going out there."
> "Dannenmaier, do you know you're disobeying a direct order?"
> "I sure do lieutenant. Come up here and give it to me."

Apparently, a textbook means of determining the size of an artillery shell is to measure the diameter of the impact. But I seriously doubt that even the author of that doctrine wanted it done during the barrage. I never heard a word about my refusal to go.

• • •

June 9, 1953

Dear Eth:

I didn't get much written in the way of letters yesterday—and so far today I haven't done too well either. To tell the truth, I have a headache and a slight cold so I don't feel too much like writing. I think that when I go into reserve I shall get some new glasses. My eyes have been giving me a little trouble recently.

I turned in some film today to be developed. It should be ready in about a week. Then I'll be able to send you a few more pictures.

The weather has been very nice over here the last couple days— but I have been in no mood to enjoy it. I expect that tomorrow I shall feel better. These things seldom last more than two days.

• • •

One of the few occasions when I knew I had goofed and the goof really irritated our sergeant occurred at this time. We had been on a squad-sized patrol when we reached a particularly dangerous sector. It was by agreement that in such situations I always went last.

There were three reasons for this. First, carrying the radio on my back made me the slowest in a dash through a gauntlet. Second, the radio made me a prime target for the Chinese. And third, if I were killed, my body wouldn't trip anyone else up when it was their turn to run.

With eight men in front of me, I had time to kill and I noticed some pretty little red and green frogs unable to get out of a shell hole. I saw no reason for them to die, so I hopped down and started catching them and turning them loose. In the process of doing this, I looked up to see Stan O'Connor glaring down at me. He had gone first, followed by each member of the squad. Then they waited for me. I didn't show up, so Stan came back to find out what had happened and caught me playing with frogs. Poor Stan—he ran the gauntlet three times. He was one really angry sergeant, though he never mentioned the incident to me afterward. He had every right to be angry. I was wrong and I knew it.

That incident occurred on the morning of June 10 during a patrol that, though I didn't know it at the time, marked the end of my casual summer-camp-with-a-bit-of-danger attitude, which until that day had characterized my approach to Korea. The future would be exciting, but the fun would be gone.

9

OUTPOST HARRY

The battle for Outpost Harry was trivial and insignificant, except to the men who fought it—most of whom would agree with Willy, an infantryman in a Bill Mauldin cartoon, who said: "The hell this ain't the most important hole in the world. I'm in it." For us it was a high-intensity, eight-day battle for a hill we would abandon three months later with the signing of the truce. By reputation the bloodiest battle of the Korean conflict, and one in which an unusually large number of units received official citations for heroic work, it was certainly the most ignored by the press and, later, by historians.

No one knows exactly how many men were killed or wounded in the battle for Outpost Harry. The Fifteenth Infantry Regiment yearbook reports only 102 Allied dead with 533 wounded and 44 missing in action, but Ernie Kramer's *Siege of OUTPOST HARRY*, published by the Outpost Harry Survivors' Association in 1995, reports 1,863 Americans killed or wounded, 412 members of the Greek Expeditionary Force killed or wounded, and 147 dead from other nations, which would include Koreans attached to the U.S. Army (KATUSAs). The difference between the two is great, but all evidence favors the higher figures.

The two companies most severely injured were K Company of the Fifteenth Regiment, with 90–95 percent casualties, and A Company of the Fifth Regiment, with 86 percent casualties. All figures are suspect, however, as men able to make it off the hill on their own were sometimes not reported as wounded on Harry. Martin A. Markley, commander of K Company, was wounded just as he was about to leave the hill. The officer who'd come to replace him was also wounded. Markeley was the more badly wounded of the two, but his relief refused to leave him. The two assisted each other off the hill. As they approached the aid station, it was hit by artillery, so they bypassed the damaged and disrupted aid station. They made it to the road and were given a lift—and, to Martin Markeley, a life. Since the two men had bypassed the aid station, they may not have been included in the official list of wounded on Harry. The yearbook, in its list of members of the Fifteenth killed in 1953, doesn't include my friends Charley Brown and Joe Freeman, both of whom were killed by enemy artillery, which gives me greater reason to suspect that the yearbook seriously underreports American casualties.

It appears that the total number of casualties represented approximately half of the estimated 4,118 Allied participants, including such combat support personnel as combat engineers and artillery. The Chinese were believed to have suffered 7,000 men killed, the Seventy-fourth Chinese Communist Division being destroyed as an effective unit.

While the ferocity of the artillery duels covered the entire regimental area and Communist feints resulted in brief hand-to-hand combat elsewhere, such as at Outpost Dick, the focus of the battle was Outpost Harry.

Situated on a hill about the size of Bunker Hill in Boston or Art Hill in St. Louis, Harry was approximately 400 yards in front of the actual front line. It sat in a gap between the hills that defined the edge of the Ch'orwon valley. Whoever controlled Harry could look well into enemy lines. A ridge ran from the outpost, first down and then up, in a northeast direction, to "Star Hill"—more of a mountain, really, like those in the Appalachians—that was held by the Communists. A company of infantry held Harry, which would have been about 160 men, but only two platoons were on Harry at the time of the attack, it being too small to hold more. The other platoons came up during the battle. There were also persons from other groups, such as engineers and forward observers for the artillery, on the hill.

On June 10, K Company, commanded by Martin A. Markley, was on Harry, with I and L Companies approximately 300 yards behind, defending the front line. The Chinese decided they wanted the outpost. Perhaps they wanted a lot more, I don't know, but I do know they tried for five nights over an eight-day period to take

Harry. When they began, we had four full-strength fighting battalions holding a three-battalion sector. When it was all over, we had one almost full-strength battalion and the remnants of three others. In addition, the Fifth Regimental Combat Team had suffered serious losses to two companies of its First Battalion. The rumor mill reported Command was rounding up cooks, supply people, and other soldiers from the rear and sending them forward to help. I'm not certain about that, but I am certain we still had Harry.

• • •

June 11, 1953

Dear Folks:

The action the Fifteenth has avoided so long has finally caught up with us. I understand that at present there is quite a fight going on up around O.P. Harry and that it went on most of last night. Don't know too much about it yet, but they have had us up and alerted on our radios since very early this morning. I'll probably find out all about it through the grapevine later on today.

Outside of the fighting, today is rather a nice day out. Very typical of a Korean spring day. Warm and sunny. If we ever get off duty today and if I'm not too tired, I shall probably go swimming—whoops, that's illegal, I mean jeep washing.

Well, folks not too much else to say today—mainly I guess because I'm a little tired. At any rate I will sign off until tomorrow.

• • •

My squad visited Outpost Harry the afternoon of the tenth to get acquainted, since we were their supporting scouts. Their radiomen and I made plans to use flashlights to signal one another if our radio network was jammed—something the Chinese could do whenever they chose, as I'd learned when I was trying to radio regimental headquarters from the Greek headquarters during a minor attack. I soon discovered how foolish our flashlight idea was. It might have worked under conditions of a minor attack, but the flares, spotlights, exploding shells, and flashing and ricocheting tracer bullets of a major assault made flashlight signals impossible.

I don't really remember much of what followed, but there are some scenes that stand clearly in my mind. When I close my eyes

I can see them again, as focused and brilliant as if the intervening years didn't exist.

I have a very clear memory of taking off my boots when I went to bed the night of the tenth of June and thinking it was the first night in a month that I'd enjoyed the privilege of a night of sleep. I don't remember any particular events that would have caused so much nighttime activity, but it's possible the memory is true. Perhaps we were patrolling a lot. In any event, I do recall that on the night of the tenth my boots were off. At 10:00 a heavy bombardment woke me up. Dirt sifted onto my face as I lay in bed. I got up and dashed into the observation area and over to my large radio, the AN/GRC 46A, which rested on a table against the wall where the telephone hung. The telephone lines were out, so I raised headquarters on the radio to let them know of the attack. There was no need for my alert: the entire line was already under fire. The noise of incoming artillery was deafening and could be easily heard back at regimental headquarters. Our artillery was replying as quickly as possible, adding to the din.

Incoming artillery fire burst with roars and flashes all about us, as if we were sitting in the center of a gigantic fireworks display. The haze of smoke and dust effectively kept us from seeing what was happening for some time. Shells burst in front of and around our bunker with regularity. In between ducking when we heard the roar of incoming rounds, we were able to tell from the location of firing and the bursting of shells that the line was holding, but K Company on Harry was in trouble. Myriad tracer bullets flashed about and artillery and airplane flares, drifting earthward, revealed hundreds of enemy soldiers moving toward the outpost through the smoke and debris. Nothing in our training had prepared us for this; indeed, nothing could have. The attackers were everywhere. As one of the members of the Outpost Harry Survivors' Assocation said, "The flares lit the attacking Chinese up beautifully, they made great targets."

Headquarters needed to know as much as possible, and I was able to maintain steady radio contact. The shell fire was intense as the Chinese tried to destroy our infantry while the American artillery set up a protective screen in front of the infantry and simultaneously tried to take out enemy artillery. A soldier near me, who, as a member of the German Army, had been captured by the Americans at Normandy when he was only fourteen years old, shouted, "This is hell, just like Normandy." Remembering my teaching disaster, I shouted back, "You think this is hell, try teaching kindergarten."

Slowly the Chinese were able to silence the other radios along the line, until I was the last direct link with headquarters. I didn't leave my post throughout that long night.

Between messages I watched and wondered. The Chinese were engaged in hand-to-hand combat in the trenches, and if they successfully overwhelmed the defenders of Outpost Harry, we would meet them next. In the interim, the Chinese artillery was reducing our numbers, trying to defeat our fighting ability. I remember thinking wryly that on the morrow, with my college degree, I would probably be the best-educated piece of meat on the field.

Wave upon wave of Chinese troops attacked, and by morning I didn't see how anyone could be alive on Harry—except that the Chinese and Americans continued to struggle for control. The Catholic chaplain, Father Harvey Kochner of St. Louis (who had forty-four points and should have been sent home months earlier) heard of the problems they were having rescuing the wounded and with his assistant, Charles S. Scott (who was also eligible to leave with thirty-six points), joined the action, searching in the dark for the wounded among the dead and carrying them to safety. Scott said there was complete confusion as Chinese and American artillery wounded many men on their way into battle as well as those actually engaged in fighting, leaving dead and wounded scattered all over the hill. There were also problems with the wounded, some asking to be left to die in peace, others insisting they could continue to fight.

As the sun rose, I watched a skirmish line of seven Americans form and drive a group of Chinese off the hill and up the ridge. One of the Americans, the second from the right, fell to his knees but then rose in answer to our prayers and continued in line. Suddenly, one of the Chinese went straight up into the air like a rocket, stiff and straight, like an acrobat launched from a teeter-totter. When he was six or seven feet above the ground, his feet clearly higher than the following Americans' heads, he began a slow cartwheel, still ramrod straight. Then, suddenly, he burst into flames and crumpled back to earth. I thought it a strange but beautiful sight.

One of those seven men may have been Master Sergeant Ola F. Mize of K Company who received a Congressional Medal of Honor for his actions. During that first vicious night, Mize learned that one of his men at a nearby listening post was wounded. Braving enemy fire and artillery explosions, he and a medic went to help, returning with the wounded soldier. Later that night, Mize noted that the enemy had overrun a machine gun post; he attacked, killing ten of them and scattering the rest. He also secured assistance for those in the command bunker who had been wounded, and, as dawn approached, organized a group that went from captured bunker to captured bunker, killing the invading enemy. In the morning he led a group that drove the remaining Chinese soldiers from the hill. If anyone ever earned a Congressional Medal of Honor for continued valor and action over time, it was Master Sergeant Mize.

About ten in the morning, headquarters asked how many rounds were hitting Harry per minute. I asked the operator if he'd ever hit a puffball mushroom and seen the dust. When he said he had, I said that was what the outpost looked like—it was so bad that I couldn't count the rounds. Still later, as the artillery fire lessened, I watched two medics carrying a man on a stretcher off the hill. They were almost to the bottom when a large shell landed, sending up a great cloud of dust and debris. When the area cleared, all were gone: medics, man, and stretcher no longer existed.

Everything quieted down about eleven o'clock. We'd lost several hundred men, either killed or wounded; the Chinese must have lost several thousand. We heard rumors that K Company had been destroyed by midnight and that the relief company, E Company, was in trouble. Then we heard that C Company had been sent to the hill about three o'clock in the morning. The fighting had been hand-to-hand in the dark throughout the night.

Following the truce, I worked briefly with a fellow, I think his name was Kelley, who said that of the approximately 160 men in K Company, he was 1 of only 7 to walk off the hill unwounded. As a machine gunner, he never should have lived through the night except that his gun jammed, forcing him to abandon it. When the gun jammed he joined others in the hide-and-seek, hand-to-hand fighting. He was wounded when he arrived at a safe point later in the morning. He said he was upset and resisted when a nurse tried to undress him because he'd messed his pants. Without asking why he was upset, she looked at him and said, "Don't worry, you all do it."

The sacrifice of the men on Harry kept the Chinese from making a direct attack on those of us along the line. But the men on the front line received a lot of incoming artillery, and many were killed and wounded. We heard that I and L Companies, which held the front line behind the outpost, suffered 50-percent casualties and that the observation post we had built up and recently left had been severely damaged. I never asked, nor was I told, about casualties among the scout squad that had replaced us there. Official estimates were that we received somewhere around twenty thousand rounds of enemy artillery fire that night, which didn't include the heavy small-mortar fire. Of course, we were shooting back with everything we had. Official sources later estimated 3,600 Chinese Communist Forces (CCF) attacked Harry during that first night.

My letter home must have been dashed off about noon, as in the early afternoon I was told to grab my small radio and gear. Other radios had been knocked out and regimental headquarters wanted me nearer the action. Consequently, I put my things together and O'Connor, Barker, and I moved closer to Outpost Harry.

The place they chose to send us was an abandoned bunker on a slight ridge about a hundred and fifty yards in front of a roadblock tank. Not only did we have a clear view of Harry, which was another hundred and fifty yards or so in front and off to the right, but from our vantage point we would provide an excellent advance warning in case the Chinese decided to attack around the west slope. A long trench ran from the road through the ridge and across the plain to our new home.

Like most other bunkers, this one had a sleeping room with two wood-bottomed bunk beds and a covered trench leading out to a small observation point. We were soon joined by a very green lieutenant, an artillery observer, and his sergeant.

I went up on top to put up my radio antenna. Not liking to work alone, I teased Barker into coming up and giving me a hand. We could see two tankers standing in the hatch of their tank in a gap in the ridge behind us, watching us work in the between-battle silence.

In the quiet of that late afternoon, we heard the "pop" of a mortar being fired and watched to see where it would land. It came down about halfway between the tank and us. I commented to Barker that the tankers had better get down and close up, otherwise the Chinese would drop one through their turret. There was a second pop and, suddenly, Barker and I had the same idea. There was a shell hole about seven or eight feet from us and we both dived for it. I got there first; Barker landed on top of me. The Chinese blew up my antenna. I remember telling Barker that he could have gotten a medal for saving my life if they'd been better shots. I don't remember his exact reply but it had to do with his opinion of the relative value of our lives.

Fortunately, I had some copper wire and was able to jury-rig a second antenna, but more cautiously this time, making radio contact with headquarters before dark.

As nightfall approached on the eleventh of June and with B Company replacing the remnants of C Company on Harry and replacements along the line for I and L Companies, fighting resumed with the same intensity as on the preceding night. The artillery lieutenant managed to get the best view, elbowing past O'Connor.

I know he had his heart in the right place, but the lieutenant was really wet behind the ears. During the early stages of the fighting, he told me to report that the enemy was firing red star flares. This would have indicated that signals were being sent for one reason or another. Then he said a second set had gone off, then a third. This made O'Connor suspicious. That was just too many signals.

The aperture was small and the view less than we needed if we were to keep our colonel informed as to the progress of the battle. O'Connor left the bunker, climbed out of the safety of the trench, and stood in front, near the observation aperture. From there he called out information, which was relayed to me by Barker. I then radioed it to headquarters. (Stan continued this extremely dangerous practice the entire time we were at this position.) It was a heroic act, bravely done over time, with full awareness of the danger. He never received any recognition for it—but there were many unrecognized heroes in Korea.

As it turned out, the lieutenant was mistaking the ricochets of tracer bullets from 40-mm guns for flares. There was a lot happening. As the fighting raged, B Company of the Fifteenth Infantry required assistance and B Company of the Fifth Regimental Combat Team climbed the hill to relieve them, which caused temporary confusion. The defense of Harry continued all that night as the Chinese advanced through their own artillery and entered the trenches. Some 2,850 CCF soldiers participated in the attack that second night.

Fighting slowed down as daylight approached, and by about 10:00 in the morning of the twelfth we were able to stretch out for some sleep. I grabbed the top bunk and slept for the first time since I was awakened on the tenth.

The battle started in again soon after dark, with A Company of the Fifth defending initially. It was supported by L Company of the Fifteenth as the night wore on and A Company's casualties became too great for its continued defense of the hill.

Most of the fighting slowed down or ended with daylight, but that didn't mean the artillery and mortar fire stopped. Night after night the Chinese charged through our exploding artillery shells, and their own attacking artillery, to force their way over the barbed wire and into the trenches. There the fighting became a mass of men using bullets, knives, clubs, hands, and teeth—anything—to fight, overcome, and kill each other.

On the second or third night, I was talking to the operator on Harry who was telling me, in a calm radio voice, that they badly needed "medics, ammunition, and reinforce—." I waited and hoped during that sudden silence. Then the same calm voice returned and said, "Sorry for the interruption, I needed to shoot a couple of guys. Hope you can get us some supplies and reinforcements."

That same night I got a call saying that medics were needed badly at Observation Post Howe, my "Castle on the Hill." I hoped the wounded didn't include that former German soldier I mentioned earlier, the one who was captured at the age of fourteen, who'd been at Normandy, but I never asked. Although I'm not certain, I think that was when Buckner, a member of my squad, was hit. He was a tall, slow-speaking dependable guy from the mid-South, a thoughtful and helpful person. I don't believe he ever really liked the constant wisecracking that Barker and I engaged in, but he tolerated it nicely.

On our third day in that location, after three nights of fighting, some artillery colonel came up to see for himself what was happening. As he walked about, trailed by the lieutenant and the sergeant, he commented on the odor in the place. Finally he stopped, looked at the lieutenant and said, "Lieutenant, there's something dead in this place. I've been trying to locate it but it seems to be everywhere. You need to find it and dispose of it or you'll all be sick."

Barker and I, who were nearby, choked back our laughter. On the first night we were there, the artillery sergeant had messed his pants. No wonder the colonel couldn't locate it—wherever he walked, the smell was always close behind him! Barker, O'Connor, and I had avoided being in the same area as the sergeant—which was easy enough to do, just by going up to the observation post— but with the colonel there, the sergeant went everywhere.

• • •

June 13, 1953

Dear Folks:

Don't worry about me. The reason I have been unable to write is that as radioman I have been sitting on the radio about twenty hours a day. When I haven't done that I've slept. I have a feeling that we are about to be pulled off line. I will write more later.

• • •

It's certainly true that I was spending a lot of time on the radio; in fact, I saw little of the fighting on the second, third, and fourth nights, being busy reporting news relayed to me by Barker from O'Connor. Later, the rear echelon watchdogs, who monitored our radio behavior, criticized me for broadcasting in the clear, that is, for not encoding my messages. What idiots. Worse than that, they were authoritative, ignorant assholes. Code books or code machines weren't permitted where I was. And even if they were, would I have been so foolish as to strike a match or light a candle to figure out how to code a message while under enemy observation? The only question would have been who would have killed me first: O'Connor, Barker, or the Chinese. If it had been O'Connor or Barker, and if they'd moved fast enough, before the Chinese could sight on the light, they might have lived. People who monitor and critique the radio traffic of combat radiomen should first spend time in combat.

On the fourth night, the night of June 13, C Company of the Fifth Regiment was on Harry. While heavy artillery continued, the attack was by a minor force and the outpost held without need of assistance.

Chaplain Kochner and Charles Scott continued to work throughout these first four nights of the battle, helping with the wounded. During daytime lulls, Scott assisted with carrying American dead off the hill, occasionally finding still-living, wounded Americans (the searchers simply rolled the bodies of dead Chinese over the side of the hill). On one occasion, Scott recalled a newly arrived major—at least a major with a clean uniform—telling him the Chinese dead had to be taken also, to which Scott replied, "First we'll take care of our own, then we'll worry about enemy bodies."

The following day, O'Connor, Barker, and I were ordered back to Howe. I was really tired by that time. As I walked down the trench, back to the lines, I watched the ground and tried to step without my feet touching fragments of steel shrapnel. In that one- or two-hundred-yard walk, I was unable to take such a step.

When we arrived at our pickup point at the end of the trench, we leaned against boxes of ammunition and grenades and waited. At the time, I marveled at the ability of the military to move all those supplies to where we needed them so quickly.

I remember looking at the hills opposite and thinking about how beautiful they were. Shell fire during months of fighting had blasted to different heights the dams of the rice paddies that shaped their sides into irregular patterns of flatness. Different levels of water in each paddy creating different stages of growth in each paddy, each paddy a slightly different shade of green. In the morning mist these colors blended into each other, creating an ever-changing, ever-renewing symphony of color.

As we waited, we watched a line of new troops being brought up to support us, perhaps headed for Outpost Harry. Our regiment had lost a lot of men. Later, I heard these were fresh troops rushed up from the south. They looked like parade-ground soldiers. Their helmets weren't dented and burnt from use as scoops or pots, they wore clean, crisp uniforms, they carried shiny rifles, and they exhibited good posture. Then a shell came in. It was easily seventy-five or a hundred yards away when it exploded, but they all hit the dirt, face down in the mud. We stood and laughed, or more likely grinned, only thinking we were laughing. They didn't know a "hello" round from a serious one. They'd learn.

When we got back to "the Castle on the Hill," we found shattered and scattered equipment and sandbagged inner walls. The first night, according to counterfire reports, some 340 artillery shells had hit our hill, including 13 direct hits on Howe. Most of our three feet of sandbags and rocks on the roof had been blown away—which is how I know there were 13 direct hits, because I counted the impact areas during a lull the next morning. None of them caused any significant damage. During our absence, enemy gunners had gotten better and slipped some shells into the place. One piece of shrapnel—more than a foot long and razor sharp—had sliced completely though my large radio, pinning it to the log wall against which it was leaning. Had I not been sent to a "more dangerous" forward outpost, it would have gone through me first. Chest high.

I had an opportunity that afternoon to talk with Poy. I found out that he'd made a significant impact of his own the second night. While scanning different frequencies, when the issue was much in doubt, he had intercepted a radio message in which a Chinese commander was asking someone why his battalion had not attacked. The man questioned had replied that the "moonbeam" was holding up his advance, shining on an area that his men had to cross. At the time he spoke, we had only one spotlight on, and it was covering a valley leading to the northwestern slopes of Outpost Harry. When Poy reported the conversation, Command ordered the spotlight turned off, waited briefly, and then filled the valley with proximity-fused artillery shells. These are set to explode downward within a few yards of the ground. That interception probably cost the Chinese eight or nine hundred fighting men. It may also have saved the battle for the Americans.

On the fifth night, G Company of the Fifteenth Regiment was on Harry and received the brunt of an attack by a much smaller CCF "search and destroy" group. E Company was sent to relieve them in the early morning hours. While E Company wasn't one of the two most heavily damaged companies the first night, the effects of the fighting are clearly indicated in a report by Fredric Knepper. He arrived in Korea on the ninth and on the thirteenth was moved up to Harry as a replacement member of E Company. Every man in his squad was new except for the squad leader, the other eight all having been killed or wounded on Harry or transferred to other squads within the company. Knepper said he had no idea what was going on and was really grateful for the limited action (mass attacks may not have occurred that night, but there was still artillery and mortar fire and a light assault). When he told me this, at a meeting of Outpost Harry survivors, he confessed that he was embarrassed because he'd had it so easy compared to others. It was as if he felt guilty for being alive and unwounded. He wasn't alone in that feeling. I think many of us who weren't wounded felt, and still feel, that if we weren't hurt we weren't really part of the battle.

The sixth and seventh nights there were no attacks by the CCF, and enemy artillery fire was greatly reduced. A Company of the Fifteenth was on Harry on the night of June 15, and P Company of the Greek Expeditionary Force was there on the night of June 16. The commander of P Company reported that his men had to hold wet cloths over their noses to mask the stench of mangled, rotting corpses and pieces of flesh that filled the trenches and covered the ground. He said that at one point he was lying next to the body of a Chinese youth of sixteen or seventeen who had short black hair and a series of bullet holes in his belly. He wondered why youths such as this had to die and whither this one's soul had fled.

There was some concern that the numerous, well-fed rats might spread disease. The Tenth Engineers spent the daylight hours rebuilding trenches and bunkers and burying Chinese dead in bulldozed pits in the valley behind Harry, but they couldn't remove all the body parts. One member of the Outpost Harry Survivors' Association told me that he specifically remembers one bloated CCF corpse hanging on the barbed wire. Another spoke of a single arm, he couldn't tell if it was Chinese or American, tangled in the barbed wire, swaying in the breeze.

On the night of June 17, at about 2:00 A.M., the Chinese Communists renewed their mass attacks. As the battle began, the Greeks sang their national anthem. Initially, P Company's defense held, but the Chinese were able to force their way into the trenches for hand-to-hand fighting, at which the Greeks excelled. N Company, also of the Greek Expeditionary Force, was sent to assist. Colonel Koumanakos stayed with us, as was his custom when his men were on the line, and a visiting Greek general spent the night on Outpost Harry. I don't remember his name, but I recall that he had a black patch over one eye.

On this fifth night of intense hand-to-hand combat, there was much less Chinese artillery—we assumed they were running out of shells—and much more American artillery, the army having hurried all available artillery and rocket launchers into our area as Command realized we were the focus of a major assault. Either because the four earlier nights of mass assaults had seriously weakened the Chinese or because the Greeks were so good, the issue on this night was never in doubt, despite the intensity of the fighting. By dawn, the battle was won.

There would be no sixth night of mass attacks, though we didn't know it then. During the eight-day battle, we had received an average of approximately eleven thousand rounds of enemy artillery fire each night, not counting the more numerous small mortars. In reply, our artillery had fired over forty-six thousand rounds per night, for a total barrage, both sides, of almost half a million rounds of heavy artillery. We had also received the attacks of an estimated thirteen thousand enemy soldiers.

On the morning following this last night of attack, I was leaning on the parapet overlooking Harry when I saw a Chinese soldier rise up from a group of dead and dash for cover behind a large rock. He was hidden from Harry but not from me. I aimed my rifle at him, but then stopped and put it down. A minute or two later, I watched him dash back to his lines. I was tired. There were enough dead.

10

AFTER THE PARTY

The Fifteenth Infantry Regiment remained on the front line for a month following the battle for Outpost Harry, and my squad continued to overlook Harry from our now-battered "Castle on the Hill." It was a chaotic month for me emotionally and one of disoriented thought processes—though I didn't think so at the time—as I reassessed, perhaps not always consciously, my values and beliefs in light of what I had experienced. A combination of anger, fatigue, belief in the justice of our defense of South Korea, strong Christian beliefs, and a loss of faith in the military and political leadership all contributed to my inner turmoil. Until this battle, the war had been a very exciting game to me, a mixture of boredom and adolescent conflict with authority, spiced with the excitement of patrols. True, people were hurt, but accidents occur everywhere, and except for my friends Charley Brown and Joe Freeman, most of those casualties were either strangers or temporary acquaintances. But the battle for Outpost Harry changed that. The slaughter destroyed the fun—forever. The excitement remained, a natural phenomenon as I prepared for one action or another and the adrenaline rush began, but the game attitude was replaced by weariness, by a detached cynicism. The unexpressed awe in which I'd held the higher-level commanders had also been tempered by analytic evaluation.

The eight-day battle for Harry seriously reduced our strength—both manpower and energy. Sensible people knew we were bruised and needed time to recuperate. But that wasn't our opinion in the final days of the battle. We were on a fighting high. We were also angry. The Chinese had punished us badly and the people I knew, including me, all wanted to return that punishment. We believed the CCF had used up its best men; certainly, the Chinese artillery had been much weaker the last two nights. Also, we knew we were good—we'd beaten them when they attacked, their many to our few, and now we wanted to attack and drive the remnants back. We believed we could gain ground, could make them pay for their attack and regret their policy of small ground-gaining assaults. We chaffed at the political decision that kept us in place, angry at the leaders who prevented us from repaying our enemies for the deaths of our friends and comrades. But there was no reprisal. We remained in our positions.

My squad was given a day off and sent back to headquarters for some rest and a good night's sleep. By that time, my anger had been replaced by a deep fatigue. I was really pleased to go back. I had been up all day on June 10, all that night (except for one or two hours of sleep early on), the next day and night, and part of the morning of June 12. After that, snatches of sleep during the days, resting fully clothed on a platform of wooden planks, kept me going. The idea of a day with uninterrupted rest and warm food was truly welcome.

• • •

June 16, 1953

Dear Ethel:

We had it kind of rough here for about a week but now things have quieted down so we are loafing around sleeping and eating and catching up on our bull sessions.

Our regiment was pretty well chewed up in the recent fighting and we were afraid we'd be pulled into reserve. However, I understand the same thing has happened all across Korea so maybe we'll get to stay on line.

The mail has been fouled up as per usual the last few days. However I hope that today we start getting our mail through again. Yesterday a few letters leaked through and that is usually a sign that the next day we get a load of it, surprisingly enough, my newspapers have been coming through.

I am going to try to catch up on my writing today. I've fallen rather badly behind in the last ten days. Perhaps I am fortunate in that I haven't gotten any mail. That way I have fewer to answer. . . .

• • •

This letter and the one that follows were probably misdated, though they may have been written during a lull in the battle. Exhaustion had replaced the excitement and anger that had driven me. I needed a break. I suppose we all did. As with most army rewards, our break had both good and bad elements. On the good side was the opportunity to see people I knew from other squads and areas—Red Curry, for example. When he heard about the action we were in, he went AWOL (absent without leave) from the hospital and hitchhiked back to the front. He figured we needed him. He told me his ears were still ringing, but otherwise he felt fine. He was angry with us about one thing: we'd thrown away his ruined rifle with its bow-shaped barrel. He said that he'd wanted the remnant as a souvenir—but, as I said earlier, we hadn't expected to see him again.

On the bad side, it must have galled someone to see enlisted men relaxing. Anyway, the grass in front of the colonel's tent was suddenly too long and, goodness, there were the First Squad scouts doing nothing. Soon we were sitting about hacking disinterestedly at strands of grass with our bayonets and knives, our only available cutting tools.

As we sat there, we saw our first sergeant with two civilians standing a few yards away looking at us. After a moment, all three turned and left. Later, we heard that two men from *Life* magazine had come to interview people who'd seen action at Outpost Harry. The sergeant, unhappy with our make-work assignment, told the reporters that, as luck would have it, we were available, that we'd been right in the center of everything. Then he brought the reporters down and pointed us out, mentioning that we were resting before returning to action. But the reporters decided they didn't want to interview us and, I heard, went instead to the marines on Pork Chop Hill, where there had been fighting too.

We were told that while our squad was having its "day off" at headquarters, one of the other squads escorted our colonel, with his fatherly concern for our welfare, and a visiting colonel up to Harry so they could see the damage for themselves. The scouts involved said Colonel Akers cried and that the visiting colonel threw up when they viewed and smelled the mess—the wreckage of the bunkers, the remnants of bodies, those still uncollected pieces that had so recently been men, men with their own hopes for the future, Chinese and American alike, enemies now mingled in death.

I couldn't understand why they were so upset. We'd done the job they'd ordered us to do, defeating an enemy against overwhelming odds, and we were ready to do it again. What more did they want?

• • •

June 16, 1953

Dear Folks:

Last night we had another very peaceful night. Good thing, for I was able to get some rest. We also got some "A" rations starting again yesterday and our movies began again last night. For a few days there things were a little rough, but it appears to be all over now.

Yesterday I received the three rolls of film you sent. I shall probably use them when I get to Japan—which will be in another month. I expect to go some time in July. So you know that there will be one period of about ten days coming up in a month or so when you shall receive no letters from me. At that time, however, I shall be either traveling or in Japan. With that in it, the month of July shall go very quickly. Then from August on the next question will be one of building up points until I go home. I should leave here by the end of January.

I thought I would like to save the Greek stamps enclosed to give to some stamp collecting kid later on.

• • •

The reference to A rations meant hot food, but my parents probably didn't understand that. And I don't know why I kept mentioning movies and USO shows, because we never saw them, at least not until after the truce was signed—which was when they became a point of contention. Perhaps some idea was going through my mind that if the folks thought I was going to movies and watching USO shows, my life couldn't be too bad. I wasn't the only one who played such games; in fact, mine were trivial. A friend and member of the Outpost Harry Survivors' Association managed to convince his family that he was in Japan throughout his time as an infantryman in Korea.

Another happening during our day of rest was a chance meeting with a new volunteer for the scouts, a sergeant transferred from the air force and newly arrived in Korea. I was on my way back to the bunker from the outhouse, grumbling, when he asked me what the problem was, why the muttering. I complained that there was no toilet paper, only newspapers. He replied that I needed to learn to tough it out while in Korea. I never saw him again—I believe his squad rejected him. I would have agreed with that decision. First, he wasn't smart enough to know you took comfort when you could get it. There was plenty of hardship to share without enduring it unnecessarily. Second, by that time I'd developed the firm opinion that a loudmouth makes a poor fighting man. If he tells you how tough he is, he isn't.

● ● ●

June 17, 1953

Dear Ethel:

I received your letter last night and am answering today, pretty good service huh. Rumors say the armistice will be signed this Saturday—June 20. In a way I hope it goes through—I am mighty sick of war. Still I am afraid that if we have peace I will be stuck here as an occupation soldier until I finish out my time. That would not fit in with my plans at all. If the war goes on, I will be home by Christmas—if it doesn't I don't know when I will get home. . . .

● ● ●

My thought processes had become completely fatalistic. On the one hand, I had complete faith in my own survival. I developed, and I suspect many of my friends did also, though we never discussed it, a curiously hysterical approach to life. Like a good hysteric, I had *la belle indifférence* toward death. Death and destruction were all about. I'd seen both on an occasional and a mass basis. Helicopter flights carrying the seriously wounded to the rear from areas of active fighting were daily occurrences. A close friend, a buddy I trusted, had died. Acquaintances had been wounded or killed. It didn't matter. Death and injury happened to other people, not to me. My letters reflected that thinking.

Still, during quiet hours, lying in my bunk waiting for something to happen or some duty to perform, I often calculated how many close calls I'd had and how many patrols I'd completed. And I wondered how many more before my turn came, before I joined the wounded or the dead.

I was also troubled by a constant refrain of "Thou shalt not kill." I couldn't remember any addendum that said, "Unless told to." I didn't mention this to anyone. Nor did I mention the thought that perhaps God had some later purpose for me. I had no minister to whom I could write, and I never saw a chaplain on the front line— if any chaplain ever took time to visit front-line troops while I was in Korea, he missed my squad, not to mention the communications platoon when I was with them. I recently learned of Chaplain Kochner's work on Harry and his help with the wounded during the fighting, but that doesn't alter the fact that no chaplain ever visited a squad I was a member of during my time in Korea.

June 19, 1953

Dear Ethel:

The first day of my thirteenth month is almost over. So half of my Army time is gone and I'm starting on the second half. If we stay on line for two more days, half of my Korean time will be long past also. We need 21 days on line to get 4 points and so far we have 19. . . . I am on orders for R&R to Japan the second shipment in July. . . .

• • •

Once again life was calm along the front, considerably calmer, in fact, than it had been in the weeks preceding the battle for Outpost Harry. Boredom ruled, but it wasn't the same. Gone was the laughter and lightheartedness with which we had once entertained ourselves. After Harry, we were different.

The credulous youth who had praised the vision and steel of General Douglas MacArthur now saw a man who had permitted those soldiers for whose welfare he was responsible to fall out of shape and become poorly equipped while he gloried in ruling Japan. All of us—the privates, corporals, lieutenants, and captains, the Americans, Chinese, Greeks, and Koreans—had been used for meaningless struggles, struggles whose ideals were hidden, if not lost, in the mist of politics. Life was transient, ludicrous. Was I, alive and unharmed, an accident of fate or a bit of God's plan, destined for some future purpose? I didn't know. I still don't.

Since Harry, the world hasn't been the same for me. Always there's been that undercurrent, that shadow of the past that invades my present, that despises those who would be important, those always willing to harm others for their own power and glory. Many political leaders, business executives, and union bosses would share the same trash bag were I their judge. But also, there's always been that search for those leaders who live in truth and place the value of man above their own—and, too often, the failure to find.

• • •

June 21, 1953

Dear Ethel:

Another day has arrived. While it is not by any means perfect at least it is not raining as it has been for the past couple of days. For a change, old Joe is not bothering us on these rainy nights. I suppose he wore himself out for the time being in this sector. At any rate, our boy Rhee ruined the peace talks. As far as I was concerned when that happened we should have pulled out of Korea.

No mail yet today, so I really have nothing much to talk about. Usually the hardest work I do in a day is gathering together the material for a letter.

Since I am still on line today, I am guaranteed my four points for this month. Thus at the end of June I will be the proud possessor of 21 points. That puts me past the halfway point. Now I just hope we stay on line for July. Of course, I'm sort of a pig in that matter as I actually want to stay up for the next four months. At any rate, next month I'll go to Japan on my R&R so that time will surely fly. I am going to try to surprise the folks by calling them up from there.

As to other news—well, there isn't much. About seven men from the company are leaving for home today and we got a few new replacements in last night. Tonight O'Connor is due back from Japan having had his five days in Osaka. The three places to which we may be sent on R&R are Tokyo, Osaka, and Kokura. Of the three, Kokura is the cheapest and Osaka is the most expensive. Actually I hope to go to Tokyo but just about everyone else wants to also.

• • •

We were into the rainy season. All the hits our bunker had taken had absolutely destroyed any waterproofing. We could, and did, replace the rocks and sandbags, but how do you repair holes torn in tarpaulins by fragments from shells when the tarps are buried under sand and mud? If it rained for three days outside, it rained for five inside. Most of us took to wearing only shorts, socks, and boots. When we went outside, we put on our helmets and flack vests. Skin was both more comfortable wet and quicker to dry than cloth. Only the artillery observer, an officer, bothered to stay fully clothed, and he was probably considerably less comfortable than we were.

My sister couldn't have understood the comment about the unusual quiet on rainy nights. Our artillery ruled the front. We could put lots of shells, quickly, on any enemy we sighted. Consequently, cloudy or rainy nights with limited vision were favored by the enemy for patrol action. Such nights usually required more artillery as well as extra work on our part, but the enemy was taking time to recover also, so even our rainy nights were quiet.

Korean President Syngman Rhee freed fifty thousand captured enemy soldiers who said they didn't want to go home. His actions stopped the peace talks. Today, I've read how many of those soldiers had been pressed into service and I'm more sympathetic to their plight. At the time, I and my comrades would gladly have rounded up them or their replacements and marched the whole lot back to the Chinese lines.

I was once again taking time to count my points—now at twenty-one—and daydream of the required thirty-six for return to the States. Four more months at four points each, maybe even just three months on the front line, would have sent me home. All I had to do was stay alive.

Our line time was interrupted only once. All scout squads were recalled to regimental headquarters. There we stood in slovenly formation in the pouring rain, rifles hidden under our ponchos with muzzles toward the ground to keep water from entering the barrels, while we watched our lieutenant receive a Bronze Medal for bravery. I couldn't help but wonder what he might have received if he'd ever joined us on patrol or visited us on the line—even once.

June 22, 1953

Dear Ethel:

. . . Today, I heard from S-2 that the following was said by Gen Taylor. "The 15th Infantry regiment will remain on Harry because I consider them the only Regiment capable of holding it." What a blow to the other Regiments. At the present time, three of our Battalions are in reserve and the Greeks are on Harry. Naturally, as long as one of our battalions remains on Harry we will stay where we are.

You know Sis, our regiment is one of the proudest outfits over here and with some good reason. We still have our Regimental colors (most of the regiments lost theirs in the early stages of the war), as part of the 3rd Division, we have more line time than any other division in Korea, and our Regiment itself has never lost a foot of ground to the Chinese. Thus, in a place where Regimental pride is the rule rather than the exception ours is notorious.

At any rate, everyone is very happy over the present situation. Who wants to go into reserve? Actually, I have now lived here longer than I ever before lived in one spot in the Army. Five months in one spot. My previous high was four months at Ft. Riley.

• • •

A factor I didn't mention in my bragging about my regiment was our understanding that we had also set the record for losing the most men in the shortest period of time in the fight for Outpost Harry. We lost a lot, we killed a lot. Harry was an extremely bloody action. Perhaps if our first sergeant hadn't tried to make a political statement to the reporters, people would have known more about it. But I can't blame him. He was right.

The three battalions in reserve were being rebuilt as fighting units. The slightly wounded were being returned to duty, and replacements for the dead and seriously wounded needed to be acquired and integrated into the various units. Reserve duty gave time for this to happen as well as for newcomers, returnees, and survivors to get to know one another. Buckner returned from the hospital during this period.

• • •

June 24, 1953

Dear Ethel:

Another day is about over and it has been a rather pleasant one. Things drained and dried off a little and, with another such day tomorrow, the countryside should be back to normal.

The battalions that moved off line last week are now moving back into position—however this time to the right of our former sector. Rumor has it that we will spend about four months in this position. If we do, I'll spend most of the month of November at home. Such a thought, naturally, bothers me no end.

In our sector tonight, all is very quiet, however, we have heard the sounds of heavy fighting over to the west around White Horse. However, that is too far away to be of any practical interest to us.

As you have probably noticed on the letter, I have developed the habit of lighting my cigarettes from the candle. Thus on most of my letters these days can be found a few stray drops of wax. I think it adds that "homey" touch—although I assure you it is completely accidental. . . .

• • •

The rains, the clouds, and the searchlights created a night landscape of vivid blues and blacks. Picture the dull black of the trenches with pools of slime glistening at the bottom. This darkness slowly changing as the blackness of the parapet reflected the brilliant blue-white searchlights, this in turn fading into the somber void of the night sky. Outside our bunker this created a uniformity of levels of blues and blacks relieved only by the silhouette of the trunk and limb of a shattered sapling, leaning at an impossible angle from the top of the parapet. The canvas was broken only by the occasional bright flashes of distant shell fire followed by its rolling thunder.

Quiet had returned. Many a night I simply leaned on the parapet, under the single, leafless branch of that shattered sapling, watching the sky.

The movement reports indicate that the Sixty-fifth was once again being withdrawn from the line. Whether this was because the troops were in disarray, as we believed, or because Command wanted our reorganized battalions to have a taste of line duty in a quiet sector, I don't know. The latter would make sense. The move was supposed to be a secret, but friends told me they were greeted by loudspeakers from the Chinese side saying, "Men of the Fifteenth, welcome back. We have found you honorable opponents in the past."

• • •

June 27, 1953

Dear Ethel:

I received two letters from you today. I'm glad to hear that young Johnny is getting a little more confidence. I think that will help immeasurably when he gets started to Kindergarten—of course, that is still pretty far in the future.

Your storm in Peoria sounds pretty vicious. I'm glad we have nothing like that to put up with over here. I bet big John was worried about the whole thing though.

Your latest letter (June 17) speaks of truce talks again and I notice that the latest Stars and Stripes [a military newspaper for overseas personnel] says that a bunch of Swedish negotiators are on their way over here. Peace talks—or reports on them—seem to have been pretty well squelched over here. We have been hearing all about Rhee though and most of us are building up a first class hate for him.

These days it is more dangerous for Americans in South Korean cities than on the front-lines. G.I.s are required to carry loaded weapons in Seoul for self defense and many of our boys tell of being stoned while there by our South Korean friends(?). Most of us are ready to say the hell with Korea and pull out. . . .

Incidentally R&R to Japan has been canceled for the present. I don't know if I'll get to go or not. At any rate, the less said the better. . . .

• • •

The concern about the severe storm in Peoria was sincere—no sarcasm was intended. I knew my world, but I didn't know my sister's. Now, years later, this paragraph fascinates me. I'd grown so completely accustomed to my front-line world of bunkers, artillery fire, and patrols that I could write I was glad I wasn't in such a dangerous place as Peoria!

My comment on the problems between our soldiers and the

Koreans in the rear areas reminds me of some things I'd forgotten. We had dual relationships with the Koreans. On the one hand, we had Koreans who were attached to our unit, either formally, as KATUSAs, or informally, as with the elderly Papasan who took up residence in our supply room and simply lived and worked with us in exchange for food and a place to sleep. Kim Shi Han, a tall, bespectacled, scholarly young man was formally attached to our squad. Yo Han Yoon, a magnificent athlete who was always ready for action, was with Curry's squad. These men earned our respect and our friendship, as did Papasan.

On the other hand, there were hostile South Koreans. Perhaps they were Communist sympathizers. I don't know if they were or were not. But I know that there were many South Koreans who didn't like Americans and didn't want us in their country, and they showed their feelings at every opportunity. Soldiers who visited Seoul would return saying that the Koreans would cheat or rob them whenever possible. However, it must be said in the defense of these Koreans that not all Americans serving in the rear areas were para- gons of virtue. Some of them were sincere workers—like us—doing the jobs to which they'd been assigned. Others were loudmouthed, bullying braggarts who used every opportunity to demonstrate their superiority by intimidating a battered and homeless people.

On my way back to the States, a soldier who'd been stationed in Japan bragged to me that he'd never paid for a woman in Japan. When he wanted one, he simply walked down the street at night until he saw one he liked. Then he'd pull her into a back alley. We had too many of the same type in Korea. Animals like this never got to the front line; or, if they did, they were the type who "got lost" when action was near, showing up later full of excuses. Units with sense didn't give them second chances.

• • •

June 28, 1994

Dear Ethel:

The month of June is rapidly drawing to a close. Two more days and I'll be starting another month in Korea. I don't think I'll go on R&R in July anymore, possibly however—if they start it back up— I'll go in August. I think that the cancellation was one of the lower tricks they've played on us. Anyway, what can we do about it?

I will be very glad to see payday roll around this month. For the first time since January, I find myself flat busted at the end of a month. A horrible and unaccustomed feeling. I just bought too much junk during the month. Next month I think I shall try to hold on to it better. Of course I sent $60 home and put $70 with my R&R money, however, I still spent almost $20. That is too much in Korea.

Today, last night, and yesterday afternoon were marked by very heavy rains. It started about two o'clock yesterday in a downpour and has simply kept up the downpour right on through. . . .

•   •   •

Officers must be taught how to destroy morale. Too many of them were too good at it to chalk it up to coincidence. Every good manager I've ever known has always said, "If you can't deliver, don't promise. Better to promise little, and deliver it, than to promise much and deliver little." Perhaps rear echelon troops, fatigued by paperwork, received the promised rest and recreation every four months, but the infantry sure didn't. Time and again we were disappointed.

I've included the bragging about money because I'm not sure people realize how much is for free, of necessity, when you're on the front line. For me to have spent twenty dollars, we must have been near or with the Greeks, where we could purchase American beer and Greek cognac.

•   •   •

June 29, 1953

Dear Ethel:

. . . Tomorrow is the end of the month so another month bites the dust. I am on my way to finishing my seventh month in Korea. I always dislike the period of time from the 21st to the end of the month. Mainly because after the twenty-first my points and pay for the month are assured and you have that period of waiting for the next month to start so that you may again begin building on your points and pay. I am glad that period for June is finished. I had hoped to be in Japan during that stretch in July but now I don't think I will be.

A beetle just had the audacity to fly into this bunker. I fought it out with him using a DDT bomb. In the course of the action, one rifle, one flak vest, some stationary [*sic*], a cup of coffee and one face (my own) was sprayed. Incidentally I got the beetle. I hit him with a newspaper.

At any rate, Sis, what I want now is a stretch of four more months on line—as peaceful as possible. If it gets too rough I won't mind a little reserve time. A little action like we had on Harry will go a long way. I want no more of it. . . .

• • •

At about this time an unpleasant incident occurred involving one of our men. I've forgotten his name, but I remember that he was different from the rest of us, and we knew it. While each man normally carried a rifle, a bayonet, about forty-five rounds of ammunition, and a few grenades, he carried a rifle, a Thompson submachine gun, a pistol, several bandoliers of ammunition, and at least a dozen grenades plus knives. He looked more like a Mexican bandit, as portrayed in the early Hollywood cowboy movies, than a soldier. You knew he was different the minute you saw him. As a World War II paratrooper, he'd been trapped without ammunition at Bastogne, and he lived in terror that he would run out of ammunition again. Beyond that he was absolutely fearless. Often he'd take off on his own for solitary excursions into the no-man's-land between the two armies. None of us understood why he was still alive.

Once, this heavily armed fellow decided to visit Seoul, and he proceeded to hitchhike down there. While he was walking along a city street, a couple of military police recognized him as being different, which wasn't difficult, and stopped to question him. When they tried to take him into custody, he got the drop on them, disarmed them, and returned to the unit as quickly as possible with their weapons added to his collection.

Of course, the MPs soon caught up with him. We were amused by the incident and unconcerned that he'd been caught. We knew he needed hospitalization, and we thought he would now receive the help he needed. After all, the army had made him what he was.

We heard later that he received a prison term instead.

• • •

July 1, 1953

Dear Ethel:

   Once again the rumors have sprung up that the Third is to go
to Japan and that the First Cavalry will replace us in Korea. The
main basis for the rumor seems to be the fact that as yet they have
not regained their colors and as long as they are in Japan they are
in no position to do so. However if they come to Korea they can
regain permission to fly their regimental colors by victorious combat. The 15th has never had that disgrace.

   Today another group of men rotated home and the fourth of this
month there will be a second shipment out. With so much line
time to our credit, we now have a great many men leaving each
month. If we move back into reserve this would dip down rather
sharply. I have worked my way up to the top half of the list. . . .
At any rate Eth, I'll be there when I get there, no sooner and no
later. . . .

July 3, 1953

   Today I loafed around most of the morning and then went and
took a shower this afternoon. Rather a lazy day but still find myself tired at the end of it. I'm just getting too used to sleeping
twenty hours a day and when I have to stay up all day I'm dead
tired. . . .

• • •

   As this and other letters show, we were doing very little work,
and the Chinese seemed to be doing the same. Many of my letters
simply recycled rumors, hopes, and plans. We were still on an
outpost. We still overlooked enemy lines. The occasional artillery
or mortar shell reminded us of this. There were still watches to be
pulled and patrols to be run, but it was generally quiet.

   Boredom returned as a leading problem. Boredom and tension—unlikely but constant partners on the front.

   There was one bit of excitement. Most of us were in the bunker when a guy came running in from the toilet and said, "Come
look at the air attack. Our air force is attacking our mortars." We
ran outside and across the top of the hill to watch. A heavy mor-

tar unit was located in the valley behind us, and because the U.N. totally controlled the skies, the mortar men had not bothered to conceal their position. Their four tents were in a nice straight line with nothing in the way of camouflage. The gun emplacements were out in the open, also in a nice straight row, as were the stacks of ammunition.

We sat and watched while three American fighter planes flew back and forth strafing the area. They didn't seem to do any damage to the guns, but one small stack of ammunition was set on fire. We later heard that no one had been injured, but all the tents were now full of holes. A real blow to that unit during the rainy season. I've often wondered what the pilots reported when they returned to their base.

• • •

July 4, 1953

Dear Ethel:

Today is very hot and sultry. . . . I haven't done a thing all day.

I got a letter and a picture from this one girl in Memphis that I've been thinking of stopping writing. What a babe! I wrote her a three page letter immediately—will probably write her again tomorrow. . . .

As for life back here at regiment, well, it is the same as always. Some rumors say we will be on line until October. I hope it is true. . . . If we are still on line next month I shall write the folks to expect me for Christmas . . .

July 9, 1953

It seems that I owe you a letter. Unfortunately I have several good reasons for being delayed in writing—the main one being rain. Over here when it rains everything leaks, consequently as much stuff as possible is stored away to keep it from being destroyed. One of the best things to put away as quickly as possible is stationary [sic], you know what water does to that. Consequently a four day rain—such as we just had—means no letter writing for four days—if we can help it (and we usually can).

Last night we heard a lot of fighting going on over to our left—and later found out that the GIs were trying to push the last of some Chinese attackers off of Pork Chop. Tonight we hear the same

sound again so I guess the battle has been continued. Luckily our
sector remains very quiet. It is my hope that it stays that way for
the next three months. . . .

• • •

It rained outside, it rained inside. The rain, the mud, and the
humidity would have created problems for normal people, but
after so many months on the front line we were well past that. We
worked at keeping our rifles and personal possessions dry, but we
didn't worry about much else.

• • •

July 10, 1953

Dear Ethel:

Yesterday was the hottest I have as yet experienced over here,
but today promises to be just as warm. Actually I was made a little
sick by the heat yesterday, but a little medicine and a good rest have
made me feel like a new man today. This morning I'm taking it easy,
but I expect to be back in the grind this afternoon.

There was no mail yesterday, but we heard the railroad was
bombed, so that would account for the disrupted mail service.

The war continues to roll merrily along. Our sector has been
very quiet of recent, but I hear there has been heavy fighting over
to our left on Pork Chop hill. I also hear that they are getting back
to work on the truce talks. This doesn't bother me anymore. . . .

• • •

At the time of these letters, I was convinced that the Communists were playing games with the truce talks. The talks effectively
prevented our political leadership from mounting the type of propaganda campaign at home that was required to build support for
an offensive against the Communists.

The Chinese used nighttime intervals in the fighting to move
troops and supplies down the trails from Manchuria. When they
had sufficient men and materiel, they would open a charge and,
perhaps, gain a mile or two. Having secured more territory, they'd
proceed with truce talks. While such a policy seems a waste of men,
they may have used troops who had originally fought for the Na-

tionalists in the Chinese civil war and whose loyalty was questionable. By using them, they could eliminate a potential threat at home and blame their deaths on the American devils, thereby increasing the loyalty of the dead men's families.

If our political leadership had had the nerve to counterattack following each of these small enemy offensives—not only to drive them back, but to take territory—I believe the North Koreans would have become much more serious, much faster, at the truce table. Perhaps thousands of men—Americans, Chinese, and Koreans—would have been spared death or dismemberment as a result.

• • •

July 11, 1953

Dear Ethel:

Unless something happens to save us the trouble we will probably move into reserve within the next couple of days. I'm not exactly eager to go—but in a way I wouldn't mind a month of reserve too much. At any rate I don't have too much to say about it.

I shall probably go swimming again today. We have found a very nice spot in the river way up stream. It is very wide with plenty of deep water. Unfortunately, the main current is very swift and leads to a small waterfall and a series of rapids. You have to watch yourself while swimming in that sector or you'll "shoot the chute." The boys who have done it are usually sadder for the experience.

July 12, 1953

There is nothing so impressive as an Army on the move. We are leaving in the morning for somewhere—way the hell back. Remind me to tell you of this when I come home. I don't have time now. Don't expect letters from a me for a while—not til we settle down—maybe 10 days or two weeks.

• • •

The enthusiasm of the letter of July 12 to my sister completely contradicts the who-cares attitude of the first letter: I was pleased to be moving into reserve. Note, too, that because of the timing of the move, we wouldn't receive four points in July, nor would the men of the regiment that replaced us—since no one in either regiment would have the required twenty-one days on the line. Perhaps those of us who believed that Command would ignore or manipulate its own policies to the disadvantage of enlisted men were right.

11

THE KUMSONG SALIENT

I looked forward to reserve duty for a number of reasons, not the least of which was that one of my boots had been slashed open by a bit of shrapnel and I had a small cut on my foot, perhaps two inches long. Not sufficient to impede my work or take me off an outpost, the cut nonetheless provided an opportunity for me to plead injury while on reserve. I bragged to Barker about my anticipated rest in a hospital, eating good food and watching the nurses—to the point where he was ready to kill me. I also hoped to get a new pair of boots, which I couldn't get through my supply sergeant.

None of us expected reserve duty itself to be any fun; we assumed that rear echelon types would appear and try to make us look and act like garrison soldiers, rather than the combat soldiers we were proud to be. I planned for my injury to enable me to avoid garrison-type soldiering, but I needn't have worried. Garrison life wasn't in my immediate future.

Arriving in the rear, we had about an hour to wait before receiving a promised hot lunch. To pass the time, I began cleaning my ammunition magazines. This was an important task, one that hadn't been taught to me in basic training. If the ammunition becomes jammed in the magazine because of sand, dirt, or just plain contrariness, it has the potential to be a real problem—that is, if you need to shoot, you can't. At the time, I had two fifteen-round magazines that were taped together so I could empty one and then quickly reverse to the other, so I'd have a loaded rifle without fumbling in my pockets. I also had a couple of five-round magazines. I had just emptied these and finished cleaning and oiling them—but not reloading them—when we received an emergency alert.

A Chinese force, perhaps three divisions strong, had crushed the Republic of Korea (ROK) Capitol Division in the central mountains on the night of July 13 and were headed south. The Fifteenth was ordered into the breach. Our colonel wanted his scouts out. My squad was to locate the nearest functioning unit to the east of the breakthrough and report back. This meant we had to cross through what had become either no-man's-land or Communist-controlled territory until we found allies on the eastern side.

There was a wild run to supply to get bulletproof vests. My tasks were to get my radio, spare batteries, and a case of grenades. Someone else, probably Barker, grabbed a couple of cases of food, assault rations. We raced to the jeep and headed north and east. I sat in the back trying to reload ammunition into my magazines, bouncing all over, while O'Connor drove at full speed on the rutted dirt road.

What young idiots we were, racing into a fluid combat area, struggling to be the first ones there. While we were still in the rear, we encountered a military policeman in the middle of the road trying to make us slow down to the speed limit. We passed him on the right. At the same time, another scout jeep, racing to beat us to the action, veered around and passed him on the left. The MP was probably pleased to survive—and if he wasn't, he should have been.

We were absolutely cocky. The lassitude and doubt of the month following the battle for Outpost Harry disappeared, and we were again pulled into the excitement of the hunt. We had beaten the Chinese at Harry, and there was no one better to meet them in Kumsong, in the central mountains. What Colonel Akers wanted, Colonel Akers would get, at least if we had anything to do about it. We returned his concern for us with our love and respect. O'Connor drove while Barker, Kim Shi Han, and I held on for dear life.

We drove steadily north and east. Not until several hours later, when we were winding through, and always farther into, the craggy mountains and cliffs of central Korea did the thought cross my mind that we were highly unlikely to get out of this situation alive. It would be difficult and expensive in lives to push a determined enemy out of those tumbled masses of boulders and cliffs. Still, I was more impressed by the foaming, rushing white water of the streams crashing down the mountainside than by any specific fears. It was my first glimpse of these mountains, and I loved them.

A more poignant memory is of long lines of infantrymen, who had been trudging toward safety and reserve duty only to be turned around on the road and sent to block a major Chinese break-through. Tired men in faded gray-green uniforms, spaced four to five yards apart on each side of the road as far as the eye could see, silently, inexorably moving forward through a faded, dusty, gray-green, isolated countryside to a future whose only certainty was pain. We slowed as we passed them. My heart went out to them. They were the muscle, we were only the eyes and ears. They had the work, we had the excitement.

Not all of them had the strength to carry on. One soldier squat-ted, crumpled, in the road, head bowed, crying, as the lines moved slowly past him. No one looked, everyone saw, no sound was made. We could give compassion but not assistance. His war was over, ours wasn't. I prayed that it was truly over and that he would re-turn again to life. He had reached a limit all of us knew we had. It was simply that no one of us knew exactly where ours was, we just knew that we hadn't reached it yet.

• • •

July 17, 1953

Dear Ethel:

A great deal has happened in the last few days. A group went into reserve twenty-four hours early to set up tents etc. The rest of us arrived at 11:00 the following day.

At 12:00 we were headed back for the front with the news that the Chinese had smashed the Capital ROK Division and were still coming. We were pretty busy for the next two days finding out where our friends were and getting units on the MLR [main line of resistance, or front line] (reorganized behind the old MLR) in touch with one another. The next day, the chief problem was finding where the Chinese were. At present we are pretty well or-ganized. The Chinese are still trying, but not so successfully against us as against the ROKs.

The roads have been a mess with scattered bands of soldiers trudging back from the front lines—new units moving forward, and a steady flow of material, tanks, guns, and ambulances. Our platoon has been rounding up the scattered ROKs—many wound-ed and having spent days dodging the Chinese without food. We bring 'em in, feed them, and send them back to their units or the hospital, whichever they need.

At present things are getting slowly back to normal. As it is I wouldn't mind staying up here for three more months. Well, Sis, so much for today, will write again tomorrow.

• • •

It took about two days of roaming narrow mud roads through the mountains in the jeep to find the nearest functioning unit. The colonel in charge at an ROK command post located in a truck that had been pulled off the road briefed O'Connor on the location of his troops. Because it was late, we decided to get some sleep before heading back. We pulled the jeep in front of the Korean command truck so no one could retreat without us knowing it. We didn't want to be left alone to face a charging enemy.

We headed back in the morning. It took us another day to find our unit and give our report to Colonel Akers. Later, we were told that we'd been reported to division headquarters as missing in action but that we'd returned before further action was taken. I was glad, because it would have really worried my folks and told them more about my duties than I wanted them to know.

I was impressed by the changes between the time we drove into the mountains and when we returned to our unit. Going in, once we'd passed our own troops and entered the mountains, the only people we saw were occasional groups of men, often weaponless and hungry. We didn't know if they were retreating South Koreans or advancing North Koreans or Chinese who had strayed from their units. As long as they didn't interfere with us, we didn't worry about them.

On the trip back we drove past massive numbers of artillery guns lining the mud roads, with trucks and jeeps bringing in supplies and engineers working to improve the roads and carve new ones with names such as "Mule Trail" and "Goat Trail"—which should give you an idea of their qualities—through the mountains. For the most part, the artillery was simply pulled to the side of the road, pointed north, and set up for firing. Hundreds of guns now lined miles of dirt roads that had been empty two days earlier.

I don't remember specifics from the days following the mad dash to locate the South Korean command post, but I do recall a lot of walking and a lot of rain. Korea seemed to be the only place in the world were it could be pouring rain and still have the trucks and tanks throwing up dust as they rushed past. One night, everyone in our squad was so tired, soaked, and cold that we simply stripped off our wet clothing and huddled together for warmth as we slept nude on the wooden platform of a surviving Korean hut. We would have been easy prey that night.

The cut on my foot was a constant source of irritation. A yellow pocket of pus would form underneath the scab, and whenever I had the opportunity, I'd pull off my torn boot and sock, which peeled off the scab. The pus would drain out, and then I'd let my foot dry as well as I could until it was time to wring the water from my sock, put it back on, and go. It was never a real problem, just ugly.

• • •

July 18, 1953

Dear Ethel:

Today I went down to the creek and helped wash the jeep. At the same time I washed my clothes and myself. My clothes and I needed it worse than the jeep did. An old papasan came along and helped us so we gave him a couple packs of cigarettes for his efforts.

We are slowly getting this new area into shape—having used three cases of DDT in a day and a half. It still is pretty filthy but it's better than it was. Maybe another month and five hundred cases of DDT from now and it will be livable.

I read in the newspaper how the ROKs stopped the big Chinese drive on the east central front. They don't mention the fact that within twenty four hours of the initial attack the entire Third Division was on line along with the ROKs. But then, having the newspapers ignore the Third is no new experience.

Well Sis, three more days and I'll have my four points for the month. That will give me twenty five at the end of the month. A pretty fair total, especially if we stay on line just three more months.

• • •

The scouts had moved into a former Korean army mess hall. It was a long hut, thatched with rice straw. There were tables and benches, with tin plates nailed to the tables. When we ripped up the plates we found the tables were covered with maggots. Consequently, we pulled out the tables and benches and burned them. Then there was the problem of bugs dropping from the ceiling. We had canvas cots at this time and we'd wake up covered with different types of worms and beetles. We sprayed the roof, which was a terrible mistake. Our thatched hut was the home and hunting ground of vast numbers of assorted animals. What had been a stream of life falling on us before became a flood of dead and dying insects. As a last resort, we pulled out our cots and set fire to the place. That night we sat near the dying blaze singing college and campfire songs. As the embers dwindled, someone suggested that we set fire to a large brush pile next to us, but the idea didn't pass. Good thing, too. Exploring the brush the next day, we discovered a concealed ammunition pile. We would have ended our careers then and there.

We moved our cots onto the ashes and slept there until we received tents. Soon, however, our squads moved back on line, coming back to the tents, bunks, and hot meals only for occasional rests.

• • •

July 19, 1953

Dear Ethel:

Today begins my fourteenth month in the Army. Thirteen down and eleven to go. At least I'm now past the halfway point in the Army—as well as in Korea. Of course, my constant hope is that we stay on line for just three more months. That would suit me perfectly.

There was no mail today so that means I don't have to answer any this evening. We have been following a very simple routine recently. We work nights, sleep mornings, care for equipment in the afternoon, write in the early evening, etc. Keeps you busy and makes the time pass that much swifter,

They seem to be whooping up the peace rumors again—but I have no faith in them anymore. However, if we do have a peace, I should be one of the first to leave here. I'm getting to be a high pointer now. At the end of the month I'll have twenty five.

Well Sis—so much for now—I have to eat and then I'm going

to try to get Dave Henze on the telephone. He is in Chunchon. I'll write again tomorrow.

• • •

We were doing lots of patrolling during this period, primarily short evening or night patrols. We had a new lieutenant named Rinklemeyer (I think that's how he spelled it). Rumor had it he'd played basketball for the University of Oklahoma. We liked him. He volunteered us for lots of patrols, so many that we, privately, began calling ourselves "Rinky-Dinky's Rangers." It was a term of affection. Rinklemeyer spent time with us and wasn't afraid to go where we went.

Nor was the lieutenant afraid to listen to us. One afternoon when we were on patrol we came under artillery fire. Rinklemeyer said to move up to the slope of a hill in front of us. This is a good textbook tactic as the enemy gunners have difficulty seeing or hitting you in such a position, even though you are closer to them. But when we pointed out that it was American artillery shooting at us, and that going up there would give them a clear shot at us, he told us to stay put. Finally, someone with some sense stopped the shooting.

That was the second time Stan O'Connor was really angry at me. He had all the points necessary to go home, but he'd insisted on coming with us. Lying there, I was reminded of a Bill Mauldin cartoon in which Willy shouts, "I can't get no lower, Joe, me buttons is in the way." I looked around and saw Stan about twenty feet away, as flat in the mud as I was. I yelled over something like, "Gee, Stan, aren't you glad you're here rather than back at headquarters?" He was short on humor that day and yelled back, "Dannenmaier, someday someone is going to kill you for one of your wisecracks."

A lot of learning goes on in combat. In a major battle, as at Harry, your life is up for grabs, but otherwise you have some control. An important thing to learn is the sound of artillery. We'd gotten pretty good at it. From the sound the shells made coming in, we could tell about where they would hit and to what degree we needed to protect ourselves. In a way, mortars were more dangerous because they arrived in silence, but if you were alert, you could hear the "pop" when they were fired and, judging from your own location, be prepared when they arrived. I never did learn to tell where rockets were going from their sound, which was why they always worried me. The U.S. gunners who were working us over on that one patrol were really bad shots. We were out in the open and they should have killed at least some of us.

Dave Henze, the person I told my sister I was going to try to telephone, was an artilleryman in nearby Chunchon. He was also a close personal friend and college classmate of mine. Contacting him brought a touch of home.

• • •

July 20, 1953

Dear Ethel:

The hottest rumor off the press today is that we are going to Japan. Of course I've been hearing that one for the last eight months, but it is still impressive. Anyway, next month this time we'll know for sure.

Seven months ago today I arrived in Korea—so I'm now starting my eighth month over here. If you add on my travel time I've been gone from home about eight and a half months now. As of tomorrow I'll be assured of four points for the month—bringing my total up to twenty-five points. All I need is three more months of line time, or six months of reserve.

I got quite a letter from Joe today. A nice long one—of course, any letter from Joe is news. He told me all about his trip up to see the folks.

Also, Dave Henze finally got in contact with me last night on the telephone. We talked for about fifteen minutes, but there wasn't too much we could say, both of us—especially me—being bound by censorship. . . .

• • •

Right around the time I wrote this letter, I heard that Joe Freeman, a friend of mine and one of the seven men who'd sat in the snow waiting for a truck to take us to our company, had been killed. Rumor had it that he'd been crouched over when an artillery shell landed. They said he simply slumped over dead. I was sorry to lose another friend but glad that it was quick. He'd never been as close to me as Charley Brown, but our little group of seven had maintained a steady friendship. Like Charley, Joe had become a lineman.

Of our original seven, two were dead, one was wounded, and one had frostbite. It made me, occupying the theoretically most dangerous job as a radio scout, think.

Much less serious was another incident that I still remember with a smile. Our squad was given a night off. We'd been working every night and they told us we could stay at headquarters and sleep. There was only one catch: guerrillas were operating in the area. As was explained to us, the security platoon had no real combat experience, so we were to back them up as needed. After all, we were the ones with experience. We had to keep one man awake and on the telephone; the security platoon would occupy foxholes in the hills around the camp. If they called for help, we were to go. As usual, Stan O'Connor took the first shift. Sure enough, no sooner had we gone to sleep than the call came. It was jump up, grab helmets, vests, rifles, and grenades, form a skirmish line, and go. When we arrived, we found that the men in the security platoon had been shooting at each other.

We quieted everyone and returned to our interrupted rest, Stan returning to the telephone. Again, just as we fell asleep, a call came in. This time we were more casual in going to the top, but it still meant helmets, vests, rifles, grenades, and a long climb. Again, they'd been taking potshots at one another.

This time Stan gathered them together and said, "Look, guys, the next time you call we're going to assume the Chinese have killed everyone up here and taken your positions. But don't worry. We'll avenge you. We'll kill everyone up here."

We slept through the night.

• • •

July 21, 1953

Dear Ethel:

Another day is here and that is about all that can be said about it. We had a light rain this morning to settle the dust and it has stayed cloudy and cool. Now, if it just doesn't rain any more we'll be all set.

The trouble is at present we don't have anything to do and time is going very slowly. So you see at times work is welcome. Next year this time, however, it will be different. I'll not only have some work to do—I'll also have something to do in my free time.

I have a lot of work to do around the house, then I have some visiting to do—you and Joe—and then I shall take a trip to the West Coast. Probably driving.

I may insist on Dad taking his vacation about that time and drive him, Mom, and Skipper—first up to visit you and then down to visit Joe. . . .

• • •

The letter prattles on. I can't recall specifics of what was happening at that time. Perhaps it was nothing, perhaps something I didn't want my sister to know about. It was about this time in late July that we were on one of my least favorite kind of patrols, a combat patrol. We led an infantry platoon out to see if we could stir up trouble. We turned out to be quite successful. We were hit front and side.

The platoon leader, the first black officer I'd worked under, did a really excellent job. He got on my telephone and called in artillery, surrounding us with white phosphorous. As the artillery died down, we got out.

On the way back, the scouts split off from the platoon. As we neared the American lines, we discovered that someone had forgotten to tell the roadblock tank that we were out. Our first knowledge of this was when a grenade exploded near us. We yelled and identified ourselves and they let us walk in. They told us we were really lucky, that they'd had us in their machine gun sights and were just about to fire when they heard us call out to them. Having been out most of the night, we were really thirsty and drank all their water once they said they could easily get more.

One reason I remember that patrol is because it had been so difficult for me physically. It was a long patrol, in both distance and time, and the radio had become a burden. I was just plain exhausted from the excess weight and was considering dropping out to rest, figuring that I'd come in alone the next day, when a "buddy" behind me pushed me out of the way so he could move faster. I was so furious that I literally ran up the mountain trying to catch him. I didn't think about shooting him, I just wanted to get my hands on him. But as we reached the top we encountered the tank and I calmed down. It was the last of only a few patrols I was on with him.

• • •

July 23, 1953

Dear Ethel:

Didn't write yesterday because I ran out of envelopes. However, I got some back at Red Cross today so I'm all set up in the writing business again. . . .

The last of our equipment is being moved up now—that is, what hasn't been stolen. I haven't gotten any of my personal gear yet but I still have hopes.

Our dogs rejoined us last night. Boy are they happy to be back with the outfit again. They jumped all over everyone when they first got back.

Our place is getting fixed up a little better now and is a little more comfortable. . . .

• • •

This was the move I mentioned earlier during which I'd lost the last of my personal gear. When we left the reserve area to race into Kumsong, we were ordered to leave behind all unnecessary items, such as cameras, writing paper, and letters. We were told that it would be guarded and forwarded to us later. I didn't have much; it all fit into a wooden grenade box, which is about the size of a case of canned soda pop, but it was mine and all that I had. We also had to leave our unofficial squad equipment, such as our Coleman lantern and our frying pan. We lost all of this. I also lost my spare clothing, including the extra socks my parents routinely mailed to me.

In addition to my camera, stationery, and pens, I lost my list of addresses. I had to wait for people to write in order to answer them, the exception being those whose addresses I knew well, such as my parents, brother, and sister. Of all the girls I'd been writing to, only Nell Fallon of Memphis continued our correspondence. I truly appreciated it. Her letters were pleasant, friendly, and humorous.

As I told my sister in this letter, our outfit had dogs. They loved us and we loved them—most of the time. When they started fighting with one another in the tents, we didn't appreciate them at all. They never came up on line with us, staying back with the headquarters squad, so we saw them only when we were visiting.

• • •

July 25, 1953

Dear Ethel:

You guessed it right in your letter, the 15th is still on line—and busier than ever. We did move further east but that's about all. The territory in this sector is much more rugged than in our old sector, as is the warfare. However, as often as our cooks can provide it, we continue to get hot food. That makes a big difference. But don't worry, I seem to carry a horseshoe around in my hip pocket.

I now have twenty-five points and it looks as if we'll still be on line through August. I hope so for that will put me right up close to the top of the list for rotation with twenty-nine. With that many, I'd be sure of getting home for Christmas so long as I stay in Korea. Of course, with the truce talks, we never know what will happen. However by the end of next month, I should be able to predict quite accurately my month of departure. Anyway, I still have six waste days in this month to go before starting on my points and pay for August. I just hope we stay on line through August and September. Then October wouldn't really make much difference. Well, Sis, it looks as if my time is getting closer—and I expect yours is too. How is this youngest one behaving himself or herself these days? I haven't heard much on the subject. . . .

• • •

At this time, all the squads were at headquarters. We slept there during the day and patrolled at night, moving to jump-off locations by jeep. There was risk in all elements of these patrols. The roads were narrow mud tracks carved into the mountains by the engineers. Often, we could look over the side and see the crumpled, burned-out hulks of vehicles that had slipped over the edge and crashed down the mountainside. It wasn't a concern, just a curiosity.

With all squads living at headquarters, we learned much more about one another's activities. One day I slipped into a small cave dug into the clay hillside to see three men from another squad deep in conversation. A flickering wick in the shell of a Chinese grenade filled with oil provided the light. Silence met my entrance. Then one of the guys said, "This isn't your business." I nodded and listened as they continued their conversation. He was right. It wasn't my business. Their sergeant had irritated them, and he wouldn't be returning from their next patrol. I barely knew him and didn't especially like him. What I'd seen made me think he was a bully and a braggart. The men in the cave were my friends, so I left without a word. We didn't know that we'd been on our last patrols. That sergeant was lucky.

My sister and I had rather different ideas, as expressed in our letters, on the desirability of line time. The truce talks had gotten quite serious. Ethel's neighbor, in a backyard conversation, said that she hoped the truce wasn't signed anytime soon because her husband was making a lot of money working overtime at the Caterpillar plant. After I came home, my sister told me about that conversation and said it was the last one she and that neighbor ever had.

• • •

July 26, 1953

Dear Ethel:

Today seems to be my day of leisure. This morning I went to church and this afternoon I've been writing letters. Pretty soft. I didn't get any mail today but that just means I get that much more when it does come. So long as no one gets any mail I don't mind not getting any.

What I'm looking forward to right now is a package Mom said she sent of cookies. I'm afraid it went down with that ship load of mail. I'm so hungry for some of those cookies I can practically taste them—and they are overdue now.

There is a slight chance that I may get down to Chunchon the first week of August to see Dave Henze. The boys from the Air Force liaison group are driving down there and if I can get permission I'll go with them. If I get there, I'll try to buy another camera to replace my old one. They should have some big P.X.'s there. If I can get two days off, I'd either spend the night at Dave's or at the air force base. Next week this time I'll know if I can go or not.

My foot is about healed now from the slash I gave it a couple weeks ago. Also I found a new pair of boots (new to me) so I threw away the ones I'd cut open. Thus I'm back in pretty fair shape again. Actually I was never stopped by it—nor slowed down—but it did bother me at times.

I just made a bet with O'Connor. He bet me $5 that he'll be married within a year of his discharge, although at present he doesn't have a girl. I'd say it was a pretty fair bet.

The radio just said the truce will be signed tomorrow morning at 10:00. If so, I think I shall get drunk tomorrow starting at 10:00. I have enough beer to do it. I still don't believe it, but if it's true there will probably be an attack all along the line tonight. Boy, that will really foul up my rotation plans. If that's true I don't know when I'll get home.

Well, Sis, as usual the best we can do is wait and find out. So I'll write again tomorrow.

• • •

The visit to church was discouraging. Early in the service the chaplain prayed for God to "protect and guide" the officers of the regiment—enlisted men weren't mentioned. Anger welled up inside me. In my world, the enlisted men went into danger while the officers partied in the rear. I stopped listening and didn't attend another service until one Sunday, following the truce, when I wanted to avoid some make-work.

O'Connor was the one who acquired some boots for me. The supply room was never able to get any, so Stan went to the morgue, where he was able to get a used pair. They were too wide for me, which I ignored at the time. In the happiness of getting dry feet, I threw away the old pair, which was a mistake. I soon discovered that walking up and down mountains in boots that didn't quite fit left me exhausted. Exhausted and with tired feet. At every opportunity, I'd strip off the boots and cool my feet in the cold mountain streams. It was wonderfully refreshing. I wasn't able to obtain a pair of boots that fit until I was on my way home.

I was able to visit with Dave Henze, whom I listed as my cousin, just to make it easier for Lieutenant Rinklemeyer to explain if I were missed. I rode down with the air force team, and Dave drove me back the next day. This was when I discovered how luxuriously the artillery lived, at least compared with my squad. They had bunks and pillows and electric lights. They even had a small bar where you could buy a cold beer. When Dave drove me back to regimental headquarters, I offered to borrow a flak vest for him if he wanted to come up to the outpost and see what the Chinese lines looked like. He declined with thanks, dropping me off at HQ and getting out of there as quickly as he could.

• • •

July 27, 1953

Dear Ethel:

There is no longer much doubt about the truce. It has been signed. At ten o'clock tonight we are to unload our weapons for the final time. It will be sort of a relief. They are taking the excitement out of the game, but I don't think I'll miss it too much.

I think I will leave here in October, but there is no way to tell for sure. I still am not giving the folks any encouragement until I see how the wind blows. I expect that by the end of the first week of August I should be able to write them something definite. If rumor is true, I should leave here about the third week of October depending on what ship is leaving about that time. Rumor says we'll spend the next three months getting the same number of points we do now. If that's true, I'll be leaving in October. Anyway, we shall see what we shall see.

• • •

There was no drinking that night. We all expected the Chinese to use as much ammunition as possible, so, individually and in pairs, we hunted for the safest holes we could find and climbed in. No one wanted to be the last casualty of the war.

Our predictions were fairly accurate. The artillery was heavy, both theirs and ours, heavier than it had been in days. Then, about nine o'clock, our artillery gradually diminished as unit after unit quit firing. At last, not a gun was to be heard, just the explosions of incoming shells. Finally, at ten, these also stopped.

The silence was startling. So was the darkness, no longer broken by the lights of exploding shells. Then, slowly, lights began appearing, a cigarette here, a flashlight there. On the road in the valley behind us, a truck turned on its lights, then another, and another. I climbed out of the hole I'd found and watched as the darkness below became laced with ribbons of light from vehicles moving on our backup roads.

I never felt more desolate or empty in my life. My meaning was gone, my life was without purpose. There I sat, alone, terribly alone, my mind blank, in the darkness.

My comrades must have shared my feelings. There were no cheers, no laughter, not even quiet conversation. We just sat, nine isolated beings, not reaching out to one another. Finally, I got up and went to lay down, to try to sleep, to bury my loneliness in oblivion.

12

THE TRUCE

My squad's brief line time following the truce resembled a sit-down strike more than a military defense. This is easily discerned in the three letters I wrote during this time. We'd spent months training for combat. Every step from the beginning through the trip to Korea, by design or by chance, prepared us for the life we were to lead. Even our experiences in combat had been a gradual descent into the maelstrom of war. Now, suddenly, it was over. The necessity of our existence was diminished. Innocent partners in a marriage of conflict, we'd been deserted, and we knew the pain of that desertion. Basically, we quit being soldiers.

Scouts were again sitting on mountaintops, watching an enemy we no longer considered dangerous. It was a time to relax and get to know one another. Stan O'Connor was gone, as was his leadership. Barker was either gone or going. Hashimura, another long-time squad member, had left. New people had arrived, but the necessity of knowing how they would perform in emergencies was gone. Of the newcomers, the one I remember best was Hank Talbot, who'd joined us during the final days of the fighting.

My introduction to Hank occurred when we were still patrolling and occupying cots in the Korean mess hall. He sat down on the cot next to mine, and the conversation went like this:

"You're Dannenmaier, huh?"
"Yes."
"Is that a German name?"
"Yes."
"I don't suppose you like to be pushed around."
"No."

"My name's Talbot. It's Dutch. We don't like to be pushed around either."

Hank had transferred into our squad under unusual circumstances. His sergeant, in another company, had placed him in an isolated outpost three nights running—a good way to get a man killed, if you wanted to be rid of him. We heard that when he returned to his company following the third night, Hank had methodically emptied his rifle and then used up some additional ammunition by shooting into the sergeant's bunker. Hank wasn't trying to kill him, he was just sending him a message. Someone decided that the scouts might be a better place for such an independent spirit.

Hank fit into our squad. He was a bright, thoughtful man with a keen sense of humor. He differed from the rest of us in a couple of respects. First, he had a bodybuilder's physique—something the rest of us couldn't claim. Second, he had a tremendous work ethic. That's what really made him different.

The morning following the truce brought its own, special surprises. From our lookout we watched hundreds of enemy soldiers come out into the open, looking for God knows what kinds of treasures. They even had carts pulled by horses. To this day, I can't understand how they were able to keep horses and wagons in front of us without us knowing about them. I sat there holding my rifle and speculated as to how many Chinese I could kill before they were able to get out of my line of fire. I wondered if others had the same thoughts, but I didn't ask. We didn't discuss it, just like we didn't discuss all the men who were missing in action.

Gradually, life returned to normal. Without thought of the future, we simply hollowed out shallow depressions in the soil as sleeping places. We covered these with our shelter halves, which were held in position by rocks and dirt placed along the edges. [Each man was issued half of a two-man (pup) tent. We didn't have tent poles, so we couldn't put the two halves together to form a tent.] At night, or for protection from the rain, we would creep into these backwards so that we were lying down facing the enemy, our rifles by our sides. These hollows were snug, warm, and surprisingly comfortable.

While we held that position, we lived on assault rations, which was when I learned to enjoy cheese and ham. Assault rations came in cans about the size of a six-ounce can of tuna. Each ration consisted of two cans. The first held the meal, my favorite being cheese with chunks (bits, really) of ham. There was also a fairly decent meal of lima beans. The one I never could finish eating contained two patties of some approximation of meat in a greasy, congealed gravy.

The second can held a pack of matches, a fuel pill for heating the first can, sufficient instant coffee for one cup, along with packs of sugar and creamer, two crackers, toilet paper, four cigarettes, a piece of candy, and a pill for purifying water. If you were really lucky, the piece of candy was a chocolate-covered caramel. There weren't many of those. In some, the type of candy was difficult to identify.

In order to use the heat pill, we would crawl into our sleeping holes headfirst to get out of the wind. Probably the only reason we weren't poisoned by the fumes that were given off was because the pills didn't work that well. I never succeeded in getting one to stay lit long enough to melt all the grease in the cans that contained the meat patties.

If the void in our lives created by the truce was tragic, the days following became a farce. Only Hank worked; the rest of us did nothing. We had the worst attitudes possible. We saw ourselves as combat scouts, but now there was no combat.

During the time we were on that mountain we saw only two officers, a young lieutenant, an artillery observer newly arrived in Korea, and a visiting lieutenant colonel who spent about an hour with the artillery observer. Afterward, we were told that the lieutenant colonel was President Eisenhower's son. It wasn't the sort of visit normally portrayed in Hollywood war films.

If officialdom didn't come to us, neither did we go to them. We sat on our mountaintop watching the Chinese in the valley below us and the passing days with equal disinterest.

• • •

July 31, 1953

Dear Sis:

This peace is harder than war, at least we have less time to ourselves. Thus my letters—I'm afraid—shall be few and far between in the two months to come. But then since I'll be leaving here in

October a couple months shouldn't be too bad. I told the folks I'd
leave here some time in October—however I didn't tell them that
I'd call them from Japan before then. R&R has been started again
and within thirty days from the time you receive this I should be
in Japan. Now that the truce is on, I'll receive seven days R&R instead of the old five. Thus I'll have from twelve to fifteen days
knocked out of my working month when I go. That will be a distinct pleasure. . . .

At present it is raining very hard. That makes everything just
ducky. My raincoat is up at the Outpost and I'm here at Regiment.
In the next fifteen or twenty minutes I'll be driving up there. I just
hope it stops by then.

Well, Sis, there's some stuff I want to do before I leave here, so
I'll write again when I get the chance.

• • •

Rain wasn't a blessing when we traveled. In a combat area, you
need to move quickly at all times. If you have to bail out of a jeep,
there's no time to open doors; nor do you want windshields that
might shatter from a nearby explosion. So our jeeps were open: no
doors, no tops, no windshields. Driving in the rain meant we, and
our weapons, got soaked—a problem of comfort when our only
clothing was what we were wearing. This was magnified by the fact
that we were living in scattered, shallow holes. The sole sources
of warmth were our own bodies and the weather. Dry clothes just
weren't available.

We also wanted dry rifles. Our rifles weren't pretty, but they
worked. Rust in the wrong place could be a problem if we needed
them again.

Our squad had been ordered to dig in where we were, a mountaintop we shared with the artillery observer, who had pre-empted
the only safe bunker. We'd already done a lot of digging, and we
were in no hurry to start again, orders or no orders. Contributing
to this was the fact that, in our opinions, the necessity was gone.
To meet orders, however, we measured and staked a twelve-foot-
square bunker with the idea that we might dig it out if anyone
bothered to make us, which we really didn't expect would happen.
[None of our officers visited that mountaintop while I was on it.]

The only person I recall who truly worked at digging the bunker was Talbot. While the rest of us watched, he put in eight hours every day, digging into the sandstone to build a new bunker. The only day he put in less time was the day he pounded so hard on the rock that he bent the point of his pick into a hook. Hank was strong, but even he couldn't straighten it out, so he had to wait for another pick.

Hank was busy digging the day we met Lieutenant Colonel Eisenhower. The eight of us were all sitting in the sun watching Hank wield the pick. We noticed an officer climbing up our mountain and, as he got closer, we thought we saw a lieutenant colonel's emblem; but he wasn't our concern—we answered only to our colonel, not to stray officers. When he reached calling distance, he shouted up that the beer ration had been reinstituted and that our platoon sergeant was at the bottom with our beer ration, one case per man.

Seven men leaped to their feet and left, but Hank was digging and I was in the middle of a conversation with him. As the lieutenant colonel got closer to the two of us, he called, "I suppose you men didn't hear me. Your sergeant wants you down below to carry up your beer."

Hank's reply, cleaned up a bit, went something like this: "I've been digging this damned hole all day while these lazy bastards watched. Now if you think that I'm going to climb this damned mountain carrying a case of beer so these sons of bitches can get drunk tonight you can go fuck yourself."

The lieutenant colonel passed by without a word, proving to me that he had intelligence and knew when to use it. After he left, the artillery observer came running over and said, "That was Lieutenant Colonel Eisenhower you talked to like that." Hank said he didn't really care.

That artillery observer was new to Korea. He'd just arrived and had little or no combat experience. Consequently, while our war was over, he was impressed by being on the front. He kept complaining to us about our wandering about in white T-shirts, saying the enemy could see us. We didn't care; the green fatigue shirts were too hot and white T-shirts were all we had. That night we upset him even more. Eight of us drank nine cases of beer—Hank didn't drink—and we built a bonfire with the boxes.

• • •

August 2, 1953

Dear Ethel:

I received your letter today talking of your last visit downtown with Johnny. From the sound of things going out with small John is an adventure—whether you want it to be or not. I guess Johnny could have a lot of fun at the farm.

We have been having a lot of rain the last few days, however it cleared up last night and today it is very nice out. I suppose I should be working but it's too nice a day to spoil with labor.

Kim Shi told me the rainy season usually ends this month. All I can say is that it is the driest rainy season I ever saw. True we have had a lot of heavy rains but we've had a nice day for every rainy one. I've seen it worse in St. Louis in April and May.

My time grows shorter here in Korea with every passing day. I'm really on the down hill drag now with almost eight months behind me and less than three (I think) to go. I'll be glad to see the cold weather arrive in Korea. . . .

• • •

Johnny was three years old, and all parents know about three-year-olds. My sister had kept up a lively account of her adventures with him through a second pregnancy. These reported escapades were read aloud and enjoyed by all members of the squad. Today, Johnny is a respectable professor of German who could probably be blackmailed with some of the stories my sister told me about him.

This letter reports the malaise that had infected most of the squad. On rainy days we couldn't work; on sunny days we wouldn't—except, of course, for Hank, who always put in his eight hours. A few of the others, occasionally including me, driven by guilt, would assist Hank every so often.

It was about this time that Hank, in his own way, resolved the problems we'd been having with the lieutenant, who seemed to feel, despite our opinions and actions, that he had some authority over us. In addition to this bad attitude, the lieutenant had bright red pajamas. Each day he hung these on a line he'd tied between two trees. If our white T-shirts disturbed him, his pajamas irritated us.

Hank, mostly by himself, had managed to dig a hole through the sandstone that was about twelve feet square and three feet deep. The day he bent his pick into a hook he admitted that he needed some assistance. The solution was to ask the antitank and mine platoon to send up a demolitions expert to blow out the hole for us. When the explosives expert arrived, we explained the need to loosen up the sandstone to help Hank dig. We also discussed the lieutenant. At the time, those red pajamas of his were flapping prominently in the breeze. Our newfound ally promised to help right our imagined wrongs when he returned with the required explosives.

Upon his return, the demolition man used his authority to require the lieutenant and his men to walk down the mountain for their own safety. To save us the long walk, he told us privately to sneak over to the far side of the hill and find a place to hide in some abandoned and decaying bunkers that were there. He also warned us to be careful, saying that he'd brought enough dynamite and plastic explosive to make one hell of a blast and it would collapse those bunkers. He was right about the blast. Sand and rocks flew everywhere. The hole Hank had excavated so carefully was now completely filled with loose sand, and one of the trees holding the lieutenant's clothesline was blown down. The red pajamas could be seen lying crumpled in the dirt. I don't know what the flying debris did to the pajamas. We never saw them again.

Best of all, the lieutenant never spoke to any of us again.

• • •

August 3, 1953

Dear Ethel:

My plans for an early return home were shot today. I received information that we are moving into reserve in the next day or two. I hear we are going "way back," probably to Kojedo. You know we were going to stay on line and get four free points for two months—but now we'll be going back into a two point area, so that will add months to my time in Korea. What a blow.

I had certainly planned on being home in November—but I don't know now. August and September are critical months over here and instead of getting my four points I'll be in reserve. Two months without danger and four points so we have to move in reserve. Well I suppose all we can do is grin and bear it.

Well, Sis, I don't feel much like writing tonight, I'll write again later.

• • •

We were an exhausted squad and we made no effort to carry out our assigned duties. Perhaps this was recognized by those in command, who chose to move us into reserve duty. Another possible reason for the move to a two-point area would have been to keep experienced combat soldiers in Korea longer by slowing their rotation. This would have made sense, even if it was unfair to the individuals involved, but it didn't occur to me at the time. Whatever the reason, the move, as we saw it, punished men who had put their lives on the line every day for months by moving them to a two-point area when there was no longer any danger in the four-point area. Our replacements were persons who had never been in danger, having come from well behind the front lines. They received the two months of "safe" four points that we felt we'd earned.

13

REST AND RELAXATION

When we received our orientation to Korea, we were informed that every four months we'd receive a five-day rest period in Japan. If the lecturer thought that was true, he was wrong. I never met an enlisted man from the infantry who was sent on R&R in four months. The usual time seemed to be between seven and nine months. Bob Maltby and Duke Glascoe, who'd been with me in radio school, had been activated with the Illinois National Guard and were now deactivated. They went home before ever receiving such a trip, even though, like me, they'd been in Korea for eight months. Other friends, such as Charley Brown and Joe Freeman, were killed before they could go. It was, however, a prized trip, one we all looked forward to taking, the proverbial carrot dangled ever before our noses.

A common joke was that those who went on R&R were too tired to work after they returned. Standard practice permitted returnees to get a few days to rest after their trip. In Japan, food and alcohol were readily available as well as inexpensive, and women could be had for ten or twenty dollars for twenty-four hours. The enlisted men's acronym for R&R was I&I, for intoxication and intercourse.

Not everyone indulged in both women and alcohol. Some did both, but some chose one, some the other, and some neither. One of the men in the communications platoon said he never left his room during his five days. He had a girlfriend back home and was afraid of being tempted. He said he had food and drinks sent up and simply stayed drunk the entire time. Another friend said he didn't touch a drop of alcohol during the entire time. He also claimed he didn't leave his room in the hotel during that period.

For most of us, R&R was eight months of social life and shopping squeezed into five days. Each day started early and ended late. When it was all over, we were broke and tired.

• • •

August 4, 1953

Ethel:

I'm going to Japan on R&R tonight. Will write you all about it when I get back. Don't expect any letters till I get back.

In the meantime, the Regiment is moving into reserve. Don't know just where—I think some where near Pochong.

Will write in a couple of weeks.

• • •

R&R came as a complete surprise to me—a bit more of a surprise than I wanted, as I didn't have all the money I thought I would need. Bob Maltby, who was on his way home, came to my rescue by lending me seventy dollars. Bob was from Mattoon, Illinois, and I told him to stop in St. Louis on his way home and my parents would pay him back for me. Bob had been one of the Christmas Eve seven who attended radio school with me. A tall, good-looking guy with brown eyes and black hair, Bob shared my level of maturity. During thaws, while I was still in the communications platoon, we used to make toy boats and race them in puddles we created by damming ditches. He was a trustworthy friend and a good radioman. I was glad he was headed home, but sorry to see him go for my own sake.

I discovered I would be going to Japan with Jim Gay. As the regimental electrician and controller of electricity for headquarters, Jim was placed at the top of the list when R&Rs resumed and used his influence to arrange for us to go together, which pleased me. Jim was a pleasure to be with, especially as he laced a low opinion of the military hierarchy with a dry wit.

Personalities aside, we both needed a rest. Jim and I had lived a long time in a difficult situation without any kind of break. We were beginning our ninth month in Korea, the last six of them with our regiment in combat.

From the time I heard we were leaving, I quit eating. We'd been on C rations for some time and, since moving to our newest mountain, assault rations. Several weeks of that diet made me decide to fast until I got to Japan. No more garbage until I could taste real food! I was to regret this decision. It took almost two days to get there and by then I was one hungry soldier.

Those of us leaving were assembled and the chaplain lectured us on how to behave in Japan. All I remember about his talk is that he began with the expected, "Now men there are other things to be enjoyed in Japan than alcohol and women . . . ," and that it lasted the rumored forty-five minutes. Supposedly, the only time it was cut short was when one of our guys, an acquaintance I knew as "Kon," interrupted the chaplain with, "You should know, you run the black market"—it being our belief that the chaplains had divided the black market in services and goods between them. That may not have been true, but when Kon said it, the chaplain stopped talking and walked away.

Following our lecture, we were trucked to the Kimpo Air Field near Seoul. I don't remember the ride, but I do remember being hungry and regretting that I had rejected all army food after I'd heard I was headed for Japan. I would have broken my promise if I'd had the opportunity, but no food was available.

Our plane was a two-engine job. We sat on two long benches facing each other, windows at our backs. I figured it was an old World War II bomber, no longer safe for carrying bombs but still useful as a ferry for enlisted soldiers. From the outside, it certainly looked like an aircraft that had seen lots of years and lots of miles. But none of that mattered to us, because we were headed for R&R.

At some point in the flight, I think when we were over the Yellow Sea (considering the color of the water), I looked over my shoulder and noticed that I could see the propeller, all three blades, just as if the plane were parked. I was pretty sure it wasn't supposed to be motionless, but it was.

Soon the door to the cockpit opened and one of the crewmen came out and said something like, "Guys, each one of you has a parachute under your seat, and I'm going to show you how to put it on. First you . . ." He was interrupted by a voice from behind the door. He listened and then turned to us and told us not to bother. I looked out the window and noticed that I could no longer see the propeller's blades. It was turning again. I was glad all things were working. Japan would probably be a bit too far regardless of my swimming ability.

When we landed in Osaka, Japan, we were immediately taken to a warehouse where we showered and were given new, class A clothes, including clean underwear and socks. All we kept of our own were our wallets and our boots. The clean dress uniforms made us feel dressed up, but the worn combat boots marked us as men on R&R and targeted us on the street. Every shopkeeper who saw us knew we would be there only five days and that we had a lot of money. [In Japan, only soldiers on R&R wore dress uniforms and ties combined with worn combat boots.] We were told we would be given a meal while our passes were prepared. When we were finished eating, we would be free to go.

We were taken into a large building with windows, a high, vaulted ceiling, and electric lights. We sat at tables for four, with tablecloths and two or three flowers in a slender vase in the center of each table. Pretty little Japanese women served us shrimp cocktail, bread and butter, steak, and French fries. I sat there and fought to keep from crying. I'm not sure I succeeded, but if I didn't, my tears were ignored by the others at the table.

I remember that I kept looking at the electric lights and windows. It had been a long time since I'd seen windows or electric lights or sat down at a table for a meal. It had been a long time since I had been a human, a long nine months during most of which I had lived as an animal, with water, food, and survival my main concerns; nine months during which friends had been hurt and some had died. It was hard to control my emotions then. Remembering, it is still hard. They were very gentle with us there; they must have seen a lot like us.

Following the meal, we were given passes and turned loose. Jim and I walked through the gate and into Japan. A long strip of bars lined both sides of the road. Whores stood at every entrance, each more delicate and lovely than the next, calling and beckoning to us. An acquaintance from the plane dived into the first bar on the right, the Texas Bar, not to be seen again until time to leave.

Jim and I went into Osaka and then took the train to Kyoto. There the military had taken over several large Japanese hotels and converted them for use by American military on R&R. We went first to the hotel with the most surface appeal. It was gorgeous, with marble-lined American-style toilets and clean, thoughtfully decorated lounges. Once again we were besieged by young ladies willing to escort us around Japan. They were beautifully gowned in semiformal attire and their English was good, but the price was high—twenty to thirty dollars a day. This was too much for an escort service for corporals. We went on to a less-exclusive, dingier hotel, one with fewer entrepreneurs roaming the halls, though I remember a group of young ladies chatting with each other, as if over a backyard fence, at the end of the hall on which our rooms were located.

I met a young lady who reminded me of the girl from summer camp that I had fallen for. She had an infectious laugh and a ready smile. She approved of me as much as I approved of her, but unfortunately her protector didn't like what she saw. The two of us ran off for a few minutes, climbing out a window and onto the rusted steel fire escape, where we sat some ten stories above the street, two children escaping supervision, cuddling and laughing until we were discovered and forced to return to our respective realities.

Jim and I eventually found guides and spent the following day shopping. I needed a camera, so we searched for that first. It was a pleasure to leave the military mainstream and visit Japanese stores that existed for the Japanese, not for American soldiers. We were met with bows, seated, served tiny glasses of liquor—all before the business of selecting the correct camera began. I bought a Balsey, which served me well for over twenty-five years. After that we shopped for gifts and remembrances to mail home. I purchased some paintings on silk and a cultured pearl necklace for my sister. We were surprised to find the streets and stores so empty as we began our shopping, but we welcomed the complete attention it enabled us to receive.

On the advice of our guide, we moved to a small, two-story Japanese hotel, the Yasui Hotel, with a balcony surrounding an inner courtyard, well away from American influence. The walls were made of bamboo and the doors had no locks. We had to leave our boots at the front entrance, slipping into the sandals that were provided for each guest. The hotel was very companionable, as shouts and laughter, even giggles, could be heard between the rooms.

Following our initial worries about being robbed, we were surprised and gratified to learn that, in a land where thirty dollars a
month would pay for an apartment, we could toss our wallets con-
taining a couple hundred dollars on the beds of our lockless rooms
and leave for the evening, certain that our wallets and money
would be right where we left them when we returned. The small-
est amount of change accidentally dropped on the floor was carefully collected and placed on a shelf where we couldn't avoid seeing it.

It was a family-owned hotel; grandmother and mother ran it,
father was a bicycle racer. The daughter of the family was the only
person who spoke English and she translated our conversations.
Jim and I would sit up with the family late into the night, drinking tea and talking, sitting on cushions around a small table. It was
hot and the grandmother seldom bothered to wear a top. After my
initial embarrassment, I learned that modesty and nudity are not
necessarily contradictions. The father said he had fought on Leyte,
in the Philippines, during World War II.

One night, trying to repay their hospitality, Jim and I provided
money for two large bottles of American orange soda pop, which
was a luxury in a country that hadn't yet recovered from war. As
we all emptied our glasses, the daughter refilled hers, which
brought an immediate outburst from her father. I told Jim later, I
knew no Japanese, but I knew papa talking to daughter. He had a
lot to say. Immediately, an embarrassed, blushing young lady
apologized for not offering us more before she helped herself to a
second treasured glass.

That conversation, of which I understood not a word, broke the
ice of some of my hatreds. I knew of the Bataan death march and
other Japanese atrocities, and here I was sitting with a former Japanese soldier. But he was also a man who wanted to live in peace
with his small family and who wanted his daughter to behave properly. I realized then that there are many of us, everywhere, who
only wish to live in peace and who would—if it weren't for a few
gluttons and bullies who want more than they can ever enjoy.
Unfortunately, we let those few rule.

Staying at that hotel, Jim and I discovered that the Japanese had
an interesting and, we decided, intelligent way of coping with summer heat. They slept until ten or eleven in the morning. Arising,

they breakfasted and rested at home during the heat of the day. As the day waned, shops opened and business began. The city, which was deserted and quiet at noon, was crowded and busy at midnight. It was lively and colorful. Old ladies in gaily printed kimonos and old men in tall hats, long cloaks, and wooden clogs mixed with young men in business suits and girls in minidresses. Occasionally, a drummer led lines of solemn young men in white robes through the crowds on religious pilgrimages. It was all strange and exciting.

Jim and I had a marvelous five days. After that first day of shopping, we spent most of our time sightseeing. Kyoto, a city of temples, was left undamaged by World War II. Along the streets, between the shops, we periodically noticed walls of cement or stone topped by long rows of paper lanterns with Japanese characters painted on them. The blandness of the walls was interrupted only by a small door. Our guide told us that inside the walls were Buddhist temples and that the lanterns were prayers.

Once we were fortunate enough to be able to look through an open door. The entire yard, which could not have been as large as the typical motel swimming pool, had been converted into a garden. An elderly priest clothed in gray was standing on the winding pathway that led through it, searching for the one weed that may have been overlooked. Graciously, speaking no English, he permitted us to visit the garden and take his photograph.

Our guide led us to several other temples and parks, the parks normally being the grounds of the temples. One was described as being among the most famous Shinto temples in Japan. Large flights of steps led up to the entrance, which was marked by mammoth wooden pillars, their fading red testifying to age and endurance. At the entrance, we were diverted by the fact that publicity pictures were being taken and Japanese men, dressed in the armor of medieval Japan, were guarding the gates with bows and arrows and swords. In between picture taking, they laughingly threatened spectators with these weapons of the past. Inside, all was cool and serene with carefully tended gravel paths winding amid trees and shrines. It was an oasis of tranquillity and singing birds in an otherwise hectic world.

Our daily routine took us to the military hotels for our meals, where we dined often on steak and lobster. We also used the military hotels for other purposes. Since the only person who spoke English at our hotel was a young girl, we were too embarrassed to ask her how to use the Japanese toilet, which was quite different from Western toilets, so we took a cab over to the military hotel whenever we felt the need. We also erred by washing ourselves in the tub: we were supposed to bathe outside and then soak in the tub after we were clean. We ruined an entire tub of hot water that was meant for all.

I also managed to telephone home during this time. I remember my father asking me over and over again if I was all right, if all was well. Perhaps our connection was a bit fuzzy. Then again, perhaps I was. We'd been sitting in the hotel bar for more than four hours waiting for the call to go through, during which time we were drinking Manhattans, I think, or perhaps it was Asahi beer.

When our time was up we headed back to the airport, only to be told that our leaves had been extended to a sixth day. This sounded great, but our cash resources were low by that time. Jim and I headed back to our little Yasui Hotel. (Our cab driver laughed when we told him where to go, informing us that "yasui" means "cheap.") Our last day in Japan was anticlimactic. We were tired, nearly broke, and ready to return to Korea.

The next day, returning to the base, we passed the Texas Bar and the comrade we had lost on the way in rejoined us. He said he'd spent the entire time drinking beer with a whore. He said he hadn't gone to bed with her, that he just talked. He said she would leave, when she got a customer and then come back to sit with him. She made arrangements for him to sleep in back once she understood that he didn't want her, that he wanted to stay faithful to his wife. He said he just needed a woman to talk to—which was a common need for all of us. She told him she was a widow, that her husband had been in the military and was killed fighting in World War II. She cried when our comrade left.

I can't be critical of those lovely ladies of the evening. They lived at a time and in a country that had been devastated by war. Tens of thousands, perhaps hundreds of thousands, of their men had been lost or killed. Many of the girls came from families that were destitute and starving. By being friendly with American soldiers they were able to earn money to support families that would no longer speak to them. I don't know that there are any winners in a

war other than the leaders of the winning side and the arms mer-
chants. Certainly, the winners don't include the dead and wounded
or the families that mourn them—of either side.

Our return was uneventful. We exchanged our class A uniforms
for the clothing we'd arrived in, now freshly laundered. Then we
boarded the airplane and flew back to Korea; the propellers turned
all the way. After landing, we were trucked back to our units.

Jim and I found that our regiment had moved in our absence.
We were now in deep reserve and would drop down to receiving
two points per month.

Tired, I threw my gear under my assigned cot and went to sleep.
When I awoke the next morning, the pearls I had purchased for my
sister were missing. I'd gotten too accustomed to that little Japanese hotel where everything was safe. It was good to be back with
my squad, but it was clear that during the short time I was away
I'd lost touch with reality.

14

GARRISON LIFE

Returning from R&R exhausted, I entered a new area and found a different type of military than the one to which I had become accustomed. Here, a neat, double row of tents lined a mud street on a small hillock. At the upper end were toilets—toilets with seats—protected from the weather by a tent. At the lower end, a winding path led down past circles of foundation stones overgrown with weeds, the only remains of a Korean village. Then the path crossed a small stream with pools of clear water, which became a favorite place for our illegal bathing. The pools saved us the problem of obtaining time and transportation to get to the shower point in the rear.

Below the stream was a large open area where Jim Gay's electrical generators and small tent were set up. The mess hall for enlisted personnel, the supply room, and other useful tents were located here also. Beyond and below was the motor pool. To the right were the officers' mess hall and the officers' tents. The entire camp was surrounded by the rounded, Appalachian-like mountains of southwest Korea.

Deep in reserve, we were in the process of becoming garrison troops. I didn't mind. I thought I had two or three months left at most. Primarily an onlooker, I watched turmoil grow into open dissent between officers and enlisted. Finally, following a mass protest concerning our living conditions, I was transferred from the scouts to a teaching unit, designed to bring literacy to men with less than a fifth-grade education. That would be my last assignment in Korea.

We had a new colonel, Colonel Akers having rotated home. Beenick, the new colonel's driver, was an old friend from the communications platoon. He told me how our new colonel had up-braided the sentry for not standing at attention and saluting when he arrived. The sentry had waved the jeep through the gate, call-ing, "Good morning, Colonel," a procedure accepted in the past by Colonel Akers. The new colonel ordered Beenick to stop the jeep and back up. Then he stood the sentry at attention and harshly crtitcized him for not saluting with proper military etiquette. Ru-mor had it that our new leader was a Pentagon colonel who had no experience with combat troops. It augured ill for the future.

We'd been on line, in combat, for a long time and we looked it. Our clothes were ragged, our boots were scarred and dirty, and our rifles were rusty in places that didn't matter. None of us had stripes sewn on our sleeves. We were proud of the way we looked because it labeled us: anyone seeing us knew we were survivors. It was the only recognition, other than the Combat Infantryman's Badge, that most of us would ever get.

The new colonel didn't have our perspective or feelings and made no attempt to understand us. He believed in clean, pressed uniforms, shined boots, and soldiers who saluted. He wanted us to look like soldiers were supposed to look. We were to be garri-son soldiers, the very type who had looked so good in Japan and then failed so miserably at the start of the Korean conflict.

The security platoon, which occupied tents across from us, exemplified the new approach. Men who demonstrated the atti-tude and appearance of peacetime soldiers were placed in that platoon. They were all good garrison soldiers. They shouted and cursed one another and yelled about what they'd do to each other if they didn't cooperate, but when they stood at attention in for-mation they looked impressive. All of them were at lease six feet tall, all of them neatly groomed and shined. They even wore blue scarves. They amused us.

Someone—we blamed the new colonel—decided that each tent had to have a guard awake every hour of the night. We saw no rea-son for that as, in addition to the truce, we were far from the front, just a few miles north of the Thirty-eighth Parallel. Consequently, we treated this order as we did many of the orders we received—we ignored it. Late one night, the colonel was inspecting the en-listed area. In tent after tent he found everyone asleep. When he and his aide reached the scouts' area and entered the first tent, he encountered our dogs. They promptly attacked these strangers amid lots of barking, snarling, and—subsequent—shouting. By the time we grabbed our flashlights and were able to ascertain who had entered our tent, and then quieted the dogs, the noise had awakened everyone in the platoon, not to mention the occupants of other tents. When order was restored, the colonel still asked, "Who's on duty here?" and nine men replied, "I am, Sir."

In the tents visited earlier, the ranking enlisted man was reduced a stripe (and a pay grade) for failure to obey orders and maintain a guard, but not the scouts. We were on the alert.

The colonel also wanted a type of discipline we didn't display. No one had ever criticized us for lacking the discipline that enabled us to pick up rifles and grenades and walk into a no-man's-land in three-man teams, but we did lack garrison discipline. The lack of respect we believed the colonel had for us was wholeheartedly reciprocated.

Once the colonel came to talk with the scouts. All I remember of this was his pausing in mid-lecture and saying to Hank Talbot, "From the look on your face, soldier, it appears you don't think I know how to run a regiment." Hank replied, "No sir, I certainly don't." The colonel left.

We may not have had the colonel's respect, but someone in the military knew what we were about. The Army was organizing its Special Forces units, and a recruiter came to see the scouts. Several of us were invited to join. He told us the military was active off the coast of China and we'd be able to see some action there. I gave the offer serious consideration but decided against it. While the idea of the excitement of once again patrolling an enemy-held area was attractive, I didn't trust the leadership to keep its word. As did some of my friends, I feared the promise of more action was simply a ruse so we would re-enlist, that there would be no action, only more time in the military. Only one of our number joined the Special Forces.

Evidence of the intelligence of our commanders came with a decision to relocate the officers' liquor supply. My squad was assigned the task of moving the cases of beverages. Our friends in the second squad were assigned as guards. Understand that enlisted men, who only needed to obey orders, had difficulty getting beer. Officers, who were responsible for thinking and planning, had enough beer and liquor to drink themselves into a stupor every night. Anyway, we carried their supplies from near our area to an area closer to their quarters. I showed great restraint, limiting myself to four bottles of cherry brandy. Others were less restrained. Naturally, we shared with the second squad and other friends.

That night we threw the biggest drinking party I'd seen since receiving my orders to Korea back at Ft. Riley. At first we exercised great caution and tossed empty bottles and cans down the holes in the outhouses; but later, walking to the outhouse at the end of our street became too much effort. I know there was a lot of talking and laughing, and I think something resembling singing occurred also. I was convinced there would be trouble from this, from the missing cases if not from the rowdiness, but we never heard a word.

Finally, tensions between the enlisted and the officers reached an intolerable level. Life for the enlisted had continued to deteriorate in many ways. The food we were receiving was of low quality and horribly cooked—it wouldn't have passed a health inspection anywhere. Our normal breakfast was scrambled, dehydrated eggs streaked with green and blue, which gave evidence that they had been kept too long. Rice was a common lunch or evening meal. Even as we were eating it we knew that the cooks were likely to announce that we shouldn't eat it, that it was wormy and should have been thrown out. We joked that this was how we got our protein. We ate it of necessity; there was no alternative: no villages, no restaurants, and we could no longer obtain C and K (assault) rations.

A memorable break in our squad's diet came when Mel Lichtig, whose father was a New York importer of specialty foods, received a package from home. We decided that Mel, who was on R&R at the time, wouldn't want us to let the food spoil in his absence. When Mel came back he was pleasant about the loss, if we mentioned it to him. He told us that he'd stayed with a friend of his father's, a general in charge of food supplies for Korea, and that the general was amazed to hear about what we were getting to eat. Mel said he was equally amazed when the general told him what we should have been getting. We decided people were becoming wealthy selling the food that was meant for us.

Movies were another source of contention. According to our understanding, movies were supplied free of charge by the Holly-

wood film industry and shipped overseas to be shown to the enlisted. But the officers saw them first and often kept them so long
that they had to be returned before we had an opportunity to see
them. There were other points of contention as well, centering
around duties and supplies, but I've forgotten the specifics.

I wasn't directly involved in the protest actions, but I heard that
some of the officers left camp for their own safety. Lieutenant
Rinklemeyer, whom we liked and trusted, returned to discuss our
unhappiness with us. He was able to promise several reforms,
which were accepted. A day or two later, we were told to turn in
all ammunition and grenades, but not as much was turned in as
they thought. Quite a bit was wrapped in plastic and buried in
various locations in case of future need.

The colonel seemed to blame the scouts for this disturbance.
Later, several of us were transferred to other jobs, though no one
was punished officially.

• • •

September 25, 1953

Dear Ethel:

Received another letter from you today. Yours have been coming in pretty steady for three days now.

There is not much new to report. I have finished my first week
with the Puerto Ricans. The morning class is very enthusiastic, the
afternoon class has a distinct lack of enthusiasm. However, I find
myself getting back into the swing of things in the teaching (?)
world so all is going well. . . .

• • •

My new unit was the Troop Information and Education Platoon,
whose mission was to teach men who reported less than a fifth-
grade education how to read. We had several hundred such men,
as well as a significant group of Puerto Rican soldiers whose primary problem was a lack of English. I was selected as one of the
teachers, supposedly because I was the only enlisted man in the
regiment with a college degree—though there were several men,
such as Jim Gay, Hank Talbot, and many of the scouts, who'd had
two or three years of university study.

Teaching the Puerto Ricans to read English was an unmitigated disaster. Even those who wanted to learn had difficulty, partly because of instructors like me who knew no Spanish and had no knowledge of Puerto Rico, but the primary problem was the teaching material we used. Our textbook was based on adult concepts but assumed that the student was an illiterate farm boy from the southern or midwestern United States. One story was about groundhogs. A class of Puerto Ricans was trying to understand the meaning of the English, with little success, when I realized that they thought groundhogs were a type of bird. Viewed from this angle, nothing in the story made sense. We all had a good laugh about this. Similar, unnecessary, problems were frequent.

A second problem was the tone of the lessons. The central theme of all the stories was that a handsome young farm boy would enlist in the army and find true happiness in that best of all worlds. But there we were—living in squalor, eating poor food, and under the direction of a disinterested, repressive leadership. The contrast made the stories absurd, which detracted from the purpose of the lessons.

If the stories had taken the approach that army life was a reasonable alternative to other jobs, but that, as in other jobs, you sometimes faced really poor conditions, our teaching would have been more successful. Certainly, instruction would not have been interrupted by student laughter and discussions—in Spanish—of how the stories and our reality differed.

In some ways, our lives improved following the dissent. We were now allowed to see our movies after the officers had seen them. As the only enlisted man who knew how to run a projector, I agreed to help show the first movie. It sounded like fun as we had received our beer ration that day and many of the guys had cases of beer with them. I confidently loaded the film from the box labeled as the first reel. It turned out to be the second or third reel, which led to a few hoots and hollers and comments about the competency of the projectionist. I tried another reel, but whoever had rewound it had done it backwards. It made for an interesting picture, but now empty beer cans started hitting the movie screen as we tried to get the reels straightened out. When we finally found the first reel, we discovered that it hadn't been rewound at all. By now, some of the beer cans were being aimed at me. I don't remember if we ever saw that movie.

Needless to say, I was relieved of the responsibility of showing movies. We also asked the officers, who still watched the films first, to stop rewinding them for us.

• • •

October 28, 1953

Dear Ethel:

. . . At the present time it is raining and quite unpleasant out—as it has been for several days. However since there is nothing that compels me to stay outside, it doesn't bother me in the slightest.

We have composed an opening day speech for our illiterate classes. It goes as follows.

Good morning you gibbering idiots. You may think you are here because you can't read—that is wrong—you're here because you are stupid. You morons may not want to come, but we leave it up to you—school or jail. If you don't enjoy yourselves—don't worry about it—the instructors are having a good time.

For some reason our opening day speech was not approved by the officer in charge.

Last night someone stole our electric generator—all 750 lbs. of it, plus the trailer that it was installed in. All of the enlisted men had a good laugh about it this morning—at the Company Commander's expense I might add. He did not see any humor in it. . . .

• • •

By now, we instructors had turned our work into play. First, we convinced everyone that it took a minimum of two of us to teach each class. Next came the need for preparation time, so each pair taught one two-hour block in the morning and another in the afternoon. But then we divided up the classes, so only one of the pair taught the first two-hour block and the other taught the second. Thus, our total teaching load, counting breaks, equaled about two hours a day. Duties such as beautifying the area took additional time.

Despite our joking opening statement, we had a lot of respect for our students. A majority were responsible, thoughtful men who had never had an opportunity to attend school. I remember well one burly, blond master sergeant. I worked with him individually, with little success. He told me that he'd been born into a circus family and had never attended school a day in his life. When you consider that it takes children a year and sometimes two just to learn the alphabet, you can understand our lack of success, even though all, students and teachers, were trying.

The officer in charge was Lieutenant Haley. We liked him but caused him more trouble than we intended. For example, an order came down that we were to have our students do exercises every day. This irritated me. Anything that detracts from my teaching time has always irritated me. The next day I had the classes lined up, in formation, doing finger exercises and rolling their eyes while chanting in unison, "Ex-er-cis-es, ex-er-cis-es, we-will-do-our ex-er-cis-es." All those participating found it hilarious. Shortly afterward, Haley came roaring down to see me. His opening words were, "Dannenmaier, what the hell were you doing? No one has ever talked to me the way the colonel just did." I hadn't known that the colonel was going to drive by to check on our exercises.

Haley really didn't understand us, nor we him, though we liked him and tried to help him get a good record. He had a battlefield commission, which says a lot. You hear about these commissions, but there were darned few of them and they always indicated true bravery and leadership. Haley had no teaching background and loved the army. We were almost all draftees or short-term enlisted men who had no particular liking or respect for the army. Still, we worked for him and liked him, and I suspect he liked us. One of his favorite lines to me was, "Dannenmaier, you're a lousy soldier. How the hell did you ever make sergeant?" My standard reply: "I was a good man in combat, lieutenant."

One point of contention was my mustache, which Haley constantly harped on, telling me that I needed to shave it off. I would reply that army regulations gave me the right to have a mustache, to which he would complain, "Not one that looks like that."

Lieutenant Haley eventually won on the mustache. I had a friend who was to turn in his jeep for a new one down in Seoul. He offered me a ride. With visions of sin and corruption—those sugar plums that dance in the minds of young soldiers—I said, "Let's get a pass from Haley and spend the weekend down there." My friend argued that such passes were illegal for combat troops, but my counterargument was the military police wouldn't know that. We went to Haley, who repeated the argument about legality. I said that I knew that and he knew that but the MPs in Seoul wouldn't know that. He finally looked at me and said, "Dannenmaier, about that mustache." I said, "Lieutenant, you know I have the right to wear it." He replied, "Dannenmaier, you know that, and I know that, but do the MPs in Seoul know that?"

A few minutes later, clean shaven, I received my illegal pass to Seoul. Incidentally, the visions of sin and corruption faded when I arrived there. The Korean girls took one look at our combat boots, helmets, and worn fatigues and decided they didn't need to associate with people like us. At the USO, no one would even dance with us.

The loss of the electric generator didn't bother the enlisted. We were still living on candles and daylight. Our meals were cooked on gasoline-heated stoves, and we ate during daylight hours. The officers had electric lights, however, and were seriously affected by the loss. This was particularly true for the company commander, who had to explain to the colonel the loss of electricity and why the colonel's marvelous security platoon hadn't prevented the theft. [The generator was stolen after Jim Gay was required to sleep in the company area. Until then he had slept in a small tent next to the generator.]

The truce that was changing our work, permitting relaxed humor during the days, hadn't completely enveloped me. I began to experience blinding headaches. They usually began after lying down for the night to go to sleep. I'd bite my lips and squeeze my head, trying to use controlled pain to disguise uncontrollable pain. It worked only partially. The headaches would plague me almost nightly, only slowly diminishing over the next thirty years; the last of them occurred sometime in the 1970s. I can also recall lying in my cot and using my fingernails to try to rake the crust out of my hair and the scum from my teeth. We still had problems getting showers and acquiring things such as soap and toothbrushes.

• • •

November 2, 1953

Dear Ethel:

Things are going a little better over here now. In response to a mass protest, the Company Commander fired the Mess Sergeant and brought our old favorite "Ollie" Olson back from Officers' Mess to straighten out our mess hall. Ollie promptly fired three of the cooks and went on to improve the place. In two days he is really turning out good food.

Tonight Col. Shopshire walked in and saw Ollie serving a little Korean boy we've picked up. He told Ollie not to feed the boy whereupon Ollie turned around and said, "By gar as long as I'm in charge I feed hungry children, if you don't like it, I'll leave." Whereupon the Colonel laughed and walked away.

Ethel—I ran into a girl from Harris here day before yesterday. She is a Red Cross Worker. We had quite a reunion, but only because I have some friends in the right places.

Well, I didn't get this letter finished yesterday—it was interrupted by a small blackjack game. I was quite lucky—winning about six badly needed dollars.

There is still no word on a Santa Claus shipment but I won't give up hope on that until about the fifteenth. They are still being very stingy about letting the guys go home—making them stay until after their time is up instead of letting them rotate on or slightly before the day their time expires.

• • •

The difference between our food when Olson was in charge and that which we had been receiving was the difference you would find between a four-star restaurant and a garbage can. Gone were the green and blue eggs, the wormy rice, and the pancakes with raw dough running from the center. One meal we actually received steaks cooked to order.

The Colonel Shropshire I mentioned in the letter wasn't the commanding colonel. He was deputy commander. He dated back to when Colonel Akers had been in charge of the regiment.

The woman I mentioned, Sue Fields, had come to Korea as a member of a four-woman Red Cross team. I liked Sue and was glad to see her, but all of us bitterly resented the presence of these women. The official prohibition on bathing in the streams and creeks was now enforced to the extent possible—these ladies might see nude men—so our opportunities for cleanliness were once again reduced. We also had to put up shelters around the urinals and toilets, again to protect the ladies. In another incident, poor Jim Gay came back from lunch one rainy day to find his tent missing. The stove was still going and his possessions were laying out

in the open, in the rain. The Red Cross women needed a tent during their occasional visits, and some officer simply ordered that
Jim's tent be taken while he was at lunch.

Another reason for our resentment was that our normal coffee
routine was abolished. We now had to wait for the Red Cross volunteers, who were driven around to the companies to serve us our
own coffee—which we prepared ourselves but couldn't drink until they showed up—and doughnuts from our own bakery. A mess
sergeant in one company lost a stripe, and the pay that accompa-
nies it, when he misjudged their arrival and didn't have the coffee
ready when they drove up. In other words, three or four thousand
men had to bend their lives for the sake of four female Red Cross
workers whose only duty involving those men was to be driven
around to serve them their own coffee and doughnuts. I was un-
aware of any other responsibility they may have had. The ladies'
free time was spent with the officers.

Money was a problem for me. As long as we were on line we
received forty-five dollars a month combat pay in addition to our
regular pay, even though we had nothing to buy. Consequently, I'd
been having the largest possible allotment sent home. Now, with
peace came the opportunity to spend money, but I was receiving
only about ten dollars a month. Because of the required paperwork, I didn't believe I'd have time to get this changed before I was
due to leave, so I was always broke.

The Santa Claus shipments were something special. In the previous year, the military took men who were slated to leave in late
December or in January and sent them home in time for Christmas. I would have qualified in the past and had hopes of being on
one in 1953, but the shipments were canceled, at least for us. Worse
yet, the rotation pattern was changed. Previously, we had been sent
home in the month we accumulated thirty-six points; in some
cases, people were shipped back with only thirty-four or thirty-five
points. Since I would have thirty-five points at the end of November, I could have expected to leave in December at the latest, possibly in November (in the past). Now, we had to accumulate the
thirty-six points first and then we were placed on orders. Under
the new policy I would leave in January at the earliest, unless there
was a Christmas special.

• • •

November 4, 1953

Dear Ethel:

The days roll merrily by and as the time goes on I become more certain that I shall be here at Christmas time. This month was supposed to be the big drop month, but so far only three are leaving the company, and they go today. At the same time, there is no rumor of future drops and we always hear of them at least a week ahead of time. In order for a Christmas drop to be a reality, at least twenty five more men would have to leave this company this month. At present, however, we still have men here who are overdue on rotation. . . .

Cold weather is definitely setting in over here. It gets very cold at night and not too warm during the day. The country side is acquiring its typical bleak look and the stoves burn continuously. . . .

• • •

About this time we were informed that if we signed up to extend our time in the military we'd receive thirty-day leaves to go home. A group of young Puerto Rican soldiers, desperately wanting to be home for Christmas, took the bait. Later, they found out that their leaves wouldn't start until after Christmas. It was also at this time that I was asked to write a regimental newspaper. I wrote a long, bitter editorial about this extension, which I considered a deliberate attempt to mislead us, accompanied by a drawing of a man asleep on a bunk with the label "Officer at work." The newspaper was never published, and I was assigned the task of driving a sand truck during my nonteaching hours.

We were still living in tents, and because of their wooden floors we were always cold. Obviously intending to maintain a presence in Korea, the army was now erecting Quonset huts, beautifully insulated and warm. The first of these was to be part of our school. We teachers decided it would reduce our travel time and increase our efficiency if we simply left our cold tents and moved into the hut. The first sergeant must have missed us on his morning inspections, but he said nothing. I think he was glad to see us go, as one of our guys had accidentally broken the sergeant's arm when he threw him out the back of the tent and down the hill during a heated discussion.

For about a month we were undoubtedly the most comfortable people in the regiment, the colonel included. Then we were caught by a stray officer and had to move back to our cold tents.

• • •

November 11, 1953

Dear Ethel:

I have a little spare time today so I shall try to catch up on my letter writing. Actually I'm not behind on writing to you—but to some people—wow!

I understand that this afternoon we are to have a half day off because it is Armistice day. Probably in another hundred years we shall have so many Armistice days that we shall cease regarding them as holidays.

I see in an article where someone describes the morale in Korea as "as high as possible." This is undoubtedly the joke of the year. They should have said it is as low as possible. However, shipments home have been fairly regular this month and in just two months I'll be out of this place so the devil with it.

Today we are completing our work on beautifying the area, to my great pleasure. I didn't mind the work myself but I was tired of forcing other men to work. Since my sea voyage, I have been a radio man, a scout, a ditch digger, a bunker builder, a woodsman, a stone mason and various other things. There is no better place to learn to be a jack of all trades than in the Army in a combat zone.

The big lesson north of the 38th is to learn to take care of yourself.

• • •

We'd been given the task of beautifying the school area, which now consisted of Quonset huts. This meant rock walls, sand walkways, and a sign at the entrance. Following the newspaper debacle, I was in charge of getting sand. There were two ways to do this. One would be to back the truck up to almost any of the hills, walk to the top, and give the ground a good kick. Another way would be to drive south to the Hant'an River, near the Thirty-eighth Parallel, where sand was plentiful—the advantage to this plan being that on the other side of the river, behind some sand dunes, was a small Korean village with trinkets, booze, and women.

While I couldn't get a single volunteer to kick sand off the hills near our camp, I found it extremely easy to get eight volunteers to dig sand by the river. We'd drive south to the river and four men would fill the truck while the other four crossed to the village. It took half a day, counting driving time, to get one load. In the afternoon, the same eight volunteers would go back, but this time the four who dug in the morning visited the village while the other four loaded sand into the truck. Once, they had just filled the truck and were waiting for the last two men to return from the village when we saw them running at full speed over the dunes pursued by military police. I hopped into the truck, backed it up into the water, and then, as the men leaped aboard, sped back to camp.

On another occasion, we had just finished loading the truck and had all eight volunteers on board when a jeep pulled up and blocked our path. Out stepped a lieutenant of the MPs, asking who was in charge. With full military courtesy, I saluted and said, "I am, sir." He glanced at my staff sergeant stripes and walked around the truck, looking up at the eight smiling volunteers. Then he looked at the truck again and said, "Fifteenth Infantry, why so far from home?" I replied, "Good sand, sir." He shook his head and walked away saying, "Damnedest detail I ever saw. A staff sergeant in charge of eight master sergeants!"

Lieutenant Haley also quizzed me on the need to go so far, but I assured him it was only because we wanted the highest-quality sand. I'll admit, however, that for a few days after the chase over the dunes we dug sand in our own area.

My last task on the beautification program was to paint the sign over the entrance to the school area. I was busy working on it when Jim Gay came down to watch me. We were trading jokes when the door of the nearest Quonset opened and an irate major stuck his head out and shouted, "You men work in quiet, we're having a staff meeting." I finished the job silently and then, as Jim was folding up my ladder, I walked over to that Quonset hut and painted the doorknob blue. I have always hoped that the major was the one who closed the door when they left.

• • •

November 12, 1953

Dear Sis:

. . . Today we had our first snow of the season. It was very light but there is the promise of more in the skies. The temperature is, of course, suitably low as we notice when we have to break a frozen crust of earth when digging.

I am now number 14 on the rotation list. So you see Ethel I am climbing to the top of the rotation list slowly but surely. . . .

• • •

The mountains continued to fascinate me. On those frosty mornings it was possible to look across at them and see a line of snow or ice halfway up, almost as if drawn with a ruler. I'd never seen anything like that before, though later, when I lived in Massachusetts, I found it to be relatively common. This was, however, the first snow that fell in the valley.

• • •

November 18, 1953

Dear Ethel:

. . . I now am the eighth man on the rotation list. This means that I will probably be leaving here the first few days of December. In other words probably home for Christmas.

Jim Gay left for home yesterday. I was sorry to see him go in some ways but in other ways very happy to see him get out of here. It was a complete surprise though he knew he was due to go. Monday morning they told him that he should check with the medics and supply . . . he was going home. . . .

• • •

Jim Gay's departure left me as the last of the seven of us who went to radio school together still in Korea. Charley Brown and Joe Freeman had been killed, and the others had spent more time in the States than I had before being sent to Korea, so their enlistments were up before mine. I felt more and more isolated as these and my other friends and associates from the scouts and the radio platoon, men like O'Connor, Ray Barker, and Red Hood, left. I was now in a platoon that included no men with whom I'd served in combat. Many of them were new to Korea and considered our current lives a hardship.

Other attitude changes were occurring in my life and seriously affecting my behavior. I'd never really expected to live long enough to return home, which enabled me to relax in many ways in what was, at times, a difficult situation. When you know the end of a book, the reading is less tension arousing. But that changed.

We had an incident, I believe it was in November, though perhaps it was October, in which several men were blown up when a jeep in which they were riding set off a mine. The free-and-easy Bill Dannenmaier of the past—the guy who assumed he would be killed, so why worry; the guy who, when the truce was signed, thought the danger was gone—suddenly disappeared. I now took precautions. I had no intention of blowing myself up during a walk in the mountains. And I wasn't alone in this. I saw other men behaving the same way once going home became real.

• • •

November 19, 1953

Dear Sis:

I had the weirdest dream last night. I think I've been playing too much rummy. At any rate, I couldn't rotate because all I had was the five and seven of spades. René had the six and wouldn't give it to me. . . .

• • •

It's easy to see where my thoughts were, and it wasn't on rummy. Actually, I spent hours playing gin rummy, mostly against René Sierra Coronado, a friend and fellow teacher. I had a perfect record against him—I lost every game.

• • •

November 21, 1953

Dear Ethel:

In the next three days there are three shipments leaving. That should leave me number two on the rotation list. Then, if the rumor I hear is true, I will leave Nov. 30th, for the people in personnel claim that there will be another drop then. At any rate, I don't figure on having over two weeks to go any longer. . . .

November 30, 1953

Payday is here and just about gone and once again I have money in my pocket. This last is definitely a good feeling.

Today, I found a good book—one of the best, in fact, the best I've read this year. When I met Hank Talbot at supper he asked me what I had to complain about. I said that for once I was completely happy due to the fact that I had a good book. He asked me which one and I said "Martin Eden" at which he roared with laughter. He said that it was on the subversive list, but that it merely confirmed his suspicions of me. . . .

• • •

This was the last letter I wrote to Ethel from Korea. I did not, as I anticipated, leave before Christmas. There were no more shipments from our area until after the first of the year, so I still had a month to go.

I never found out—never tried, really—why *Martin Eden* was on the subversive list. It's difficult to believe there was a good reason, but I never saw reason as particularly important to the military.

On Christmas Day 1953, a group of our guys went south to the nearest Korean village to give gifts to the children. I spent my day a little differently. The four Red Cross women went from one company to the next serving morning coffee to the enlisted men. Sue asked that I, a friend, be permitted to drive her. So I spent my Christmas driving from one company to another with a former classmate from Harris Teachers' College. We chatted in the jeep while I drove, it being the first opportunity we'd had to talk since we met at the time of her arrival. While she doled out coffee and Christmas cheer to the men in the front of the mess halls, I'd have a drink with the mess sergeant in the rear. It was as good as a Christmas could be, given the circumstances.

15

HOME—ALIVE

Two hundred of us from rifle regiments had been hurriedly, and mistakenly, assembled at Inch'on for shipment home, but the ship was full. Quick work by the military found room for us on a ship at Pusan, and we were on a train headed south by nightfall. The next day, we were on board ship and headed for Japan.

At Pusan, because we had been given showers at Inch'on, we were allowed to skip the showers, but we once again received a half ration of everything, plus a field ration, as we had on our arrival at Inch'on. Now we had our full ration, plus a few extras. For example, two pair of dress shoes rather than one; two overcoats rather than one. It made our duffel bags a bit heavier, but there were no complaints and no guilt. We felt we had earned the extra.

As at Inch'on, the processing of homeward-bound troops was routine and well orchestrated, with no delays. After receiving our uniforms, we were fed, watered, and put on board a waiting ship, floating alongside the dock. A low, unpainted, two-story wooden building with a balcony running the length of the second floor was opposite the ship. A band played some song, badly, a few ragged streamers hung from the roof and second-floor railing of the warehouse, and a number of Korean women stood on the dock, quietly weeping as they waved good-bye to soldiers who had been supporting them and their families. Two small tugboats pushed our transport away from the dock and out into the harbor, toward open water. Finally, Korea was behind us.

The movement out of Korea was the Army Transportation Command working at its best. There was a quiet competence in all their activities. When a mistake was made—such as 200 soldiers showing up for a ship that had no space for them—the problem was taken care of, quickly and quietly—and we weren't told of the mistake until after a solution had been found.

In Japan, that situation changed. Again, as when I was on my way to Korea, the ship arrived in the evening and we unloaded at night. It was cold and late when we arrived at Camp Drake, where we, the unexpected 200, would await shipment to the States. We were directed to our barracks, but there we found ourselves standing outside in the January cold. The doors were locked. In front of them stood a sergeant. He told us that no bedding was available at this time, that they were trying to locate some. He said that we should just be patient.

Patience wears thin in the dark and the cold, especially when you're within feet of warmth and beds with mattresses, something we hadn't seen in more than a year. Quiet became mutters and mutters became shouts. The sergeant got on his bullhorn and shouted, "Just because you guys have been in combat you think you're tough. Well, we can handle you, so you'd better quiet down."

Actually, we weren't especially tough, at least we didn't think of ourselves that way. We were simply cold and tired and within feet of warmth and comfort. We wanted that warmth and comfort.

The sergeant's comments made things worse. Shouts got louder and rocks broke a window or two. I heard later that the MPs were called out and kept on alert, out of sight behind us, in case the situation worsened. It's just as well that we didn't see them, because the situation could have become ugly. The MPs had been trained to fight to keep the peace, but we had learned to fight for keeps.

Fortunately for all, an intelligent officer showed up. He wanted to know what all the commotion was about, why we were still standing outside in the cold after more than two hours. The sergeant's obsequious reply, replete with one "Sir" after another, was to the effect that they needed to check us in for bedding and there were problems with its availability. I remember the officer's reply: "These guys have been in combat, they've slept in a lot worse. Unlock the door and let them in." I spent the night peacefully sleeping under my overcoat. I was in a warm room, on a mattress, and I had a cover. What more did I need?

I don't remember how long we were in Japan, perhaps two or three days—not long enough to leave more than one memory. One night, they had a "Two Dollar" night at the Non-Commissioned

Officers' Club. This meant that for two dollars you could have all you could drink and a full dinner. I had lost my wallet and my dollars in Seoul, but since my change added up to two dollars, I could take advantage of the offer. With an acquaintance, I rode the post bus to the club. I started on whiskey sours and, after nine of them, if I recall correctly, decided it would be a good idea to eat something. I had a sixteen-ounce sirloin steak with French fries and salad. That much I know for certain. I also remember thinking that I'd best keep drinking whiskey sours, even though I didn't want any more, because I'd heard that if you mix drinks you might get drunk. I have no recollection of when or how I got back to the barracks that night. I do have vague memories of a striptease show featuring an amazingly acrobatic woman that started about the time I finished eating. I've never had the slightest desire for a whiskey sour since that night.

At Yokohama, we boarded a U.S. Navy ship. All three of my previous trips had been on merchant marine ships, which had all had certain things in common: they were rusted and dirty—"filthy" being a better word; it had been difficult to take a shower and impossible to wash clothing. We ate standing up, the food normally ranging from passable to poor. The U.S. Navy, I found, lives differently. This ship was spotless. You could have been served food on the deck because it was cleaner than many of the things we'd eaten off of in the past year. And the food—it was magnificent. I remember getting all the butter—real butter—that I wanted. The sailors serving the food laughed at us as we loaded up on pats of butter. There was also plenty of fresh milk. We were kings, sitting at tables laden with all we wanted to eat.

Discussing navy life with one another, we decided that the navy had some real advantages over the army and only one major disadvantage—namely, in case of combat, there was no place to dig a hole. This made most of us think we'd rather be in the army even if the navy ate better and lived a cleaner life.

As on the merchant marine vessels, there was work that needed to be done and soldiers were conscripted to do it. Now, however, there were so many of us who were sergeants that they were afraid they'd run out of privates and corporals to fill the work details. So instead of assigning staff sergeants, which was my rank, to oversee work details composed of privates, they assigned master sergeants to the task. By working toward the middle, with the lowest enlisted men doing the work and the highest supervising it, if they needed more people at the bottom to do the work they could use staff sergeants. Those of us at the beginning sergeant level found ourselves in a bureaucratic paradise. Before they got to us, all work requirements were met, all jobs were filled. Privates, corporals, and master sergeants worked while we relaxed. I really enjoyed that.

On the merchant marine ships we'd been encouraged to stay in our compartments throughout the day, but the navy closed the compartments for inspection each morning. We were expected to spend the day on deck if we had no assigned duties. That was fine with me. I loved the ocean. One day I watched a thunderstorm move across the horizon, a mile or two away from our ship. It was fascinating to listen to the distant, rolling thunder and to watch the lightning flashes and the gray sheet of torrential rain. Standing there, it occurred to me that Korea didn't have thunderstorms. It was different from America. Rain, yes; thunder and lightning, no. Twenty years passed before, looking back on that memory, I realized that Korea probably did have thunderstorms but that I had always interpreted flashes and roars as artillery, going or coming, never as lighting and thunder.

We sailed from Yokohama to Okinawa, where we stopped briefly to pick up other soldiers rotating home. We were expressly forbidden to have cameras on deck or to take pictures while we were in the harbor, but I took a few anyway, though I've since lost them. Despite being homeward bound, my attitude toward the military hierarchy hadn't improved.

Acquaintances and I spent most of the short time we were in the harbor at Okinawa looking for and spotting fortifications in the cliffs surrounding the beach. As at Pusan, a couple hundred soldiers boarded the ship, a band played, streamers flew, and a hundred or so women, some with children, waved good-bye.

The remainder of the trip was smooth and uneventful. Our days were relaxed and easy. One time, three of us stretched out on the steel deck in a stairwell for a nap. I awakened enough at one point to hear some sailors stepping over us. One asked, "How can these guys sleep here?" Someone replied, "They're infantry, they can sleep anywhere."

You'd think that my mood would improve as each passing day brought me closer to home, but it didn't. I remained in the type of emotional gray that had characterized my emotions while waiting to go on patrol or waiting to leave the line.

Finally, one dawn, we passed under the Golden Gate Bridge in San Francisco, the early morning sun reflecting off the orange of the bridge, which gleamed against the bluest of skies. I, along with several hundred others, stood on deck watching as we sailed beneath it and came into port. It wasn't a sight, it was an emotion. For the first time, the realization that I was headed home invaded my mind, disturbed my soul, aroused my emotions.

Our reception in San Francisco was completely different from that accorded us in Japan. Once again a sergeant stood in front of us with a bullhorn, but the similarity ended there. The speech he gave went something like this: "Men, I know you're in a hurry to be on your way home and we're here to help you. There's a hot meal waiting for you. You may leave your duffel bags where they are, they'll be guarded. When you return, we'll have your orders ready. We'll call out your names and you can pick them up. We'll need your cooperation for this—noise will cause problems. Most of you will be going to Ft. Carson, Colorado. A train is waiting and will be held. There's no hurry. Enjoy your meal."

When we finished eating and returned to get our orders you could have heard a pin drop in that crowd of several hundred. There were no mutters and no shouts. Names were called, orders picked up. When my turn came, I ran forward to get my typed orders, returned for my duffel bag, and then raced for the train. I was on my way.

When we arrived at Ft. Carson, we were divided into two groups. Those who had three months or less to serve in the army following their thirty-day leaves weren't given new assignments, they were given their discharge papers. I had three months and seven days, so I wasn't in that group. Those of us who would be reassigned were sent to supply, where the supply sergeant began to issue us a half ration of clothing. This time we protested, pointing out that we'd received a half ration in Inch'on and another half ration in Pusan. We had no need for more uniforms. The sergeant's reply was classic army: "I don't care what they did in Pusan and

Inch'on, those are ports of debarkation. You were to receive a half allotment there. This is a port of arrival. You are to receive a half allotment here, and you will receive it." And we did.

We were then gathered in a large assembly room where our pay status was checked and we were paid any money owed to us. I received ten dollars. We also received a lecture on our future. We'd receive thirty-day home leaves and then return to Ft. Carson to pick up orders for our next assignment. Since we'd just arrived from overseas, we were entitled to medical treatment for any real or imagined problems. The person who told us this added that if we required treatment our return home would be delayed for several weeks.

At the time, if I took a bite of fresh white bread you would have seen the outline of my teeth, both upper and lower, in blood on the bread; also, I still experience those blinding headaches every night, and my hearing had become a problem. But I thought about those "several weeks" and decided not to bother reporting these petty annoyances—something I would later regret. I wasn't alone. Not a single person in our group had a medical complaint. So we received our orders, giving us leave, and were shown the gate.

By now it was either late January or the first week of February—I don't remember which, except that I was home for my father's birthday on February 8. I was wearing a clean, new uniform, I had ten dollars in my pocket, and I had the army's permission to go home to St. Louis, about a thousand miles away. My first step was to telephone home and ask my parents to wire me forty dollars for bus fare, then I hitchhiked to Denver. Once there, I went to the Western Union Office to pick up the money, only to discover that it had been wired to Colorado Springs. By the time this muddle was corrected it was dark outside, a layer of snow providing as much illumination as the streetlights. Checking with the bus terminal, I discovered I couldn't leave until morning. There was only one answer for me at that time. Who cared about winter and snow, I could hitch-hike faster.

Some hours later, huddled in my overcoat in the pitch black and wind of a winter night on the Kansas prairie, it occurred to me that hitchhiking across the plains, at night, in early February wasn't the most intelligent action I'd ever undertaken. I was lucky, however, and received rides that took me all the way into St. Louis. I arrived about the same time the bus was leaving Denver.

My last ride dropped me off at Union and Delmar. Anyone who knows St. Louis knows that this is just about the center of the city proper. I could easily catch a bus and ride to within blocks of my home in the southwest part of town, but no one would be expecting me for several hours.

I don't know how to explain the feeling I had when I stood on that street corner. Gone was the drive, the rush, that had led me to hitchhike all those miles across the West in the dead of winter. I was completely relaxed. I was also just a few blocks from the college I had attended. With all the hurry out of my system, I walked over there to visit a few favorite professors. There was no rush; there would be a tomorrow. I was home—alive.

EPILOGUE

One of my first acts on returning home was to purchase a car. I visited my sister in Peoria, took a fast trip to Memphis to meet and thank Nell Fallon for being such a wonderful penpal, and drove on to visit my brother in Oklahoma before returning to Ft. Carson. At Carson I was reassigned to the food service school at Ft. Riley to complete my army time.

My parents' house still needed painting, so when summer arrived and I was out of the army I took care of that. Years later, my mother told me that my father said I now had a much quicker temper than in the past, but he never said it to me. Years later, my mother also complained that I'd come home with wanderlust and less stability than I'd had in the past, but I denied it when she said it. The only change I noticed in myself was a great interest in food. I loved to eat in a way that never appealed to me in the past, an interest that, unfortunately, has continued to the present.

As far as family and friends were concerned, Korea was to be an ignored year in my life. I was to be again the person I had been before I went overseas, the boy next door who wondered if he should ask a girl for a kiss on a first date, who found employment, and who accepted his bosses' orders without complaint. But it was too late for that.

I now believe I had more problems than anyone realized when I first came home. Physically, my hearing and my teeth were ruined, but that was the tip of my personal iceberg. The nightly headaches continued without relief.

I was disturbed by the realization of my blandness toward death. I believed that I could kill anyone, stranger or friend, and walk away without concern. I was frightened by this attitude and by my tendency to look at those who annoyed me and consider the best way to get rid of them.

Life was transient, ludicrous, and I was meaningless in it. Sometimes, walking down the street in the evening and seeing a line of people standing and laughing, waiting to buy theater tickets, I'd fly into an internal rage. I wanted to scream at those people, Why are you laughing? They didn't know what the world was like. They had no knowledge of the pain and anguish in the world.

Gradually, the rage faded. When I taught, I compensated for my hearing loss by walking close to people who were talking or asking questions. The headaches tapered off over the years, to the point where I no longer have them. But my feelings concerning the absurdity of life and of people who think it's meaningful continued. It's not possible to see as many men die as I did—American, Chinese, Greek, and Korean; men who had hopes and plans, just as I did, whether they wanted to be farmers, businessmen, or professors—without realizing the insignificance of individuals or, for that matter, of humankind. Those feelings slowed my graduate studies at Washington University, where I vocalized my opinions concerning the triviality of much of the professors' research, an attitude not helpful for a doctoral candidate. Nor has it helped me in my relationships over the years with those of my supervisors and bosses who considered themselves and their ideas sacrosanct.

I still have a problem with my hearing, and with my teeth. I continue to prefer to work alone, and I've never gotten over being uncomfortable if I can't see what's going on around me. Perhaps I was like that before I joined the scouts, perhaps not. My sister told my wife I wasn't.

In 1985 I was working as an educational researcher at the intelligence school at Ft. Devens in Massachusetts when I noticed an advertisement for a psychologist at the 121st Evacuation Hospital in Korea. During my wanderings as a college professor, I'd continued taking a variety of courses. Consequently, the army considered me qualified in several areas: education, statistics, operations research, and psychology. After all those years, an opportunity to visit Korea again! With my wife's agreement, I applied, was accepted, and went.

What a change! I'd left a Korea where no civilians were permitted north of the Thirty-eighth Parallel, a Korea that had few standing buildings north of Seoul—and those were primarily made of corrugated tin, cardboard, and anything else that could be used to shelter people. When I arrived I kept looking for the bullet and shell fragment holes that had turned all the walls into a bizarre pattern of space and solid. They were gone. So were the multitudes of hungry urchins who'd swarmed on every corner, begging all they could while simultaneously stealing your wallet and watch. The old Seoul, my Seoul, had desolate acres of empty space, buildings without roofs or windows, cardboard and tin hovels in which people protected themselves as best they could from the elements. Later, I showed pictures I had taken of Seoul during my one weekend visit to a group of Korean officers, majors and colonels. Despite their age and seniority, they were unable to recognize the majority of the buildings or the area of the city in which I had taken the pictures. They knew only the parliament building, which still stood, maintained as a memorial. The city itself had changed dramatically.

The hills and low mountains of Korea had been treeless. What we and the Chinese had not cut for our huts and bunkers or blown to shreds, the Koreans themselves had cut in a desperate fight for survival. Antiquated, windowless trains had shuffled on aged tracks. Rice straw huts had formed small villages as one traveled south through a poor and destroyed land once peopled by prosperous small farmers who seldom strayed far from their villages, working with their oxen, in content ignorance of the motorized world. But with the war these farmers had become a hungry and restless tribe, driven from ancestral homes by barbarian hordes, one from the north and one from the United Nations.

Now all was different. Hillsides were covered with trees, planted, I was told, on Thursdays by the citizens as required by the government, with every family participating. Seoul was a huge, modern city of 11–15 million residents with numerous skyscrapers, including the tallest building in the Orient. A city whose buildings were constantly being torn down and rebuilt, larger and more functional, by men and women whose grandparents knew only oxen and the rice paddy.

Initially, waiting for my family to join me, I stayed very close to the hospital to which I was assigned, working with the children during the days and doing reports on Saturdays and Sundays. At

night I studied Korean and wandered the back alleys of Seoul, perhaps trying to establish a base in what was an unexpectedly foreign land. After a few months I changed jobs, taking a promotion,
returning to research, and conducting war games.

I was more difficult to work with than I should have been. I was
angrily and passionately insistent that only the best was good
enough. War games had to be accurate, new strategies had to be
discovered, the South must win, but win honestly.

The anger and passion confused my Korean associates, partly
because they didn't feel it themselves. Few if any of them had any
direct experience with the anguish of the 1950s. The threat, to
them, was primarily academic. Like most people who only read of
horror and despair, their passions were not involved.

And I was an American, and Americans were not supposed to
feel this way. Most Americans in our area were one-year wonders.
They were military personnel who needed an overseas tour to further their careers, but they had no desire to leave the States. They
volunteered for Korea for a year to fulfill their overseas require-
ment for promotion. Figure the year this way: assignment to Korea; a month to two months, depending on one's level of responsibility, to get adjusted; four months of work; then a month off
with your family brought to Korea or you meeting them in the
Philippines or Hawaii so you wouldn't get too lonely; then back to
work for a couple of months; and finally preparation to return to
the States. Obviously, this was not a situation designed to inspire
devotion and loyalty to a cause.

Many of the officers I knew and worked with in Korea were
careerists, interested only in achieving the best possible individual
ratings on their records with the least possible effort. Rocking the
boat by uncovering errors or problems was not the way to do this.

While my family and I were in Korea, the newspapers in the
United States reported increased tensions and the possibility of a
renewed conflict. This worried my wife's parents as well as my
sister. I reassured them by telling them that we had seventeen generals living in sumptuous villas in Seoul, within artillery range of
North Korea. If the danger had been real, I told them, the generals would be in Pusan or Japan.

I noticed that such concerns of renewed warfare always occurred at times when the military requested more money. I suspect it helped the North Korean military also. An accommodating confrontation, one might suggest.

In my own case, I believe I was much more confused and upset when I returned to Korea than anyone realized. This was Korea, but it was not *my* Korea. My Korea of death and insanity was gone—or was it? Could it be that I hadn't survived the war, that all of this was a dream, to be repeated eternally? Although most of the time I was frantically busy, there were moments when I occasionally wondered if my existence had ended long ago, as had Charley Brown's and so many others.

One thing hadn't changed. I was given an opportunity to revisit the front. When I was there I saw North Korean soldiers wandering about. I hated them as much as ever. Near me stood a South Korean sentry with an M-2 carbine just like the one I had carried so many years before. If he had handed it to me and said, "Let's go," I was ready to go. The emotion was there, the tension was there, I only needed the invitation. They were the enemy, not human, just something to be exterminated. I turned to the sentry and almost asked to hold his rifle. I had to expend effort to be quiet. It was a dangerous moment for me.

The two years I was there were semitherapeutic. I gradually came to accept that this was a different Korea. Not only the Americans but even the Koreans had only faded memories and tales of the past. Just a few of us, the old-timers of both nationalities, had those vivid memories—a child crying from a dead mother's back as refugees trudged past; a child frozen while riding a father's back to safety; a soldier captured and tied up, left to freeze in the snow. Those memories didn't exist for the newcomers, just for a dwindling few who remembered and understood and spoke only to one another.

Toward the end of my tour, I read that the U.S. Army, in coordination with the Korean government, was planning a dinner to honor Korean War veterans and any children of Korean War veterans serving in the military. The thought was warming. It was nice that the government wanted to say thank you. I telephoned the office coordinating the affair, said that I had served as a scout for the Fifteenth Infantry Regiment, and asked about the party. The young woman in charge listened and then said, "But this is for veterans' children currently serving in the military. We're not interested in the Korean veterans."

It seemed appropriate. That statement could serve as a fitting epithet on our headstones—those of us who came back from Korea.

William D. Dannenmaier served in Korea with the U.S. Army from December 1952 to January 1954, first as a radioman in the Communications Platoon of the Fifteenth (Can Do) Infantry Regiment, then as a radio scout in the Intelligence and Reconnaissance Platoon and—following the truce—in the Troop Information and Education Platoon, being promoted from private to sergeant during that time. He earned M.Ed. and Ed.D. degrees from Washington University in St. Louis and has worked in college administration and taught at Washington University, the University of Alberta, Drury College, the University of Calgary, and Austin Peay State University. A civilian employee of the Department of the Army from 1981 to 1992, he now lives in Cumberland Furnace, Tennessee, where he writes a column for the *Clarksville Leaf-Chronicle* and the *Dickson Herald*.

Typeset in 11/13 Cycles
with Stencil Display
Book design by Dennis Roberts
Composed by Jim Proefrock
at the University of Illinois Press
Manufactured by Cushing-Malloy, Inc.